HEIKIN-ASHI

HEIKIN-ASHI

HOW TO TRADE WITHOUT CANDLESTICK PATTERNS

DAN VALCU

educofin

First published in 2011 by Educofin Ltd
301 Linen Hall
162-168 Regent Street
London W1B 5TD
United Kingdom
ha@educofin.com
www.educofin.com www.heikinashi.co.uk

All rights reserved. This book may not be reproduced, in whole or in part, in any form or by any means electronic or mechanical, including photocopying, recording, or by any information storage and retrieval system now known or hereafter invented, without written permission from the Publisher, Educofin.

© 2011 Dan Valcu

The right of Dan Valcu to be identified as the author has been asserted in accordance with the Copyright, Design and Patents Act 1988.

ISBN 978-0-9569864-0-5

British Library Cataloguing in Publication Data
A catalogue record for this book is available from the British Library.

Designated trademarks and brands are the property of their respective owners.
Cover design by Virginia Valcu

To my wife, Virginia and daughter, Veronique

DISCLAIMER

This book is intended for informational and educational purposes only. Neither the information nor any opinions contained in this book, or expressed later in any discussion or correspondence, should be construed as a solicitation to buy or sell any investments or as investment advice.

The author and publisher shall not be liable for any loss of profit or any other commercial damages, including but not limited to special, incidental, consequential, or other damages. All information presented in this book is believed to be correct, and all examples have been tested with historical data deemed to be correct but not guaranteed. Variations may result from use of the information in this book with historical time series from other data providers.

The information provided in this book is not intended for distribution to, or use by, any person or entity in any jurisdiction or country where such distribution or use would be prohibited by law or regulation.

CONTENTS

FOREWORD	XV
INTRODUCTION	1
ABOUT THIS BOOK	5

PART ONE
A CRASH COURSE IN HEIKIN-ASHI CHARTING — 13

CHAPTER 1
WHAT HEIKIN-ASHI IS AND IS NOT — 15

CHAPTER 2
CONSTRUCTION AND INTERPRETATION OF HEIKIN-ASHI CANDLES — 21

CHAPTER 3
HOW HEIKIN-ASHI CHARTS WORK — 27

CHAPTER 4
QUANTIFYING HEIKIN-ASHI CANDLES   31

CHAPTER 5
VOLUME AS A NEW DIMENSION TO
HEIKIN-ASHI CHARTS   37

CHAPTER 6
RELATIVES OF HEIKIN-ASHI   45

CHAPTER 7
IN PREPARATION FOR THE SHOW   51

CONCLUSIONS   59

PART TWO
MANO A MANO: HEIKIN-ASHI CHARTING
AND JAPANESE CANDLESTICK PATTERNS   61

CHAPTER 8
ARE YOU AN ARTIST?
CAN YOU AFFORD TO USE ART
IN TRADING?   63

CHAPTER 9
HEIKIN-ASHI AND HARAMI   67

CHAPTER 10
HEIKIN-ASHI AND ENGULFING PATTERNS   79

DISCLAIMER

CHAPTER 11
HEIKIN-ASHI, PIERCING LINE,
AND DARK-CLOUD COVER   93

CHAPTER 12
HEIKIN-ASHI AND THE MORNING STAR   105

CHAPTER 13
HEIKIN-ASHI AND THE EVENING STAR   113

CHAPTER 14
HEIKIN-ASHI AND HAMMERS   123

CHAPTER 15
HEIKIN-ASHI AND DOJI   143

CHAPTER 16
HEIKIN-ASHI AND TWEEZERS   159

CHAPTER 17
HEIKIN-ASHI AND SPINNING TOPS   169

CHAPTER 18
HEIKIN-ASHI AND BELT HOLD LINES   177

CHAPTER 19
HEIKIN-ASHI WITH ON-NECK, IN-NECK,
AND THRUSTING PATTERNS   185

CHAPTER 20
HEIKIN-ASHI, THREE WHITE SOLDIERS,
AND THREE BLACK CROWS   195

CONCLUSIONS   207

PART THREE
MARRYING HEIKIN-ASHI WITH OTHER TECHNIQUES AND INDICATORS — 209

CHAPTER 21
HEIKIN-ASHI AND MOVING AVERAGES — 213

CHAPTER 22
HEIKIN-ASHI AND MULTIPLE TIME FRAMES — 217

CHAPTER 23
HEIKIN-ASHI AND NEXT DAY FORECAST — 225

CHAPTER 24
HEIKIN-ASHI AND Z-SCORE — 231

CHAPTER 25
HEIKIN-ASHI AND RELATIVE STRENGTH INDEX — 237

CHAPTER 26
HEIKIN-ASHI AND ICHIMOKU CHARTS — 243

CHAPTER 27
HEIKIN-ASHI AND MARKET BREADTH — 251

CHAPTER 28
HEIKIN-ASHI AND PIVOTS — 257

CHAPTER 29
HEIKIN-ASHI AND FOREX — 267

DISCLAIMER

CHAPTER 30
THE END OF THE BEGINNING 277

APPENDIX A
FREQUENTLY ASKED QUESTIONS 279

APPENDIX B
USING MICROSOFT® EXCEL®
TO GENERATE HEIKIN-ASHI CHARTS 287

ACKNOWLEDGEMENTS 293

RECOMMENDED READING 295

INDEX 297

ABOUT THE AUTHOR 307

FOREWORD

This beautifully written book – which I believe to be the first one written in the West on the subject of heikin-ashi – offers investors new decision-making tools and a broader, more inclusive, perspective on financial markets. Heikin-ashi is a variation of Japanese candlestick charting, which explicitly uses the pattern recognition capabilities of the human brain and focuses attention directly on reversal patterns and on evolving market trend.

This technique is still little known in the West, but Dan Valcu – who has spent many years developing it, and using it for real-time trading – is now offering it for more general consumption. There is, of course, no simple method of forecasting financial price movements, and investors are overburdened with too much information; so any trading endeavour demands hard work.

Nevertheless, Mr. Valcu describes and discusses heikin-ashi, and its relationship to conventional Japanese candlesticks, in such detail that he effectively offers investors a very straightforward methodology for coping with the uncertainties of financial markets. Indeed, the use of heikin-ashi should encourage that most elusive aspect of decision-taking in the face of uncertainty – namely, confidence.

Tony Plummer
Author, *Forecasting Financial Markets*
Director, Helmsman Economics Ltd.

INTRODUCTION

Silicon Valley vs. Florence. Analysis vs. creativity. Logic vs. imagination. Life is a continuous interaction between the left and right sides of our brains. These two giants are constantly shaping our thinking and actions. Some persons are very good analysts trying to extract structures, rules, and logic from everything. Creative people like painters, musicians, and advertisers regularly exercise the right side of their brain. The history of human civilization is a very rich synergy of the existence and collaboration of the two hemispheres. Things are less likely to change in the future. What we will see will be better use of both sides of our brains and a reduced gap between how the two work.

In technical analysis, trading, and investing, the situation looks similar. Certain people look at charts and extract information using only basic visual input such as support, resistance, trend lines, price ranges, patterns, and volume.

The beginnings of technical analysis have been influenced and dominated by the artistic and creative side, by the right side of the brain. The next stage of development allowed the left side of the brain to bring its contribution by introducing numerical methods to quantify price or/and volume action. This was the early 20th century, when Point & Figure charts and the Wyckoff method gained momentum.

Throughout the first half of the 20th century, William Delbert Gann, Ralph Nelson Elliott, and cycle researchers like Nikolai Kondratieff, William Strauss and Neil Howe, B. Berry, Joseph Kitchin, and others built the foundation of a more complete analysis using both visual and scientific components.

The computer revolution and availability of cheap processing power in the late 20th century led to an explosion of technical indicators. Statistical methods gained popularity as more financial historical market data became available. The next logical step was to use computer power to process market information using statistical methods.

Prices of hardware and software fell significantly, markets developed strongly, and more people became interested in starting their own research for profit. This was the time when classic technical indicators, such as Relative Strength Index (RSI), Moving Average Convergence-Divergence (MACD), and Stochastics, were designed to quantify trends and look for reversal indications.

Consequently, thousands of indicators and algorithms were invented, all with the same goal in mind: to beat the markets or, even better, all markets.

Technical analysis was in Left Brain mode.

The disappointment of not finding the Holy Grail in the markets using technical indicators changed this mechanical approach for many retail and even professional traders and investors in recent years. They are returning to the basics of the Right Brain period. We are witnessing a revival of simple technical analysis, such as trend analysis, cycle studies and analysis, Elliott Wave theory, Gann strategies, and Point & Figure charting.

One separate and important chapter of this short historical overview must be dedicated to the Japanese influence. The Japanese contributions to technical analysis are creative, visual, artistic, and many times subject to interpretation. The right side of the brain was and still is very utilized within the Japanese school of technical analysis and investing. More and more people are learning about

INTRODUCTION

and using Japanese candlestick, Ichimoku, Kagi, and Renko charts. They are blending this knowledge with Western contributions to the field of analysis, trading, and investing. The East is meeting the West. However, the objective today remains the same as with the Japanese candlesticks used in the late 19th century: to measure supply, demand, and finally, emotions to gain advantage in the markets.

Nevertheless, our psychological setting disrupts all nice plans. Human emotions sometimes derail our best intentions and damage our perfect trading plans. A strong mechanism with solid risk and money management to control the devil inside us is a vital add-on to everyone's desire to beat the markets.

Combining different techniques and indicators in our search for better results should logically lead to better trading, and this is the result in many cases. But in far many other situations, excessive input generates confusion—even *big* confusion. As everybody knows or should know, things must stay simple. A trading system using too many indicators and techniques is doomed to fail. Christmas trees should only be used for decoration and celebration, not for trading. Is there any hope?

Simple is indeed beautiful.

The immediate solution is the use of simple analysis tools combined with a solid psychological and risk and capital management setup. Recent revival of older visual analysis is a proof that the Right Brain period is gaining momentum. Markets are not efficient, and our decisions require a simpler, better, and more synchronized work of the two hemispheres of our brain.

This book has been written in the same spirit and is the first attempt to bring into the limelight a relatively unknown yet very promising Japanese charting technique: **heikin-ashi**.

It is a visual representation which clearly shows trends and reversals. More importantly, it is a quantifiable technique that is easy to implement and use.

Ultimately, heikin-ashi equally appeals to both sides of the brain for better trading and investing results.

ABOUT THIS BOOK

A picture is worth a thousand words.

This book was born from the idea that life can be made simpler and time can be used more wisely. As Leonardo da Vinci once said, "Simplicity is the ultimate sophistication."

With specific reference to trading and investing, candlestick trading and chart reading can be made simpler, easier to analyze, and used for better decisions. And these are the objectives of this first book on the subject of heikin-ashi.

Many people use traditional Japanese candlesticks. Thousands of books and software packages are available on the subject, and one can find courses, seminars, and webinars about this visual representation everywhere in the world. The same could be said about the number of newsletters and websites that discuss candlesticks and identify and recommend reversal or continuation patterns. Cheat sheets, like the ones we may have used in school, have been developed to help people memorize candlestick patterns.

Japanese candlestick patterns are very popular today. They have very flexible rules and interpretations "in the context." Everyone translates them, more or less, in a subjective manner. My personal interpretations may be different from yours, the reader, or from that of the top experts in this field. These facts lead to the reality that candlestick patterns are subjective, artistic, and challenging, so traders need a more objective, quantifiable tool. And this is the main subject of this book.

While it is true that things work as they are now, they could work even better with a little help from new our friend, heikin-ashi.

Obviously then, this book is intended for readers who already have some familiarity with Japanese candlestick patterns and is not intended to teach readers how to use them in trading.

Rather, the main objective of this book is to bring the heikin-ashi technique to a wider audience and consider it vis-à-vis traditional candlestick patterns. There is no competition between the two; rather, there is a *synergy*.

While traditional price candles appeal to the more artistic and subjective judgement (Right Brain people), heikin-ashi candles are a far more evident way to display trends and reversals, as shown in the figure below.

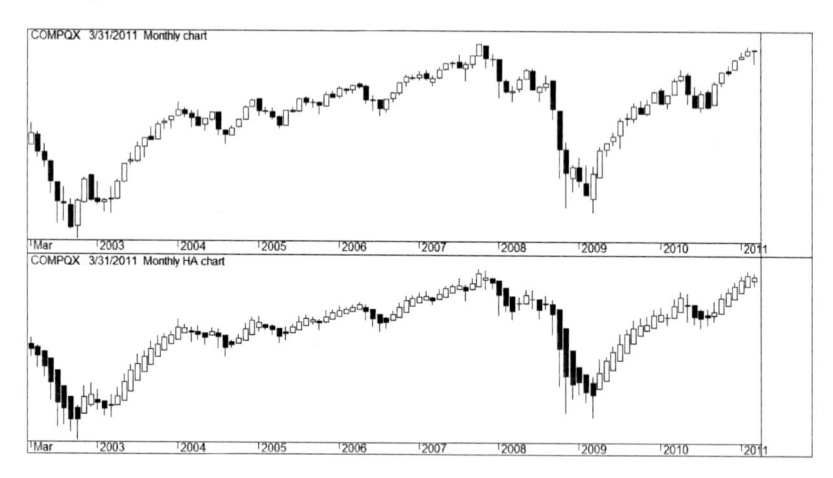

For instance, consider this compare-and-contrast example for the monthly NASDAQ Composite Index (COMPQX). The upper pane displays the index using Japanese candlesticks, and the lower

ABOUT THIS BOOK

pane shows a chart using heikin-ashi candles. Both representations cover the same period in a monthly time frame. The visual difference is the striking clarity of the upward/downward trends and the consolidations introduced by heikin-ashi charting. The color changes with the trends, and doji-like candles with upper and lower shadows point to trend reversals. Series of heikin-ashi candles with both high and low shadows define periods of price consolidation. Turning points are sharper, and trend analysis improves.

Furthermore, the very simple quantification makes the heikin-ashi technique attractive to those who tend to take a more analytical, more precise approach (Left Brain people). In other words, **heikin-ashi appeals to both sides of the brain in a complementary and efficient way.**

Throughout this book we will use terminology like ***heikin-ashi candles*** and ***modified candles*** to refer to candles on a heikin-ashi chart. ***Doji-like candles*** are references to candles with smaller bodies and upper and lower shadows.

The learning objectives of this book are intended to help you become more effective and efficient in analyzing markets and making trading decisions. For instance:

- You will learn how to trade better with a lot less time and effort.

- You will learn how to reduce dependency on candlestick patterns or how to use the two techniques together—and to your advantage.

- You will get a crash course in the heikin-ashi technique for better trading and investing.

- You will learn to quantify heikin-ashi candles, with direct and improved impact on trends and reversals.

- You will learn how to detect earlier indications of trend weakness and change.

- You will review popular Japanese candlestick patterns and learn how to easily translate them using only five simple heikin-ashi rules.

- You will walk through examples and discussions on charts using both traditional Japanese candlestick patterns and heikin-ashi candles and quantification.

- You will see charts using heikin-ashi for different instruments and time frames.

- You will learn how to use heikin-ashi with technical indicators.

- You will learn how heikin-ashi works with Ichimoku charts.

- You will learn how heikin-ashi can be used to gauge market strength.

- You will get ideas to develop your own strategies based on modified candles.

This book consists of three major parts, each of which has been organized into short chapters for easy understanding and comprehension. Each chapter concludes with a "30-Second Summary" that highlights key points.

Part One offers a crash course by total immersion in heikin-ashi charting. At the end, you should understand the essential fundamentals of this technique.

Chapter 1 defines what heikin-ashi is and is not. The second chapter outlines the five simple rules to define modified candles and applies them on charts for quick understanding and use of this technique. How are trends and consolidations identified on any heikin-ashi chart using the new rules? Chapter 3 shows the technique.

ABOUT THIS BOOK

In Chapter 4 you are introduced to a novelty: quantification of the heikin-ashi candles. The two indicators defined in this chapter are a complement to the visual side of the technique. The first indicator, haDelta, is of leading nature, sometimes too nervous and rough but easily smoothed with a moving average. The benefits resulting from using haDelta singularly or together with other analysis tools are evident.

Volume is considered by many a secondary variable used to confirm a trend. Chapter 5 describes how heikin-ashi charts are used with this new dimension.

Modified candles are a unique visual representation of trends and consolidations. In addition, there are other indicators used for trend analysis that quantify traditional price candles and their frequency. They offer another view of trends and turning points on price charts. Chapter 6 discusses two very simple, yet powerful, relatives of heikin-ashi: Qstick and psychological line indicators.

Before going to Part Two, it is time for a warm-up in Chapter 7 where we discuss some Japanese candlestick patterns vs. their heikin-ashi translations.

Part Two is the arena where traditional and modified candles meet *mano a mano* (hand to hand). We review popular Japanese candlestick patterns and compare each of them with the heikin-ashi technique in both formats, visual and quantifiable. You will see how time and money investment in Japanese candlestick patterns is significantly reduced by simple heikin-ashi chart reading. The compare-and-contrast charts will easily convince you to add the heikin-ashi technique to your trading and investment analysis tools.

Chapters 8 through 20 look at 28 Japanese candlestick patterns used by most traders and discuss the challenges of using these patterns. Although this book is not specifically about Japanese candlestick patterns, each of these chapters looks at candlestick pattern definitions, raises questions about their objectivity, and compares pattern expectations with heikin-ashi resulting signals. Most of the examples presented show the benefits brought by the heikin-ashi technique both as a visual tool and technical indicator.

Before going further, we must reiterate that heikin-ashi complements interpretations of Japanese candlestick patterns. Heikin-ashi helps to confirm, or not confirm, the expected outcome on Japanese candlestick charts.

Should heikin-ashi totally replace the traditional candlestick analysis? Should it work together with what you already know and use in terms of candlestick knowledge? Is heikin-ashi a tool that saves you time and money, and improves your trading and investing? Part Two ends with answers to these and other questions about using heikin-ashi.

Part Three is where we marry heikin-ashi with other technical analysis tools. Averages are simple, yet powerful, tools for traders. Chapter 21 describes how to use modified candles with averages.

In Chapter 22 you see how heikin-ashi works in multiple time frames. This is a powerful approach where the new technique is easily applicable, with better results. Use of time frames is very important; the correct approach is even better. Usually two time frames are sufficient; three are best. Alignment of entry and exit signals in two time frames is better than in one. The same results apply and are expected in three time frames vs. two. More identical signals in two or three consecutive time frames generate safer and better results, and the degree of confidence improves dramatically.

About forecasts Yogi Berra once said, "It is tough making predictions, especially about the future." We take a calculated risk here and discuss in Chapter 23 a simple method to compute the profile of the next heikin-ashi candle. Will it be white or black? With all risks involved and accepted, an educated computation about the immediate future is an advantage.

Volatility is an important variable to deal with in any market and time frame. The use of Bollinger bands with oscillators or ADX is already a component of many strategies. In Chapter 24 you will see how volatility works with heikin-ashi charting. As a novelty for many traders, we will discuss the use of the z-score indicator with heikin-ashi. Why z-score? It improves the visual perception of the volatility.

Chapter 25 looks at a popular indicator, Relative Strength Index (RSI), and its use with modified candles.

ABOUT THIS BOOK

The new, yet rather old, kid on the block in recent years is Ichimoku charting. It is considered a complete trading system: trend identification, trend strength, entry, stop-loss, trailing-stop, and exit, except for bring-your-own money and risk management strategy. Chapter 26 builds the foundation for a productive partnership between the heikin-ashi technique and Ichimoku Cloud charts.

Even at this early stage, the monthly heikin-ashi NASDAQ chart shown previously in this section hints that this technique can be used to measure the strength of a market or sector. Chapter 27 shows the steps to quantify the strength.

Everyone loves turning points (pivots) and especially buying and selling at market sweet spots. There are many ways to define stronger or weaker pivots. Chapter 28 shows how to associate price pivots with heikin-ashi charting.

Since the publication of my article about the heikin-ashi technique in *Technical Analysis of Stocks & Commodities* in February 2004, many FOREX traders started using this technique in its original format or with modifications. Chapter 29 covers the use of heikin-ashi as a visual and technical indicator for those interested in FX markets.

The examples illustrated and discussed in this book are part of the wide range of markets and techniques with which heikin-ashi can be used. By the end of this book, I hope that you, the trader or investor, will seriously consider adopting modified candles. Be nice with them, and they will reward you.

I am convinced that the journey that follows will benefit you; the door to better trend trading and investing is open.

Feedback is a powerful tool to improve products, services, and trading results. Feel free to drop a message at ha@educofin.com with questions, thoughts, or ideas about heikin-ashi. I am delighted to keep in touch. Great heikin-ashi trading!

Dan Valcu, CFTe

PART ONE

A CRASH COURSE IN HEIKIN-ASHI CHARTING

"I often say that when you can measure what you are speaking about, and express it in numbers, you know something about it; but when you cannot measure it, when you cannot express it in numbers, your knowledge is of a meager and unsatisfactory kind; it may be the beginning of knowledge, but you have scarcely in your thoughts advanced to the state of Science, whatever the matter may be."

Sir William Thompson, Lord Kelvin, Scottish engineer, mathematician, and physicist (1824-1907)

CHAPTER 1

WHAT HEIKIN-ASHI IS AND IS NOT

In its original form, heikin-ashi charting is a visual instrument to *quickly* identify trends, consolidations, and trend reversals. Chapter 4 reveals a new dimension—heikin-ashi *quantification*—and discusses its big impact vis-à-vis the visual aspect of this charting technique.

The heikin-ashi technique should be seen as a complement to existing analysis tools such as traditional Japanese candlestick patterns, technical indicators, and other techniques and strategies. The use of modified candles in both formats, visual and quantifiable, improves chart reading, and in the end, your trading decisions.

Heikin-ashi works with slightly modified price information (open, high, low, and close). It ignores the volume, although a solution is available and will be covered in Chapter 5.

Any heikin-ashi chart filters out price noise; as a result, trends, consolidations, and reversals are more visible and clearer to the naked eye.

Heikin-ashi charting (*heikin* means "average" or "balance" in Japanese, while *ashi* is translated as "foot" or "bar") has its birthplace in Japan. The technique was introduced to the Western trading community in an article published in *Technical Analysis of Stocks & Commodities* in February 2004. I started the research in Spring 2003 and found on the Internet only one reference in English belonging to the Japanese trader who introduced me to this technique. Since the publication of that article, heikin-ashi has gained momentum, has been adopted by many traders, and has been quickly implemented on various charting platforms.

And now the good news! **Heikin-ashi works only with three types of candles: white, black, and doji-like. And, there is no need to remember candlestick patterns.**

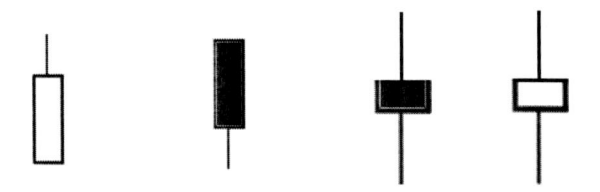

FIGURE 1.1: *Heikin-ashi charting uses only three types of candles, pictured here from left to right: white (up candle), black (down candle), and doji-like.*

Sentiment, Trend, and Momentum

Sentiment, trend, and momentum are three elements every trader should take into account—and all are addressed by heikin-ashi.

A big advantage of the Japanese candles is that they show participants' sentiment. Candle color and body length are reliable barometers for determining the degree of bullishness or bearishness. Long-body candles with no or small shadows appear as a result of strong buying or selling. Excessive shadows underscore buyers' and sellers' mood swings. A doji shows indecision or waiting for the next action. The closing price relative to the open is a clear indication about the bullish or bearish clouds hanging above the trading period.

Japanese candlesticks as such are less obvious about displaying clear trends. Sequences of mixed white and dark bodies, with their shorter or longer shadows, raise the need for more aid to filter the price noise. Technical indicators and Japanese candlestick patterns get into the picture to help. Additional candlestick knowledge and subjective judgement interfere in many cases with the need for faster, more objective, and more reliable decisions.

The analysis of candle bodies and shadows, together with possible patterns in progress, tell the story about the price momentum.

Identifying Trends, Consolidations, and Reversals

While we can say that a traditional Japanese candlestick chart contains all types of information, the challenge remains that traders need additional knowledge and effort to correctly identify trends, consolidations, and reversals. **Japanese candlestick patterns remain a foreign language that requires very good translation. We found a good translator: heikin-ashi.**

Heikin-ashi candles make it easier to identify and follow trends. White bodies with no lower shadows show an uptrend. On the other hand, dark bodies with no upper shadows represent the price being in a short or longer downtrend. A doji-like modified candle with shadows emerging after an uptrend or downtrend *suggests* a reversal. Finally, price consolidations are translated as sequences of two or more heikin-ashi doji-like candles.

The weekly chart of Chipotle Mexican Grill (CMG) in Figure 1.2 displays all these main ingredients.

With heikin-ashi candles, the sentiment is gauged by the color and size of the candle bodies together with the position of the shadows.

FIGURE 1.2: *Chipotle Mexican Grill (CMG) weekly candlestick and heikin-ashi chart for July 2010 through May 2011. In the heikin-ashi chart, trends, consolidations, and reversals are easier to spot and act upon. Traders will find it easier using modified candles instead of finding and translating candlestick patterns.*

Big white and black bodies are features of solid underlying trends. Smaller bodies warn about trend fatigue. A doji-like candle that follows a sequence of white or black modified candles raises caution about either a reversal or the beginning of a consolidation.

The height of the heikin-ashi candle bodies measures price momentum and is a visual indication of overbought or oversold conditions.

In Figure 1.2 we notice in many cases a one-bar lag between reversals on the price chart and the corresponding doji-like candle on the heikin-ashi chart. In other words, peaks and valleys on the price chart are confirmed *usually* one bar later on a modified candle chart. This is a reality traders have to live with because this is how heikin-ashi charting works. Although the Holy Grail is beyond our reach, traders should not be discouraged; the quantification described in Chapter 4 shows a way to overcome this delay.

WHAT HEIKIN-ASHI IS AND IS NOT

The next chapter defines and analyzes all price elements of a heikin-ashi (modified) candle and goes into more detail about the use of these candles.

30-Second Summary

- Heikin-ashi is a Japanese visual charting technique for identifying, at a glance, clear trends, consolidations, and reversals.
- It is a technique used to filter out the price noise.
- It works in all markets and across any time frame.
- Heikin-ashi charting uses only three type of candles, no patterns, and simple rules.
- Compared to the Japanese candlestick charts, heikin-ashi charts are very simple to translate and require minimal time and financial effort.
- Modified candles are based on modified prices.
- Although heikin-ashi can be used as a stand-alone technique, it is best used as a support for existing analysis tools.
- Normally, a heikin-ashi chart displays peaks and valleys one bar later than in Japanese candlestick charts.
- Quantification of modified candles reduces this lag and improves signals (see Chapter 4).
- Heikin-ashi is not the Holy Grail; use heikin-ashi for discretionary trading.

CHAPTER 2

CONSTRUCTION AND INTERPRETATION OF HEIKIN-ASHI CANDLES

Modified candles use a slight modification of the open, high, low, and closing prices. In their original form, they are defined by the following formulas:

$$haClose = \frac{(O+H+L+C)}{4}$$

$$haOpen = \frac{(previous\ haOpen + previous\ haClose)}{2}$$

$$haHigh = Max(H, haOpen, haClose)$$

$$haLow = Min(L, haOpen, haClose)$$

haClose is the average price of the current bar, (O+H+L+C) divided by four. haOpen starts at the midpoint of the previous heikin-ashi candle body. haHigh is the maximum between the high, haOpen, and haClose; haLow is the minimum between the low, haOpen, and haClose values.

Appendix B shows all steps required to calculate values for heikin-ashi candles using historical price data and Microsoft® Excel®.

Japanese candlestick theory quickly became very popular and carved a niche for itself in technical analysis and trading. However, developing a good level of expertise in this area takes both time and money, so it would be practical to reduce these efforts and improve results.

Used together with traditional Japanese candlestick theory, the heikin-ashi technique moves us a step forward in that regard. *Correctly* reading a candlestick chart remains a costly art. Some patterns and subsequent price action work by the books, but many more are a matter of subjective interpretation. The translation is doubtful, and the dependence on other sources adds new costs. Can subjectivity be reduced?

The strengths that heikin-ashi charts bring to your trading are a confirmation of traditional candlestick patterns and advance signals with higher confidence for better decisions.

Five Simple Rules for Translating Heikin-Ashi Candles

While Japanese candlestick theory requires many definitions and flexible interpretation rules for most common and exotic patterns, the heikin-ashi technique works with only the five simple rules outlined in Table 2.1.

Rule	Features
R1	A sequence of white bodies identifies an uptrend. A sequence of black bodies identifies a downtrend.
R2	The uptrend gets stronger with longer white bodies and no lower shadows. The downtrend gets stronger with longer black bodies and no upper shadows.
R3	The trend gets weaker with smaller bodies and, possibly, with the emergence of both lower and upper shadows.
R4	A consolidation is revealed when a series of smaller bodies with both upper and lower shadows emerge.
R5	A trend reversal is likely with the emergence of a small body with long upper and lower shadows (doji-like candle) or a sudden color change.

TABLE 2.1: *The five rules used to translate heikin-ashi candles.*

CONSTRUCTION AND INTERPRETATION OF HEIKIN-ASHI CANDLES

We apply these rules for a quick heikin-ashi chart analysis. Figure 2.2 shows the Apple Inc. (AAPL) daily price on a modified candle chart. Note that there are no Japanese candlestick patterns, no bars, and no other help. We take this minimalist approach because the easiest way to understand what heikin-ashi stands for is to understand its basic five rules as depicted on an actual heikin-ashi chart.

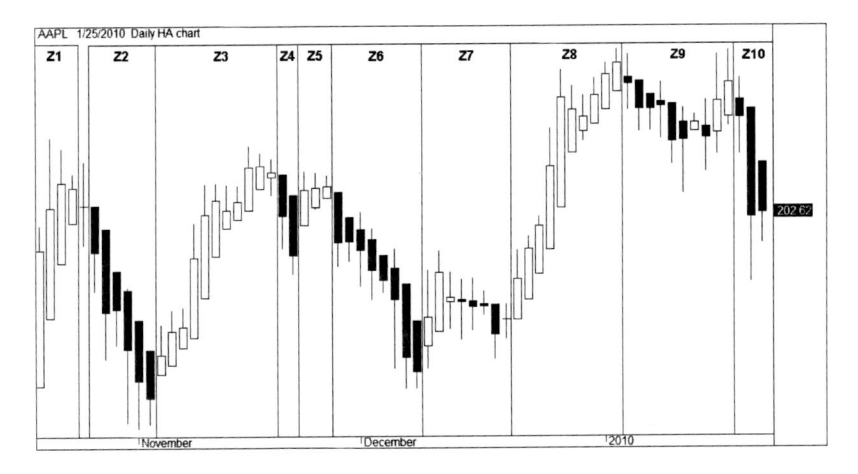

FIGURE 2.2: *Apple Inc. (APPL) daily heikin-ashi chart for October 2009 through January 2010. Ten specific zones are marked on this chart to illustrate how the five basic rules work.*

This chart is divided into ten zones, Z1 through Z10, with the objective of identifying heikin-ashi candles and translating them according to the five rules described in Table 2.1:

- **Zone 1 (Z1)**: The very long white candles with only upper shadows (Rule 2) suggest a strong price uptrend. The last candle is white, but its body size and position relative to the prior body (Rule 3) indicate a slowdown of the strong trend that dominated the first three bars.

- **Zone 2 (Z2)**: The heikin-ashi doji-like candle with long upper and lower shadows stuck between zones 1 and 2 is a

23

typical reversal candle identified with Rule 5. Zone 2 shows a new trend totally dominated by black candles with no upper shadows, a sign of a downtrend (Rule 1).

- **Zone 3 (Z3):** The period is covered by an uptrend (Rules 1 and 2). The first white candle makes the color transition (Rule 5) to a new trend. The entire period is dominated by white candles with no lower shadows, but with variable body size. The uptrend starts as normal but is followed by three longer white candles, indicating a strong price action. The seventh and the eighth candles are getting smaller, suggesting a slowdown of the uptrend. Will it change? At the end of the zone, a doji-like candle emerges (Rule 5) and warns about either a trend change or a consolidation.

- **Zone 4 (Z4):** The downtrend features two long black heikin-ashi candles (Rule 2). The message is bearish.

- **Zone 5 (Z5):** Although all three candles are white with no lower shadows, their small body size (Rule 3) points to timid bullishness. The trend change from zone 4 to zone 5 is identified by a candle color change (Rule 5).

- **Zone 6 (Z6):** The black modified candles point to a downtrend with variable intensity (Rules 1 and 2). The emergence of multiple black candles with both upper and lower shadows suggests price slowdown and consolidation (Rule 4).

- **Zone 7 (Z7):** This period shows a typical consolidation with a majority of doji-like candles and color variations (Rule 4).

- **Zone 8 (Z8):** This is a bullish time for Apple, with similar developments as those occurring in zone 3 but stronger. The first candle is a modified doji-like candle, suggesting either the reversal or beginning of a consolidation (Rules 5 and 4). The uptrend that follows features white candles of different sizes

CONSTRUCTION AND INTERPRETATION OF HEIKIN-ASHI CANDLES

and no lower shadows (Rules 1, 2, and 3), with the exception of the one with both upper and lower shadows (Rule 5). This candle and the one preceding it are contained inside the prior bodies, suggesting that the uptrend is getting consumed.

- **Zone 9 (Z9):** This period starts with a doji-like candle (Rule 5) and continues with a short downtrend followed by an uptrend. Overall, the general character is that of consolidation because a majority of candles has small bodies of both colors and with upper and lower shadows (Rule 4). Zone 9 is dominated by indecision.

- **Zone 10 (Z10):** Finally, the last segment on the chart starts with a possible reversal candle (Rule 5) and points to a short but strong downtrend (Rules 1 and 2).

These comments show how the five rules are easily used to translate at a glance a heikin-ashi chart. The next chapter compares and discusses price action on candlestick and heikin-ashi charts for Apple and General Electric.

30-Second Summary

- The original purpose of heikin-ashi charts remains to visually offer a clear image of trends, consolidations, and reversals.

- Heikin-ashi candles use slightly modified prices.

- Five simple rules are used to translate and explain price action on heikin-ashi charts.

- White candles show an uptrend; black candles point to a downtrend.

- Stronger uptrends display long white bodies with no lower shadows.

- Stronger downtrends display long dark bodies with no upper shadows.
- Small bodies tell the story of a tired trend.
- A doji-like modified candle following a trend brings caution about a possible trend change or start of consolidation.
- A change of candle color points to a reversal.
- A sequence of doji-like candles identifies a consolidation period.
- The ideal visual flow on a heikin-ashi chart is a sequence of white (black) bodies, then a doji-like candle, then a sequence of black (white) bodies, then a doji-like candle, then a sequence of white (black) bodies, and so on.
- However, the real visual stream contains alternating sequences with smaller and bigger candles of same color (trends) and a number of doji-like candles (reversals or consolidations).

CHAPTER 3

HOW HEIKIN-ASHI CHARTS WORK

The previous chapter explained how modified candles are defined and provided a short but comprehensive explanation of heikin-ashi chart translation. This chapter looks at both types of charts, candlestick and modified, and compares them. From what we have seen until now, we expect less noise on a heikin-ashi chart. As time frames are concerned, the higher we go, the less noise is expected on a regular price chart—and even less using heikin-ashi charting.

The lower pane of Figure 3.1 is the Apple heikin-ashi chart discussed in the previous chapter and divided now into the same ten zones. How does the heikin-ashi chart relate to the price action shown in the upper pane? There is no need for words to visualize the correspondence between the two charts and the result of the noise filtering on the heikin-ashi chart.

FIGURE 3.1: *Apple Inc. (AAPL) daily share price for October 2009 through January 2010. At a glance, are Japanese candlesticks or heikin-ashi candles better? You decide.*

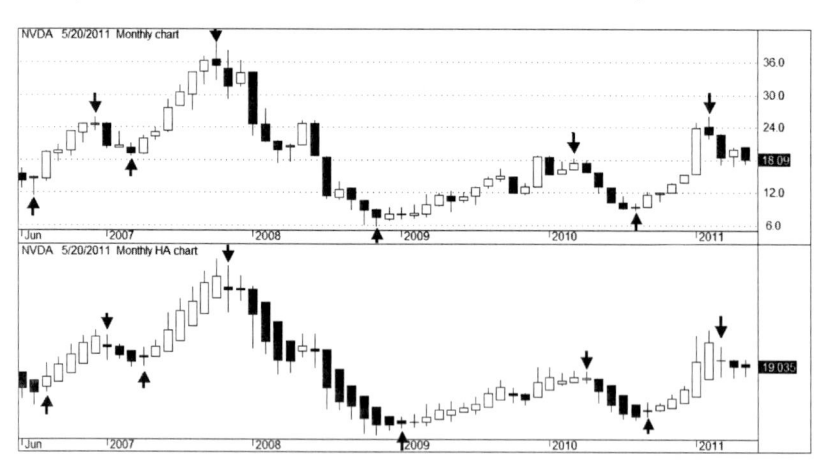

Figure 3.2 shows NVIDIA (NVDA) in a monthly time frame.

FIGURE 3.2: *NVIDIA (NVDA) monthly charts for June 2006 through May 2011. Price action is seen in a more accurate mirror using heikin-ashi charting.*

HOW HEIKIN-ASHI CHARTS WORK

Let us quickly compare the two charting techniques depicted in Figure 3.2 using the five rules defined in Chapter 2.

A perusal of the chart in Figure 3.2 reveals that heikin-ashi candles deliver again. Doji-like candles and color changes point to price reversals (Rules 4 and 5), and trends are clearly defined by sequences of white and black modified candles (Rules 1, 2, and 3).

This is another example showing heikin-ashi's main purpose as a *visual* technique for filtering out price noise and showing trends, consolidations, and reversals in a timely manner. It is easy to spot the one-bar delay between a trend change on the price chart and the corresponding reversal on the heikin-ashi chart (see the arrows on the chart). This is a known and accepted fact worth considering in analysis, trading, and investing with the visual component of the heikin-ashi technique that appeals to right-brain thinkers. Fortunately, there is great news for left-brain thinkers: Chapter 4 brings a power boost to the original the heikin-ashi technique—its quantification—and introduces a technical indicator that changes many things on heikin-ashi charts.

30-Second Summary

- A heikin-ashi chart is a visual instrument that offers a snapshot of trends, consolidations, and reversals.

- **Heikin-ashi charting is simple, easy to implement, and does not use candle patterns.**

- Consideration of both regular and modified price candles brings more confidence when you are in doubt.

- Modified candles look and work great in higher time frames. Remember that on heikin-ashi charts, there is a one-bar delay between price reversals and corresponding turning points.

- Is heikin-ashi simple and worth trying? *You* decide!

CHAPTER 4

QUANTIFYING HEIKIN-ASHI CANDLES

Everything in 2-D or 3-D can be measured, and heikin-ashi candles are no exception. *Why* and *how* can we measure modified candles? This chapter reveals a simple method that works with visual heikin-ashi charting to improve accuracy of the entry and exit signals. This technique is geared towards left-brain thinkers as well as those who want to improve the visual aspect of heikin-ashi.

The previous chapter described how heikin-ashi charts work. Heikin-ashi rules are simple and efficient, so there is no need to learn, identify, and translate100-plus candle patterns into trading decisions.

In essence, the bodies of modified candles are the main component used to indicate and assess trend direction, strength, and reversals. This simple observation leads to an indicator that measures the strength of the trend and points to trend reversals.

We define this indicator as the difference between haClose and haOpen and call it ***haDelta***. Even at this early stage, with no chart available, we can imagine how this indicator works. Longer heikin-ashi candle bodies push haDelta to extreme positive or negative values, depending on the direction of the trend. Shorter bodies, as sign of a slowdown, bring the indicator to normal values. Figure 4.1 shows the NASDAQ Composite Index (COMPQX) on a heikin-ashi chart with haDelta.

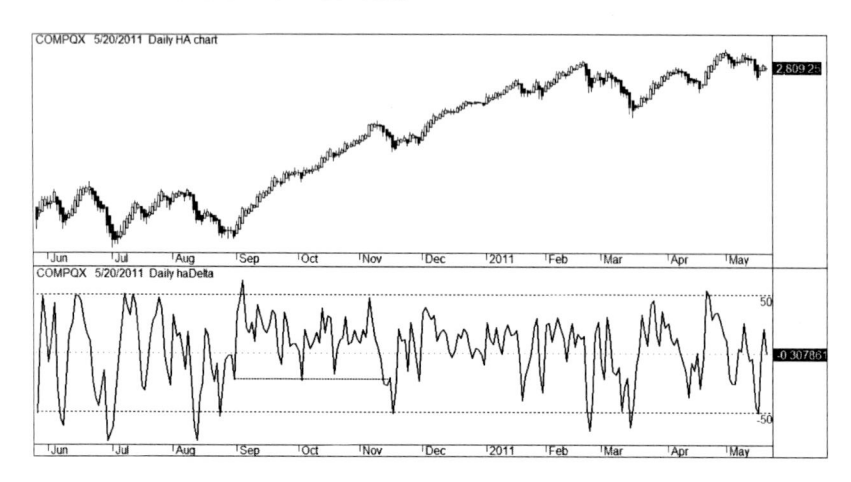

FIGURE 4.1: *NASDAQ Composite Index (COMPQX) daily charts for January 2010 through May 2011, showing the heikin-ashi chart in the upper pane with haDelta in the lower pane.*

haDelta is a sensitive and raw indicator since it measures only the height of the body. Positive values of the indicator are associated with white bodies, whereas negative values correspond to black candles. Extreme values of haDelta point to trend slowdowns (Rule 3).

There are times when using the visual technique and haDelta fail. In these cases, it is important to determine where haDelta is, relative to other extreme values reached in the past. During some periods of time, haDelta fluctuates wildly; during others, the bands are tighter. Figure 4.1 shows haDelta with oscillations inside a horizontal band defined by 50 and -50. There are cases when the floor or ceiling was broken, but in general we *expect* haDelta to warn about a price top or bottom when it hits +50 or -50, respectively.

Another thought is that price trends can be linked to the limits (and width) of the interval in which haDelta varies during a period of time. If the upper limit is higher than the absolute value of the lower limit, the trend is up (as depicted in Figure 4.1 for September through the beginning of November 2010). The opposite is valid in a downtrend (as depicted in the same figure for mid-March through mid-April 2011).

A solution for smoothing haDelta is to apply a short simple average. Figure 4.2 is a zoom-out view of March through May 2011 activity depicted in Figure 4.1, with an additional three-bar simple average (light gray) applied to haDelta. Now the landscape is completely changed.

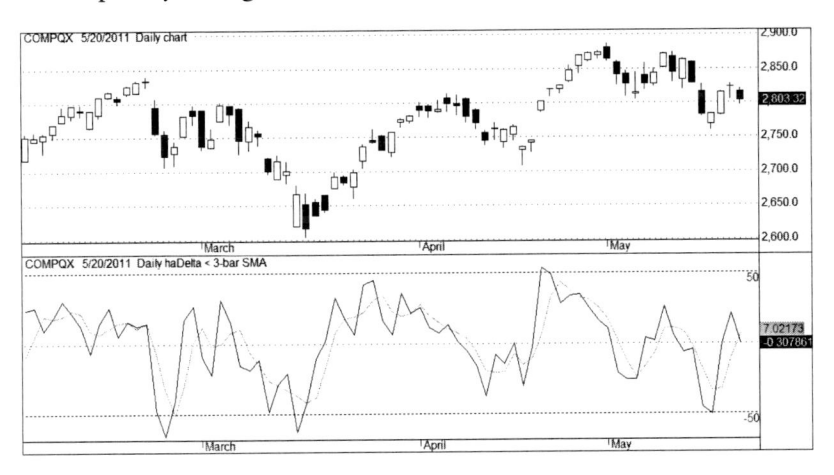

FIGURE 4.2: *NASDAQ Composite Index (COMPQX) daily chart for March through May 2011. The Japanese candlestick chart appears in the upper pane. haDelta and its three-bar average in the lower pane show more accurate trend indications.*

Using the resulting average, we can look at crossings below and above haDelta, or the positive or negative polarity of the average. The crossings with haDelta are very important, especially in stronger trends when whipsaws are rare and confidence is higher.

Positive values of the average confirm price uptrends while negative values point to downtrends.

What happens if we apply a further smoothing to this moving average? Figure 4.3 shows the new and improved picture using the same three-bar period for the second average.

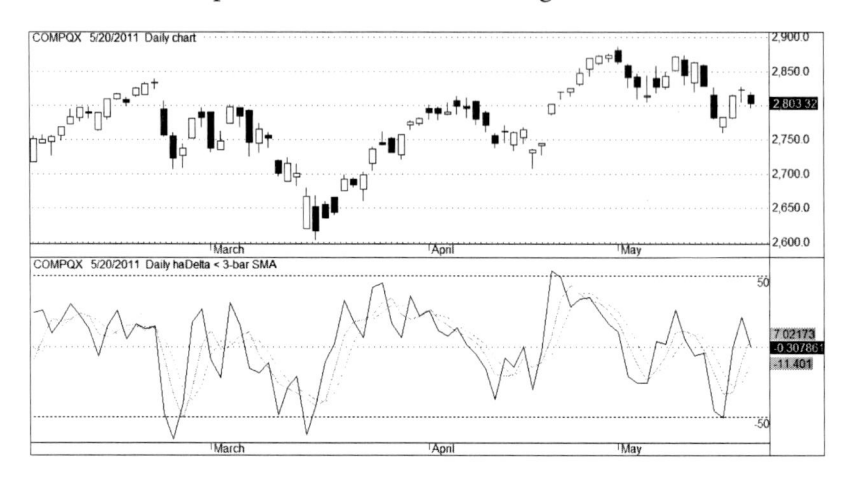

FIGURE 4.3: *NASDAQ Composite Index (COMPQX) daily chart for March through May 2011. This is the same snapshot as in Figure 4.2 with the addition of a second average (gray dashed line) in the lower pane.*

We see that crossings between the two averages confirm trend changes with an anticipated delay introduced by each average. For this example, we used simple averages. You may consider other averages with longer periods and lesser lag.

In the lower pane of Figure 4.3, haDelta is displayed with both averages. haDelta offers an initial signal when it crosses its first average (light gray line). The next indication is issued when the second average (gray dashed line) turns below or above the first one.

The quantification introduced in this chapter may suggest the idea of mechanical trading; however, remember what heikin-ashi is and is not. Personally, I use haDelta and its three-bar average with visual heikin-ashi charts as a confirmation. We will see later that the heikin-ashi quantification can be used to ignore Japanese candlestick patterns.

30-Second Summary

- Everything can be measured, including heikin-ashi candle features.
- Measuring the height of modified candle bodies leads to a simple and sensitive indicator called haDelta.
- Excessive haDelta values are generated by higher price momentum (a gap or a breakout on the price chart).
- Decreasing haDelta values reflect returns to more normal trends.
- A white heikin-ashi candle translates into positive haDelta, while black heikin-ashi candles generate negative values.
- haDelta can be smoothed with a short simple average.
- Crossings between the indicator and its average are better confirmations of trend changes.
- Further smoothing is achieved by applying a second short average to the first one.
- Any smoothing process introduces a lag but improves the confidence in the signal; it is a trade-off that works best in strong trends.

CHAPTER 5

VOLUME AS A NEW DIMENSION TO HEIKIN-ASHI CHARTS

Many traders use volume as confirmation for the price action. When prices go up on higher volume, the uptrend has more credibility than when volume is lower. Similarly, downtrends with higher volume look stronger than those with declining volumes. This chapter will address the application of volume on both Japanese candlestick and heikin-ashi charts.

To incorporate the visual effect of the volume into Japanese candles, the trader has two price-volume representations available:

- Equivolume charts developed by Richard W. Arms, Jr.

- Candlevolume charts, a hybrid between Japanese candlesticks and volume.

Equivolume Charts

Equivolume charts display price and volume information as candle bodies with no shadows. The height of a candle body is the difference between the high and low; its width is calculated using a ratio of the volume and its average value. The higher the volume, the wider the candle body of a candle, which is how healthy trends are depicted on Equivolume charts. Inversely, the lower the volume, the thinner the candle body—and this suggests suspicious trends.

Figure 5.1 shows an example of an Equivolume chart for Netflix (NFLX). Days with high volume have wider candle bodies while days with low volume are shown as thin candle bodies.

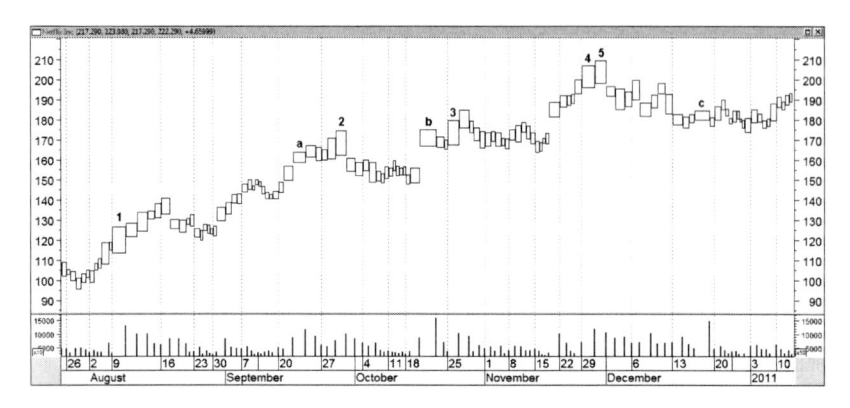

FIGURE 5.1: *Netflix (NFLX) daily Equivolume chart for August 2010 through January 2011.*

On this Equivolume chart, the most convincing days have candle bodies showing a strong price action confirmed by strong volume. In this example, such candles are tall and wide (see the candles marked 1, 2, 3, 4, and 5). The days marked with a, b, and c had big volumes (wide bodies) but small high-low ranges (smaller height). They were unconvincing; hence, the consolidations that followed shortly after. Finally, days with both small price range and volume appear as very small and irrelevant candles (as for unmarked days in September, October, November, and in the end of December through the start of January).

Candlevolume Charts

Candlevolume charts are similar to Equivolume charts, but they include shadows. For this reason, Candlevolume charts are better to use with candlestick patterns.

Figure 5.2 shows a daily Candlevolume chart for Netflix (NFLX) for the same period (August 2010 through January 2011). The bearish dark-cloud cover pattern that developed on September 29 and 30 (see boxed candles) appears *visually* stronger due to the wider dark candle on the second day when the volume played a decisive role. The downtrend brought Netflix from a high of $174.40 to a low of $147.35.

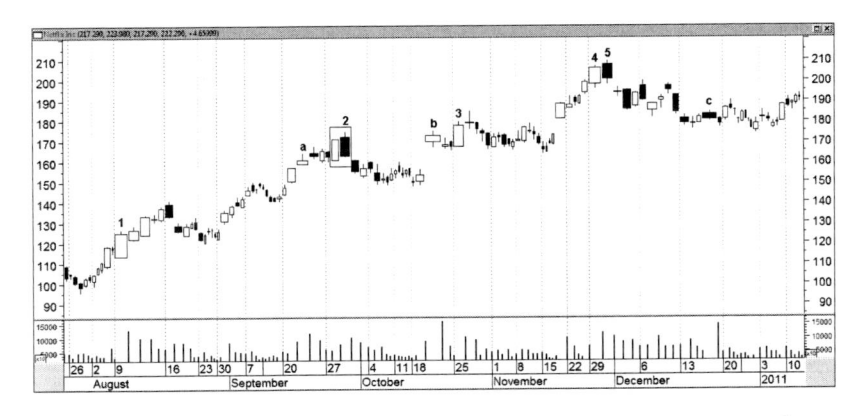

FIGURE 5.2: *Netflix (NFLX) daily Candlevolume chart for August 2010 through January 2011.*

It is easy to consider how volume can be integrated with heikin-ashi candles. Instead of open, high, low, and close, we use haOpen, haHigh, haLow, and haClose (as defined earlier in Chapter 2). The visual results are impressive.

Applying Equivolume and Candlevolume Charts to Heikin-Ashi Candles

Figure 5.3 illustrates the strong impact of an Equivolume chart generated with heikin-ashi candles, particularly when compared to the Equivolume chart in Figure 5.1. Although the period covered and the stock are the same in both figures, the picture in Figure 5.3 is different from that shown in Figure 5.1. The gaps we saw in October, November, and January in Figure 5.1 are invisible on the heikin-ashi chart, as they are incorporated into taller candles. The resulting candles on the Equivolume chart in Figure 5.3 show the real strength defined by big price moves on high volumes. Remember that the absence of gaps on a heikin-ashi chart is a reality resulting from the way modified candles are defined.

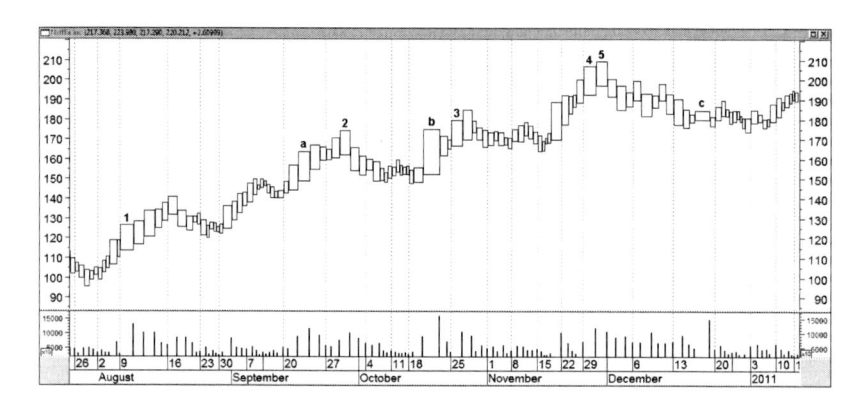

FIGURE 5.3: *Equivolume applied to daily heikin-ashi candles for Netflix (NFLX) for August 2010 through January 2011. The numeric and alphabetic markings above the candles on this figure correspond to the same markings in Figure 5.1.*

Figure 5.5 displays a Candlevolume chart for Netflix, covering same period but with heikin-ashi candles as input. This chart looks like the chart in Figure 5.3, but the candles now have shadows. This heikin-ashi Candlevolume chart has several advantages over the no-volume heikin-ashi chart in Figure 5.4 upper pane:

The volume is now part of the candle, offers better visual impact, and is used as price confirmation.

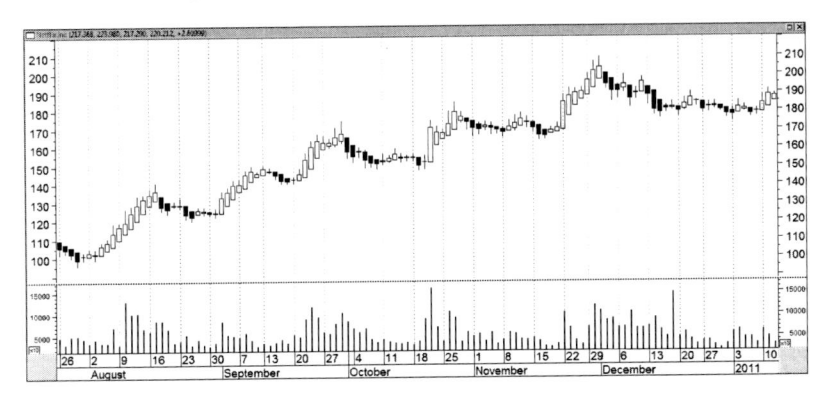

FIGURE 5.4: *Netflix (NFLX) daily heikin-ashi chart for August 2010 through January 2011, without volume applied.*

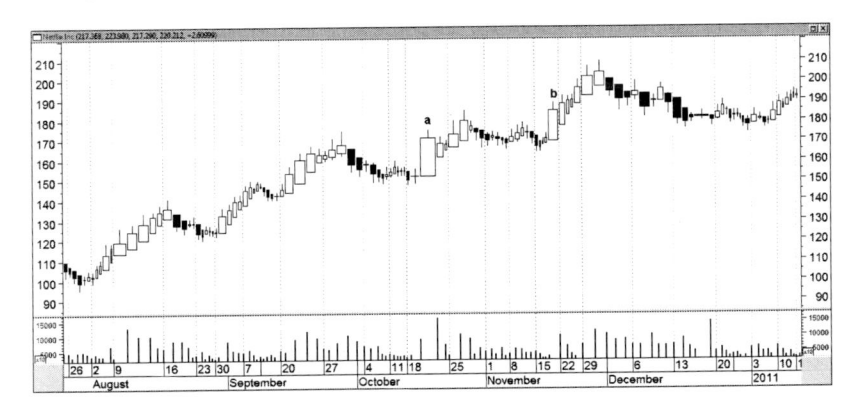

FIGURE 5.5: *Candlevolume applied to daily heikin-ashi candles for Netflix (NFLX) for August 2010 through January 2011.*

Looking at the information visible in Figure 5.5, particularly the daily candles marked a and b, we can make these observations:

On 10/21/10, the extreme height of candle a indicates a very powerful price move that occurred immediately after the reversal (indicated by the doji-like modified candle). The reason for this strong move was a gap up, invisible on the heikin-ashi chart. For those who need to see gaps, the Equivolume chart (see Figure 5.2) and a Japanese candlestick chart can aid the analysis. The powerful combination of big price movement and high volume (big price with high volume) is evident on this chart and points to an energy gap for a continuing uptrend.

On 11/22/10, candle b depicts a situation like the one described on October 21, but only with a lower volume.

In analyzing heikin-ashi trends, we should look for tall-and-wide candles or smaller-but-wide candles. Small candles, in terms of both height and width, are irrelevant and describe a wait-and-see approach. Even when heikin-ashi shows clear trends, the width of the candles determines whether or not they are credible.

All examples discussed in this chapter prove that price *and* volume can work together on heikin-ashi charts. Equivolume and Candlevolume charts serve as the glue.

30-Second Summary

- Equivolume and Candlevolume charts are powerful visual tools that incorporate price and volume.

- Since Equivolume and Candlevolume charts work with prices, they can be used with modified prices to define heikin-ashi candles.

- When Equivolume and, *in particular*, Candlevolume charts are applied to heikin-ashi candles, they add a new visual dimension by introducing volume confirmation for the price action.

- Gaps are invisible on heikin-ashi charts; they are hidden inside the resulting candles, but their impact is visual with or without the new volume dimension.

- To use volume efficiently with heikin-ashi charts, Candlevolume is the best technique for identifying tall and wide candles in uptrends and downtrends.
- The intelligent use of Equivolume and Candlevolume charts applied to heikin-ashi candles may revive volume and price cohabitation.

CHAPTER 6

RELATIVES OF HEIKIN-ASHI

Technical indicators quantify trend direction and strength in different ways. One way is to use the difference between close and open for each bar and to sum it up over a period of time. If the resulting value is positive, the trend is considered up; otherwise, the trend is considered down. This is the basic idea behind a lesser known, yet simple and accurate, technical indicator developed by Tushar Chande called Qstick.

$$Qstick(period) = Average((close - open), period)$$

Using the Qstick Indicator

It is reasonable to expect that plotting the difference between close and open results in a rough indicator. To smooth out this roughness, an average applies to this difference. In Figure 6.1 the upper pane shows the price candles for the monthly S&P 500 Index; the lower pane shows a 12-month Qstick indicator.

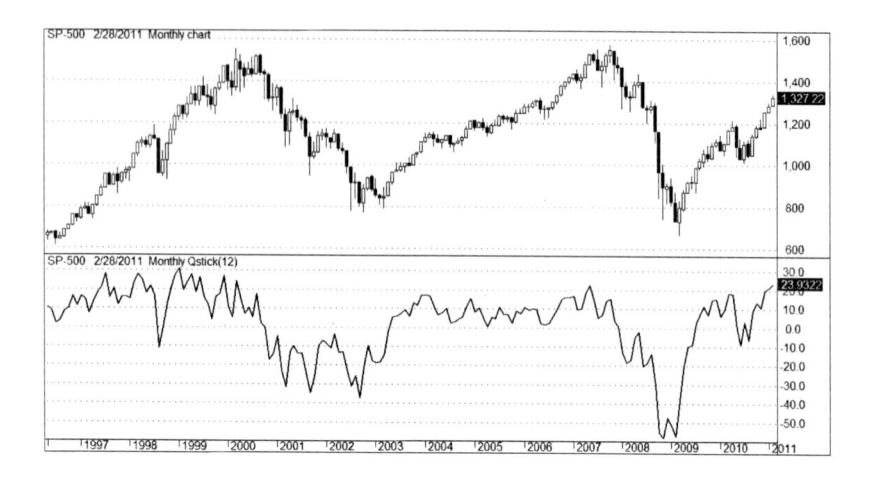

FIGURE 6.1: *S&P 500 Index (SP-500) monthly candlestick and Qstick chart for 1996 through early 2011. A 12-month Qstick indicator shows the US market is extended on the monthly chart.*

Notice in the lower pane that the current value of the indicator is almost 24 and similar to values corresponding to market tops in the past. This is a sign of possible trouble ahead, as the market looks stretched from this perspective. A second observation is related to trends: Positive Qstick values point to uptrends, and negative values identify downtrends.

What happens when we build a heikin-ashi Qstick indicator using the difference between haClose and haOpen? As explained in Chapter 2, the difference between haClose and haOpen is an indicator called haDelta. Figure 6.2 shows the S&P 500 near a potential top, with heikin-ashi Qstick over 43. Even in this case, the market looks overextended using the Qstick approach.

FIGURE 6.2: *S&P 500 Index (SP-500) monthly candlestick and Qstick chart for 1996 through early 2011. The Qstick indicator is now based on heikin-ashi candles and shows the S&P 500 near a top.*

Using the Psychological Line Indicator

Qstick is one way to quantify trend direction and strength. A second, simple way is the psychological line indicator, which can be defined as the number of bars with consecutive higher closing prices over a period of time.

Psychological line(period) = number of rising closing prices during the period

With a period of 12, the maximum value is 12 and points to a perfect uptrend. From a statistical point of view, this value is an indication of a high-probability top approaching. A psychological line value of zero identifies a perfect downtrend over the period considered for calculations and ensures exceptionally high odds for a bottom. Thresholds used with this period are 3, 6, and 9. A drop below 3 suggests an approaching low, and a crossover above 9 warns about an upcoming top. In this scenario, 6 is a neutral value and represents the borderline separating uptrends and downtrends.

Figure 6.3 shows a daily S&P 500 chart with a psychological line applied for a period of 12. The index is clearly in an uptrend with a psychological line at 8, indicating that the market still has room to run.

FIGURE 6.3: *S&P 500 Index (SP-500) daily candlestick and psychological line chart for October 2010 through February 2011. The psychological line indicator shows the S&P 500 in an uptrend with room to advance in the short term.*

Following similar logic as for Qstick, we can define a heikin-ashi psychological line indicator (see Figure 6.4). Values greater than 6 point to an uptrend starting in December 2010. Trend indication is far better than the one shown in Figure 6.3, where the normal psychological line dipped below 6 in January although the S&P 500 was in an uptrend. The current value of the indicator applied to modified candles is 7 and does not show excess on the daily chart.

RELATIVES OF HEIKIN-ASHI

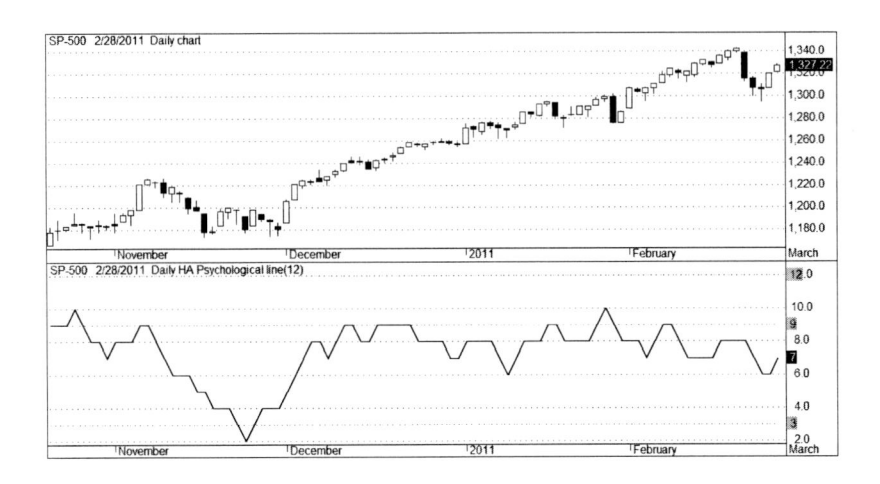

FIGURE 6.4: *S&P 500 Index (SP-500) daily candlestick and heikin-ashi psychological line chart for October 2010 through February 2011. The psychological line on a heikin-ashi chart shows the S&P 500 in an uptrend with room left to go higher.*

30-Second Summary

- Trend direction and strength can be measured by summing up the size of candle bodies or counting consecutive higher closings over a period.

- Qstick averages the sum of the difference (close-open) over a period.

- The psychological line counts consecutive higher closing prices during a period.

- Both indicators work fine with regular prices.

- Modified candle prices can be also used to generate these two indicators.

49

CHAPTER 7

IN PREPARATION FOR THE SHOW

So far, this book has delivered a crash course in heikin-ashi charting. You have seen what it is and is not, how modified candles are built, how to quantify them, how to incorporate the volume, and how to measure trend strength.

The main focus of heikin-ashi charting remains the trend, with particular attention to direction, strength, and reversals. Those same objectives are also part of the study and application of Japanese candlestick patterns—with emphasis on reversals.

The next logical question is "What would result by marrying the two Japanese charting methods?" **Can we use heikin-ashi charting to simplify the interpretation of Japanese candlestick patterns and get better indications?** The answer is positive; heikin-ashi is a strong candidate to start a candle revolution for traders, investors, and analysts.

The universe of candlestick patterns is rich (100-plus patterns), with a lot of flexibility and tolerance in terms of definitions, rules, and use. As a result, their interpretation is subjective in many cases.

With heikin-ashi charting, traders, investors, and analysts finally have an analysis tool that:

- Removes as much personal translation and interpretation as possible from candlestick pattern reading
- Simplifies Japanese candlestick pattern reading and translation
- Uses price candles in any format for faster and better decisions
- Simplifies chart reading for better trading and investing decisions
- Cuts through the heavy jungle and opens a way to simplify.

In Part Two of this book, we will discuss a set of Japanese candlestick patterns and candle patterns vis-à-vis their heikin-ashi equivalence. But first, we close Part One by looking at some examples. Figures 7.1 and 7.2 illustrate the US Dollar Index (DXY0) in a weekly time frame, with prices shown as Japanese and heikin-ashi candles in the upper and lower panes, respectively.

FIGURE 7.1: *US Dollar Index (DXY0) weekly Japanese candlestick and heikin-ashi candle charts for July 2008 through June 2009.*

IN PREPARATION FOR THE SHOW

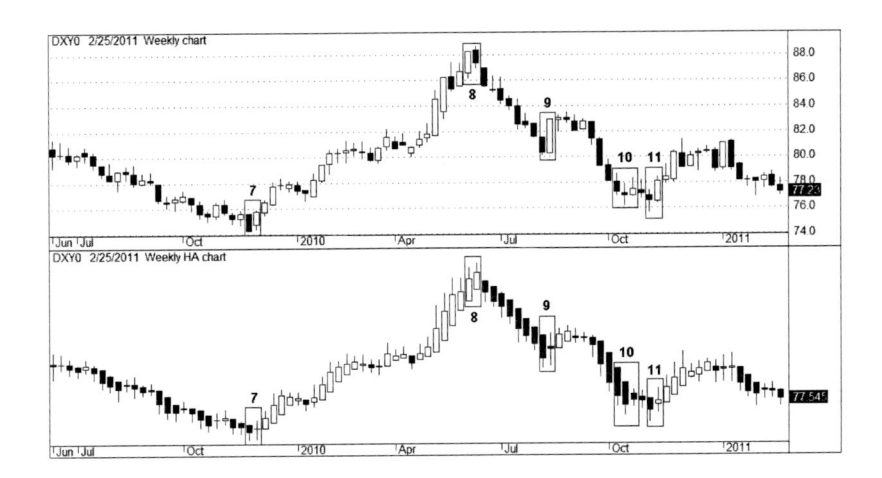

FIGURE 7.2: *US Dollar Index (DXY0) weekly Japanese candlestick and heikin-ashi candle charts for June 2009 through February 2011.*

First, we will identify candlestick patterns (marked with the numbers 1 through 11) on the price chart in the upper pane of both Figures 7.1 and 7.2. We can identify the following formations, some of them subject to further debate:

- Shooting star (1) on 9/12/08
- Evening star (2) on 11/28/08
- Morning star (3) on 1/2/09
- Evening star (4) on 3/13/2009
- Inverted hammer (5) on 5/29/09 as part of a bullish engulfing formation (6) on 6/5/09
- Above the stomach (7) on 12/4/09
- Dark-cloud cover (8) on 6/11/10
- Bullish engulfing pattern (9) on 8/13/10

- Morning star (10) on 10/22/10
- Bullish engulfing pattern (11) on 11/12/10.

Questionable patterns from my perspective are 2, 3, 4, and 10.

Next, we compare each pattern on the Japanese candlestick chart (JC) with the corresponding candle(s) on the heikin-ashi chart (HA) as shown in Table 7.3.

Numbered Pattern on Figures 7.1 & 7.2	Interpretation of JC Pattern	Interpretation of HA Pattern
1	Shooting star warns about a reversal.	The white candle shows the uptrend is intact, with no sign of reversal.
2	Evening star is considered a bearish reversal pattern.	The doji-like candle suggests a trend reversal.
3	Morning star is considered a bullish reversal pattern.	Each of the last two black candles have bodies inside the previous body (a sign of trend slowdown).
4	Evening star is considered a bearish reversal pattern.	The doji-like candle suggests a trend reversal.
5	Inverted hammer is considered a reversal candle.	There is no sign of reversal.
6	Bullish engulfing pattern suggests a reversal.	The second candle of the pattern is smaller and almost inside the previous body, indicating a slowdown.
7	Above the stomach pattern suggests a reversal.	The doji-like candle suggests a trend reversal.
8	Dark-cloud cover has a close at the midpoint of the first white candle. A reversal is suggested.	The uptrend remains intact; there is no sign of slowdown or reversal.

9	Bullish engulfing pattern suggests a reversal.	The doji-like candle suggests a trend reversal.
10	Weak morning star; third candle is not too bullish; reversal is suggested.	The small black candle with upper and lower shadows suggests a likely trend reversal; the bias remains bearish.
11	Bullish engulfing pattern; reversal is expected.	The small white candle with upper and lower shadows suggests a likely trend reversal; the bias changes to bullish.

TABLE 7.3: *This table shows the differences in interpreting heikin-ashi patterns (HA) and Japanese candlestick patterns (JC).*

Last, we can summarize some pros and cons of using heikin-ashi (HA) vs. Japanese candlesticks (JC) observed *until now* in the following table:

	Heikin-ashi	Japanese Candlesticks	Comments
Trends (visual aspect)	Excellent	Good/ Normal	HA: Heikin-ashi allows for sharper trend assessment and filters out price noise. JC: Any trend contains both white and black candles as they emerge.
Reversals	Usually one-bar delay	Candle patterns require further interpretation	HA: Heikin-ashi provides either a single doji-like candle or a change of color. JC: Japanese candle theory discusses a wide variety of reversal patterns, which in many cases is time-consuming and subjective.

TABLE 7.4: *This table shows a preliminary summary of pros and cons in comparing heikin-ashi charting (HA) with Japanese candlestick patterns (JC).*

Candlestick patterns	No patterns	Subjective interpretation	HA: There are no patterns to consider. JC: Patterns may appear clear on the chart or may look like valid ones.
Gaps	No gaps	Yes	HA: Heikin-ashi does not show gaps because of the way candles are defined. Gaps are part of the modified candle. As a solution, use heikin-ashi with regular price charts.
Prices	Modified open, high, low, and close	Open, high, low, close	HA: Heikin-ashi charting uses modified price values. It is the trade-off required to have all heikin-ashi benefits. As a solution, use heikin-ashi with its quantification and regular price charts.
Volume	Yes	Yes	Candlevolume and Equivolume charts are used with both charting techniques.
Time and money investment	Very low	High	HA: Heikin-ashi charting follows only five rules to read and translate charts. Far less resources are required with the new approach. JC: More than 100 candles patterns are available and documented. In many cases, there is subjectivity in translation. Proper interpretation requires a long learning curve.
Quantification	Simple	Both simple and far more complex	HA: Heikin-ashi provides a simple indicator, haDelta. Psychological line is also used to avoid whipsaws. JC: Qstick, psychological line, other complex algorithms can be applied.

TABLE 7.4: *This table shows a preliminary summary of pros and cons in comparing heikin-ashi charting (HA) with Japanese candlestick patterns (JC) (continued).*

30-Second Summary

- There are many situations when evaluating Japanese candlestick patterns is subject to guesswork and debate. They are either skipped because they do not pass a validity test, or they may be analyzed using other methods. We choose heikin-ashi to evaluate all candlestick patterns, regardless of their names, rules, structure, or the trader's experience.

- The heikin-ashi technique makes reading traditional Japanese candlestick patterns easier, faster, and more accurate.

- The easiest way to achieve this result is to analyze commonly used candlestick patterns together with a heikin-ashi chart.

- Remember that modified candles can be used to confirm Japanese candlestick patterns.

CONCLUSIONS

Japanese candles and associated patterns display emotions in the markets. Compared to bars, lines, Point & Figure charts, and most other visual chart-reading tools, Japanese candles bring color to a grayish world. Like old movies that are digitally color enhanced, quality is improved and, at the end, they sell better to everyone's satisfaction.

In trading, more than in life, the main focus is on *the trend* (direction, strength, and reversals) and everything resulting from it (timing, risk and money management, mechanical/discretionary approach, financial results, etc.). It is easy to understand why so much effort is channeled toward better trend analysis and finding new tools to "steal" at least one bar from the trend or to send an earlier warning about possible reversals.

Heikin-ashi is one such tool that follows only five simple rules. It can be used as such or with other techniques and indicators. Because using Japanese candlestick patterns alone is so subjective, the heikin-ashi technique in its both formats, visual and quantifiable, is a serious option to consider for trading and investing.

Part Two examines a series of well-known Japanese candlestick patterns and brings each one into the ring against components of the heikin-ashi technique. The intent behind this hand-to-hand comparison is to answer this question: **Can the influence of Japanese candlestick patterns be reduced or even eliminated from trading?**

PART TWO

MANO A MANO: HEIKIN-ASHI CHARTING AND JAPANESE CANDLESTICK PATTERNS

"I don't care if it's a white cat or a black cat. It's a good cat as long as it catches mice."

Deng Xiaoping, Chinese politician (1904-1997)

CHAPTER 8

ARE YOU AN ARTIST? CAN YOU AFFORD TO USE ART IN TRADING?

Trading is about perceptions, probabilities, and money management. The amount of information and noise surrounding any trader requires one to constantly try new techniques to trade in favorable trends with the highest probabilities the profile allows. People are different, their perceptions vary, and as a result, they have their own set of techniques for improving their odds in a trade or longer-term investment.

The Japanese candlestick patterns have been introduced as a visual technique to reveal buying, selling, and indecision in the markets. Their exotic character and artistic interpretation attracted (and still does attract) a growing number of people who clearly saw the balance of powers. As humans, we are curious and we take a smaller or bigger risk of guessing what is around the corner. Since a large number of the existent candlestick patterns cover trend reversals, it is easy to see why Japanese candlestick patterns attract so many.

In trading, the room for error is limited by your capital, which is your lifeline in the markets. To stay longer and more successful in the market, you need smaller losses and bigger gains. And to get there, you need better tools to anticipate and confirm trends and reversals.

These simple facts raise the issue of trading with artistic instruments vs. trading with quantifiable instruments. Clearly, there are two options available here: either one or a combination.

Anyone using candlestick patterns in trading sees their flexible definitions and interpretations as a potential and even real weakness. At any point of failure, there is an explanation from the specialist why pattern X or Y or Z did not work. There is always something traders did not take into account because they did not have the same knowledge as the pattern expert. In other words, if the pattern works, then the theory is great, everybody is happy, and "I told you so." If it fails, you are advised to get more education and gain more experience in learning the subtleties of the patterns. Translated, you should spend more time and money. Are you ready and willing to do that?

Following the heikin-ashi approach, here are some concerns about Japanese candlestick patterns that will be raised and discussed vis-à-vis heikin-ashi technique in the future chapters:

- **Visually, candlestick patterns look like those in the books, but they are not.** A small deviation from the basic rules creates another "exception" that can be easily explained by the specialist as a finesse or a lesser known feature of that pattern.

- **How is an uptrend or downtrend defined? How many bars are required to qualify as a trend?** The duration of a trend, in terms of number of bars, varies from expert to expert, from trader to trader. Everyone has seen candlestick analysis pointing to bullish or bearish engulfing patterns in consolidations, or after a bullish or bearish day. The answer to these questions is still open ("trading is an art"), and without an answer accepted by a majority, charts will still be full of patterns that otherwise will not be identified as such.

ARE YOU AN ARTIST? CAN YOU AFFORD TO USE ART IN TRADING?

- **What if candle colors deviate from rules?** The basic rules describe a certain color sequence for many patterns. As traders know and experience in their trading, other color combinations may occur. Will this be explained as another finesse or exception? How many exceptions are too many?

- **Certain patterns require one of the candles to close below or above certain thresholds. What if they do not?** In this case, they become another subtlety or an exception to the rule. If the pattern succeeds as expected, it is declared valid despite the failure to follow the rules. If the pattern is unsuccessful, the explanation is simply "Nothing is perfect."

- **Candle pattern recognition services skip many formations that otherwise work.** This is a big and dangerous problem for those who rely on automatic candlestick pattern identification and translation services. There are many services that either skip a valid pattern due to some pennies missing from the calculations, or they identify a pattern with no trend preceding it.

These are some of the important issues traders face when using Japanese candlestick patterns. They are reality. As long as pattern rules are not clear and "special" cases continually appear, many of the translations will be wrong.

The best way to approach market analysis is with a combination of artistic/visual and quantifiable techniques. But *even* in this case, the visual (artistic) component must be as precise as possible to reduce the level of incorrect personal interpretations. It is like comparing a painting by Rembrandt with one by Braque: Both were great painters, but it is far easier to translate how Rembrandt saw the world than to interpret Braque's cubist vision. The Dutch painter was as detailed as a photographer, while Braque challenges us to see where the guitar is in his *Man with a Guitar.*

The next chapters discuss how the heikin-ashi technique in both formats works with popular Japanese candlestick patterns and how patterns can be detached from trading. It may be a bold statement, but **it may be possible to dramatically reduce—if not eliminate—the role of candlestick patterns**.

In each chapter of Part Two, we examine known characteristics of the Japanese candlestick patterns, raise some questions to consider, examine how heikin-ashi works as a complement or option to the patterns, and conclude with a brief summary of our conclusions.

These explanations are illustrated with examples and figures displaying the traditional candlestick chart, the heikin-ashi chart, and the haDelta indicator in multiple panes for easier comparison. The layout of these figures follows two patterns:

- In double-pane figures, the upper pane shows traditional Japanese candlestick charts and the lower pane shows modified candles on a heikin-ashi chart.

- In four-pane figures, the upper left quadrant shows the Japanese candlesticks, with the modified candlesticks displayed in the heikin-ashi chart in the lower left and lower right quadrants (the latter a duplication of the former). The upper right quadrant shows the result of applying the haDelta indicator.

Within these figures, boxes are used to highlight activity pertinent to the discussion at hand.

CHAPTER 9

HEIKIN-ASHI AND HARAMI

This chapter discusses harami pattern on both traditional candlestick and heikin-ashi charts.

Facts

- Harami is a two-candle pattern.
- It must be preceded by a trend.
- It is considered a reversal pattern.
- A harami pattern comes in two formats: bullish and bearish.
- Candle 1 has a long white body in an uptrend (bearish harami) or black body in a downtrend (bullish harami).
- Candle 2 has a smaller body and is black in an uptrend (bearish harami) or white in a downtrend (bullish harami).
- Candle 2 has its body inside the body of candle 1.

Questions to Consider

- How many bars should define an uptrend or downtrend?
- What is a *long* body? How is it measured?
- How do the color combinations of white/white and black/black impact the reversal?
- What happens when candle 2 is entirely inside the body of candle 1?

Figures 9.1 and 9.2 show a daily chart of Nustar Energy (NS) with different content. Figure 9.1 contains Japanese candlesticks (upper pane) and modified candles (lower pane). In Figure 9.2 we keep modified candles in the lower pane and add haDelta, the indicator built to quantify them, in the upper pane.

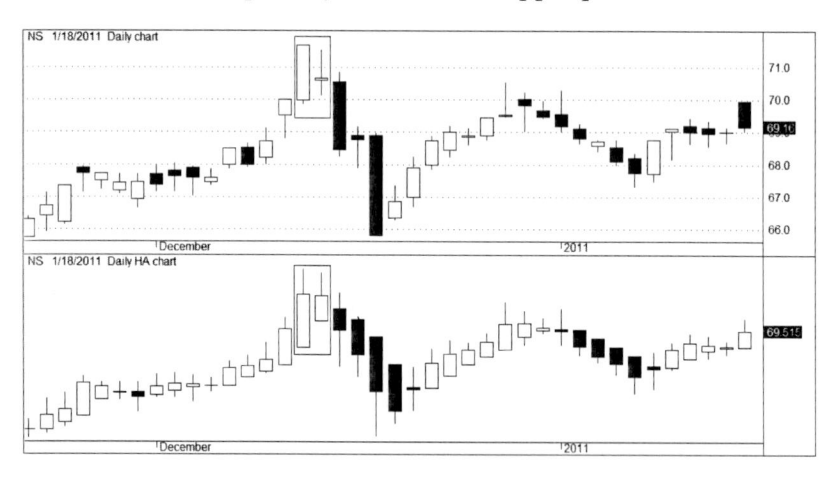

FIGURE 9.1: *Nustar Energy (NS) daily charts with Japanese and modified candles for December 2010 through February 2011. Note the bearish harami pattern in the boxed areas.*

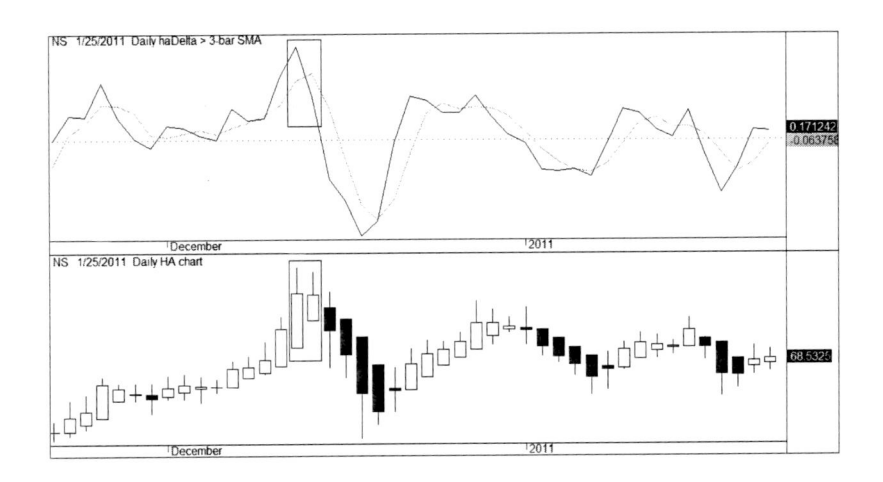

FIGURE 9.2: *Nustar Energy (NS) daily charts with haDelta and modified candles for December 2010 through February 2011. Note the bearish harami pattern in the boxed areas.*

Looking at the upper pane of Figure 9.1, we see that the first harami pattern on December 13 and 14 (see the boxed area) has a very long white body followed by an extremely small body with excessive shadows. The white/white pattern emerges in an uptrend, the second candle is contained inside the first body, and normally it is not considered a bearish reversal moment.

With this pattern in place, things do not look bad on the candlestick chart. The heikin-ashi chart for the corresponding days (see the boxed area in the lower pane) shows two white candles with no lower shadows as sign that the uptrend is still intact. However, the second body is inside the first one and indicates a likely slowdown of the uptrend.

We know that haDelta and its average improve the quality of the visual picture. We move to Figure 9.2 to find out more—eventually a confirmation on December 14, earlier than the big down day that followed the next day. haDelta peaked on December

13, exceeded previous top values, and is below its short moving average on December 14.

In analyzing these figures, the message is clear:

- The Japanese candlestick chart shows the bearish harami as an *indication* for a trend reversal. We wait for a pattern confirmation as early as the next day, January 15.

- The heikin-ashi chart shows the uptrend is intact with a warning about a slowdown (January 14).

- haDelta peaks one day earlier on January 13 and crosses below its average on January 14. Heikin-ashi brings a bearish confirmation for the price, and it comes one day earlier.

- Here is a summary of the events on the charts in Figures 9.1 and 9.2:

- 01/13/11: Nustar Energy is in uptrend.

- 01/14/11: There is more action on the charts. A pattern similar to a bearish harami emerges at the end of the day. The heikin-ashi chart shows a possible slowdown of the uptrend. haDelta falls below its average and confirms the bearish character of the formation.

- 01/15/11: This big down day confirms the bearishness of the pattern. The heikin-ashi candle is black with upper and lower shadows (a little confusing). haDelta falls deeper into negative territory, giving more bearish confirmation.

We keep same chart settings in Figures 9.3 and 9.4 and focus on the bullish harami developed some days later, on December 17 and 20.

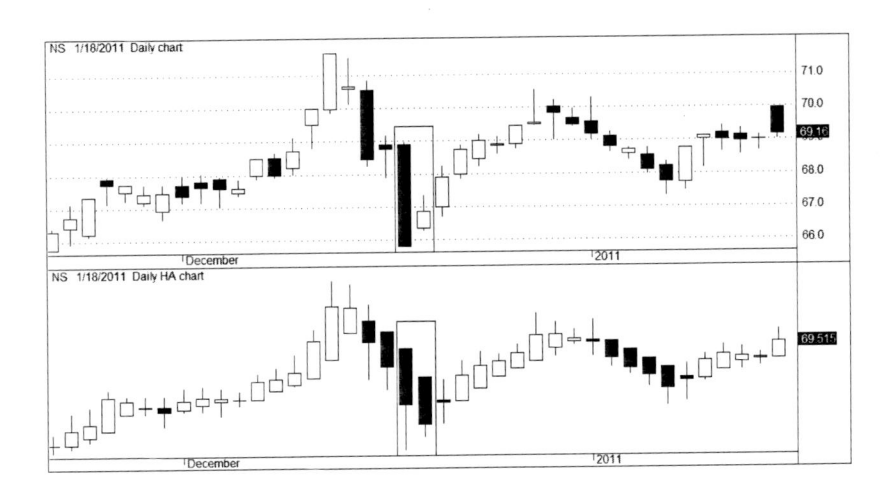

FIGURE 9.3: *Nustar Energy (NS) daily charts with Japanese and modified candles for December 2010 through February 2011. Note the bullish harami pattern in the boxed areas.*

The new pattern follows the definition with the exception of the length of the downtrend. The bearish harami (black/white) in the upper pane of Figure 9.3 has a long black body followed by a candle with a small white body and shadows. The second candle is inside the first day's body. The trend is down, and this harami is expected to act as a bullish reversal pattern.

On the second day of the pattern, the heikin-ashi chart (lower pane) shows a black candle with no upper shadow, indicating that the downtrend is intact with no slowdown in sight. When we suspect something but there is no indication on the heikin-ashi chart, we call in haDelta to bring clarity to the picture.

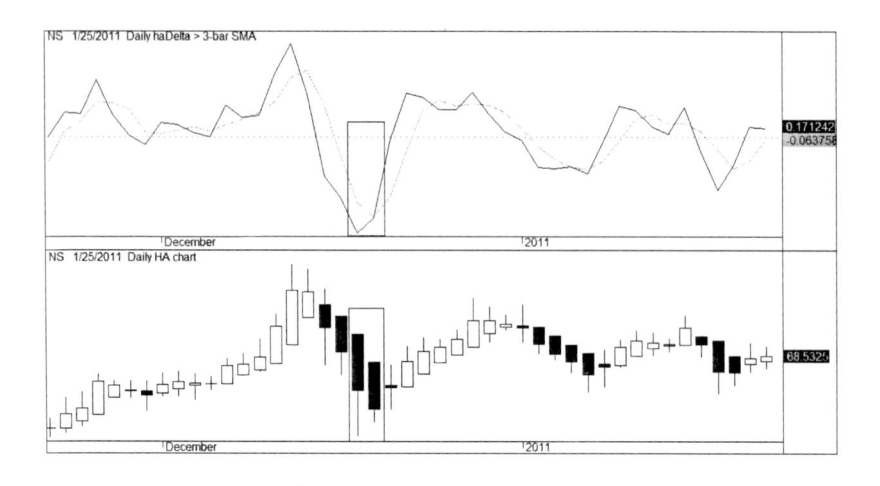

FIGURE 9.4: *Nustar Energy (NS) daily charts with haDelta and modified candles for December 2010 through February 2011. Note the bullish harami pattern in the boxed areas.*

Figure 9.4 reveals more about December 20. haDelta made an extreme low on December 17 and was below its short moving average (bearish behavior). Note in the upper pane that haDelta and its average are very close to each other on December 20, but still on a bearish note.

The next day, December 21, is bullish, but it does not close above the high of the pattern. The heikin-ashi chart (lower pane) shows a typical doji-like reversal candle, and haDelta makes a bullish crossing above its average. It is time for a bullish reversal.

Here is a summary of the events shown in the charts in Figures 9.3 and 9.4:

- 12/17/10: Nustar Energy is in a short downtrend.

- 12/20/10: There is more action on the charts. A bullish harami emerges in a short downtrend. The heikin-ashi chart shows no sign of a trend reversal. haDelta made already an extreme low on January 17 and is still below its average. Our reaction is to wait and see.

- 12/21/10: This is a bullish day on the price chart but not enough to confirm the pattern. The heikin-ashi chart shows a doji-like reversal candle. haDelta is above its moving average, which is a sign of reversal.

Patterns outside normal harami definitions are more interesting with heikin-ashi. A bearish harami is composed of two candles: *usually* the first candle has a long white body followed by a candle with a small black body. Situations when the first body is black instead of white are rare and more powerful. Figure 9.5 shows such case in an uptrend in October 2009.

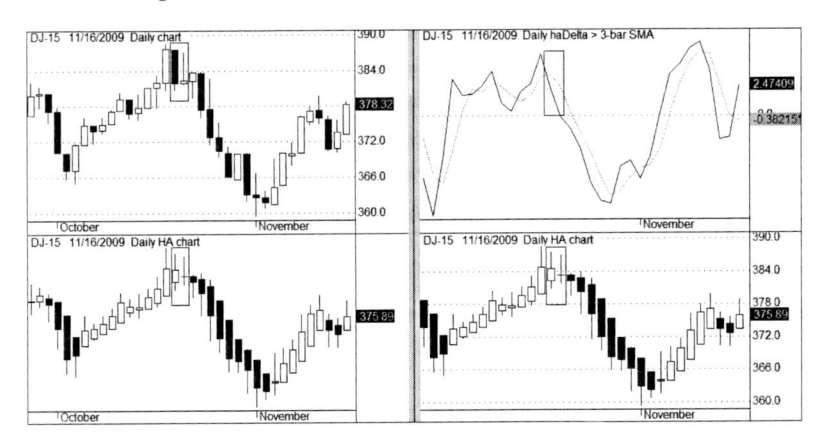

FIGURE 9.5: *Dow Jones 15 (DJ-15) daily charts for October and November 2009. The boxed area shows a less common bearish harami. Even in this case, ha Delta issues a warning before the pattern has been confirmed.*

Here is a summary of the events shown in the charts in Figure 9.5:

- 10/20/09: The candlestick chart shows a long black candle for the Dow Jones 15. The corresponding modified candle has its body inside the previous one, a sign of slowdown. haDelta is after a peak and below its average. Heikin-ashi indicates good signs for a bearish reversal.

- 10/21/09: A less common (black/white) bearish harami pattern emerges on the daily price chart. The heikin-ashi chart prints a doji-like candle as sign for a reversal or possible consolidation. haDelta is deeper below its average. Signs point to a good bet on an impending bearish reversal.

- 10/22/09: This is another day of positive price action, which does not confirm the bearish harami. The heikin-ashi candle is black, indicating a downtrend. haDelta average is very close to negative territory. Bets made on the downtrend start yielding results.

A rare occurrence of a bullish harami is shown in Figure 9.6 where the pattern is made of two white/white candles. The subsequent price action is very strong, sending the share price for Apple (AAPL) to a temporary high of $97.80 in December 2006.

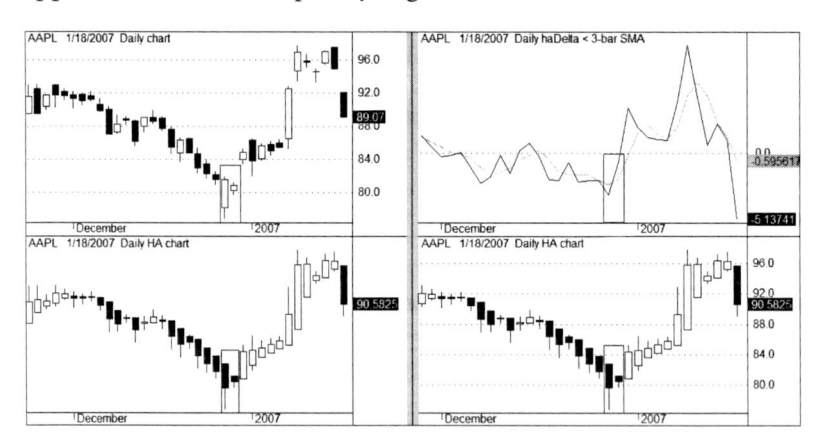

FIGURE 9.6: *Apple Inc. (AAPL) daily charts for December 2006 through January 2007. The boxed area shows a less common bullish harami pattern for Apple in December 2006, seen with Japanese candlesticks and the heikin-ashi technique. Warnings of a reversal came earlier than the confirmation of the pattern.*

Here is a summary of events depicted in Figure 9.6:

- 12/27/06: Apple is in a strong downtrend but has a very bullish day. The heikin-ashi chart shows no slowdown. haDelta is below its average. There are no signs of reversal.

- 12/28/06: A less common bullish harami completes on the daily price chart. The heikin-ashi chart shows a smaller candle with a body inside the body of the prior candle; it is a sign of trend slowdown but no confirmation of a reversal. haDelta is above the average, which made a low. There are signs indicating good odds for a bullish reversal.

- 12/29/06: There is a breakout with gap up.

We know that rules for most Japanese candlestick patterns are *flexible*—hence subjective—and involve the number of candles as well as their height, color, and relative position. One example is the harami definition in the beginning of this chapter which generates both objective and subjective interpretations. Many pattern recognition services or software packages quantify these definitions and deliver a list of trading candidates based on Japanese patterns. Unfortunately, they do not catch pattern subtleties which are reality for Japanese candlestick patterns. As a result, many potential patterns and trades are lost in the translation. This is another reason to add heikin-ashi to your analysis.

The following example shows one questionable pattern outside the orthodox definition. Moreover, it shows how heikin-ashi charting helps reduce personal interpretation of Japanese patterns.

Figure 9.7 shows the Dow Jones 15 on a weekly chart with a *false* harami developing during October 2006. Why is it a false pattern? Because the second candle has its body *outside* the previous candle body, not inside as the definition requires. Consequently, pattern scanning services would skip this formation as it stands on this chart. If you move the body of the second candle just 0.02 points lower, you may get a harami that appears as valid after a pattern scan.

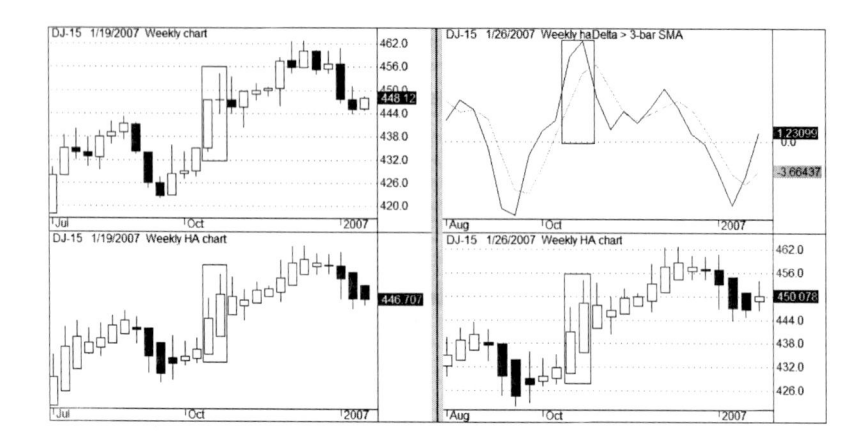

FIGURE 9.7: *Dow Jones 15 (DJ-15) weekly charts for August 2006 through early 2007. The boxed area shows a false high-price harami. Heikin-ashi comes to rescue.*

Pattern rules are very much complemented with experience. In this case, it adds another rule saying that if the second body of a harami is very close from the top of the first candle, the pattern is a high-price harami with a bullish bias followed by a consolidation. Is this also true for our false high-price harami? What does heikin-ashi say about this?

Here is a brief description of the events on both charts in Figure 9.7:

- 10/20/06: The Dow Jones 15 is in uptrend on the weekly chart. A long white-body candle emerges for the week. The heikin-ashi chart shows uptrend. haDelta is positive and above its average. The charts present a bullish picture.

- 10/27/06: The candlestick chart displays a small candle with its body slightly above the range of the previous candle. From a distance, it may look like a harami, but it is *not*. The heikin-ashi chart is very bullish. haDelta hits the level of a recent high in July; this is a sign of a bearish reversal or consolidation.

- 11/3/06: Consolidation starts. The modified candle has its body inside the preceding one (a sign of slowdown/consolidation). haDelta is below its average, indicating a reversal or loss of momentum.

- The following three weeks are in range. During this time, the heikin-ashi chart shows a series of small candles that exclude uptrend or downtrend.

This example underscores again the fact that Japanese candlestick rules are either too rigid or too flexible to define and identify candlestick patterns. Experience makes the difference. A slight deviation from the rules, as in this case, excludes a pattern that otherwise behaves like a harami. **Heikin-ashi with its quantification indicator, haDelta, helps remove subjectivity from pattern translation. This is what traders want: less time spent on candlestick reading, more time for trading.**

30-Second Summary

- Harami is a two-candle formation and considered a reversal pattern.

- Existing trend, color of the candles, and relative position of the second body vs. the previous one determine the character (reversal or even continuation) of this formation.

- Due to these variables, the harami pattern requires often a subjective judgement and translation where personal experience makes the difference.

- Heikin-ashi candles and especially their quantification (haDelta and its short average) help remove much of this personal interpretation.

- The quantification helps translate harami patterns that do not follow the definition, but still *look* like valid ones.

CHAPTER 10

HEIKIN-ASHI AND ENGULFING PATTERNS

This chapter discusses bullish and bearish engulfing patterns on both traditional candlestick and heikin-ashi charts. The analysis will touch basic and more nuanced features of these patterns.

Facts

- An engulfing pattern must appear in a trend.
- It is a two-candle formation and considered a reversal pattern.
- Candle 2 has a taller body than the body of candle 1.
- The body of candle 2 encapsulates the body of candle 1.
- An engulfing pattern can emerge in two formats: bullish and bearish.
- For a bullish engulfing pattern:
    - The trend must be down.
    - Candle 1 is black.
    - Candle 2 is white.

- For a bearish engulfing pattern:
    - The trend must be up.
    - Candle 1 is white.
    - Candle 2 is black.

Questions to Consider

- How many bars should define an uptrend or downtrend?
- Are the heights of the two bodies relevant to the quality of the anticipated reversal?
- Can these patterns have other color combinations? What are the consequences for the validity of the pattern?

Figures 10.1 and 10.2 show the same daily chart of Akamai Technologies (AKAM) with different content. Figure 10.1 has Japanese candlesticks and modified candles in the upper and lower panes, respectively. Figure 10.2 keeps heikin-ashi candles in the lower pane and adds haDelta and its average to the upper pane.

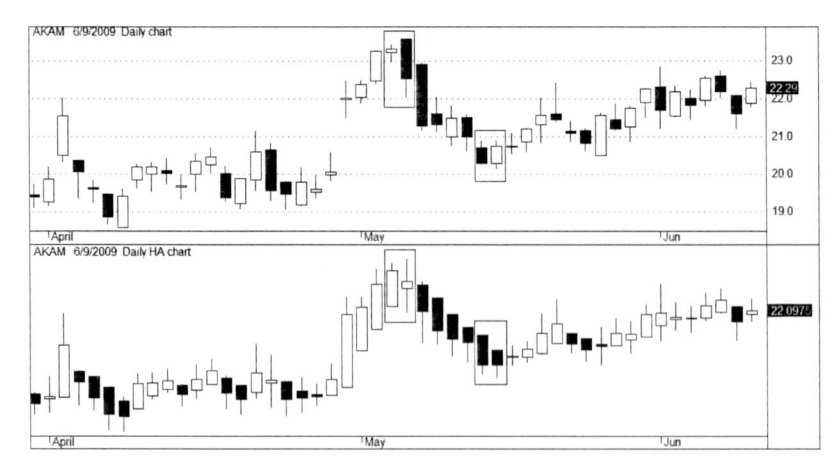

FIGURE 10.1: *Akamai Technologies (AKAM) daily charts with Japanese and modified candles for April through June 2009. The boxes indicate a bearish engulfing pattern.*

HEIKIN-ASHI AND ENGULFING PATTERNS

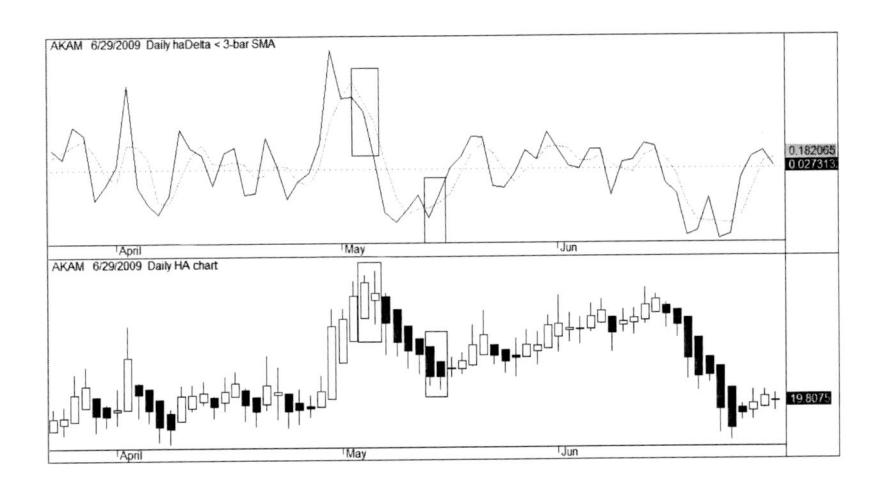

FIGURE 10.2: *Akamai Technologies (AKAM) daily charts with haDelta and modified candles for April through June 2009. The boxes indicate a bearish engulfing pattern.*

The first bearish engulfing pattern on May 5 and 6 has a very short white body followed by an unusually long black candle engulfing the whole range of the first day. This setting anticipates strong price action.

Here is a summary of the events depicted in Figures 10.1 and 10.2:

- 5/5/09: A small white body appears in an uptrend dominated by a gap and several small candles. The heikin-ashi chart displays a spotless uptrend. haDelta already made a top and is below its average; this is a sign that the uptrend is slowing down.

- 5/6/09: A very long black body engulfs the whole range of the first day. The corresponding modified candle has both upper and lower shadows and *suggests* a trend change. haDelta is lower below its average, near zero but still positive. The odds favor a trend reversal.

- 5/7/09: This is the proverbial nail in the coffin. Observe the downtrend that follows until the next bullish engulfing pattern emerges on May 14.

This bullish pattern is composed of approximately equal-size bodies, with the second body overlapping the first one. According to studies of Japanese candlestick patterns, this situation anticipates a weaker immediate price action.

Here is a summary of events for this bullish pattern:

- 5/13/09: A black candle appears in a downtrend. The corresponding heikin-ashi candle shows a downtrend. However, haDelta gives contradictory indications: It is below its average but displays a positive divergence with the price. Moreover, its average recorded a low. Therefore, haDelta shows a bullish bias.

- 5/14/09: A white candle emerges with a body that covers the body of the previous candle. A bullish engulfing pattern is complete. The modified candle is still black (confirming a downtrend is in place), but the position of its body suggests a slowdown. haDelta crosses above its average but is still in negative territory. These are positive signs.

- 5/15/09: A doji with longer shadows appears. This is not a clear confirmation of the bullish pattern. The modified candle suggests a trend reversal ahead. haDelta is still above its average; these are positive signs.

Another observation from traders' experience is that an engulfing pattern that follows a doji is a very strong formation. Figure 10.3 shows such an example for Monsato.

HEIKIN-ASHI AND ENGULFING PATTERNS

FIGURE 10.3: *Monsato (MON) daily charts with Japanese and modified candles for March and April 2009. A strong bullish engulfing pattern in March 2009 is preceded by a doji.*

Does heikin-ashi help even in this case? A look at the events in Figure 10.3 provides the following indications:

- 3/5/09: A doji emerges in the downtrend. The heikin-ashi candle shows a tired downtrend (body with higher and lower shadows). haDelta offers positive indications, being slightly below its average with a positive divergence with the price. The average made a low. haDelta offers a positive bias.

- 3/6/09: A black candle with long shadows emerges in the downtrend. The heikin-ashi candle shows again a tired downtrend (a second candle with higher and lower shadows). haDelta is almost unchanged.

- 3/9/09: This is a reaction day, with a white body engulfing the previous black body. The bullish engulfing pattern is complete. The corresponding modified candle (a doji-like candle) suggests a bullish reversal is near. haDelta is now above the average.

- 3/10/09: We see a gap up from the previous close. The following uptrend adds about $18 to the low of March 9—not a bad result.

With haDelta, positive signs were already visible on March 5. The positive divergence of the indicator with the price was another sign of possible bullish price action. The completion of the bullish engulfing pattern coincides with the classic sign of a reversal given by the heikin-ashi technique (doji-like candle). Everything falls correctly in place.

On the contrary, Figure 10.4 shows that the same engulfing pattern for Priceline (PCLN) is not consistent with the folklore.

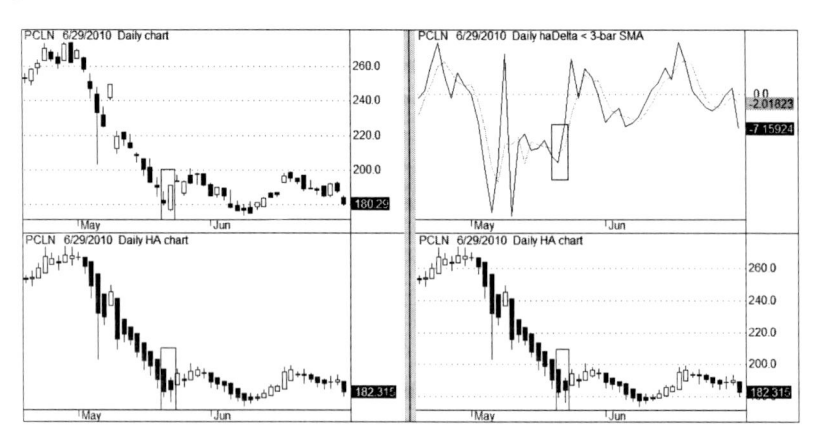

FIGURE 10.4: *Priceline (PCLN) daily charts with Japanese and modified candles for May and June 2010. The bullish engulfing pattern is preceded by a doji but fails.*

Can heikin-ashi help again? Can we get advance warnings? Figure 10.4 shows these indications:

- 5/19/10: A doji/very small body emerges in the downtrend. The heikin-ashi candle shows a downtrend. haDelta is below its average. Everything is bearish.

- 5/20/10: A small black candle with long shadows emerges in the downtrend. The heikin-ashi candle shows the downtrend is intact. haDelta is unchanged.

- 5/21/10: This is a reaction day with a long white body engulfing the previous black body (bullish engulfing pattern). The modified candle suggests a slowdown of the downtrend (second black body inside the first one). haDelta is now above the average. The picture is positive.

- There is no strong action price as expected. Priceline is consolidating for the whole month of June 2010.

In this case, haDelta acts as the canary in the mineshaft only on the second day of the bullish pattern. The bullish pattern was preceded by a doji but did not result in a strong price action as expected.

The lesson learned from these examples (Monsato and Priceline) is very important for the future use of heikin-ashi charting. Forget about what is expected. Look for indications of trend reversals using quantitative methods such as haDelta, a derivative of heikin-ashi candles.

One of the subtleties of the engulfing pattern is that the size and relative position of the two bodies from each other may generate patterns with stronger or weaker character. In the event of a bullish engulfing pattern, if the close of the first black candle is equal with the open of the second white candle, the bullish reversal is expected to be weaker. The reverse may also be true: For a bearish engulfing pattern with the close of the first white candle equal with the open of the second black candle, the resulting trend may be weaker than expected.

Do charts prove these observations are correct? Figure 10.5 shows Boeing (BA) on a weekly chart. Three real and pseudo engulfing patterns are visible. The second formation may be questionable because of the short downtrend preceding it.

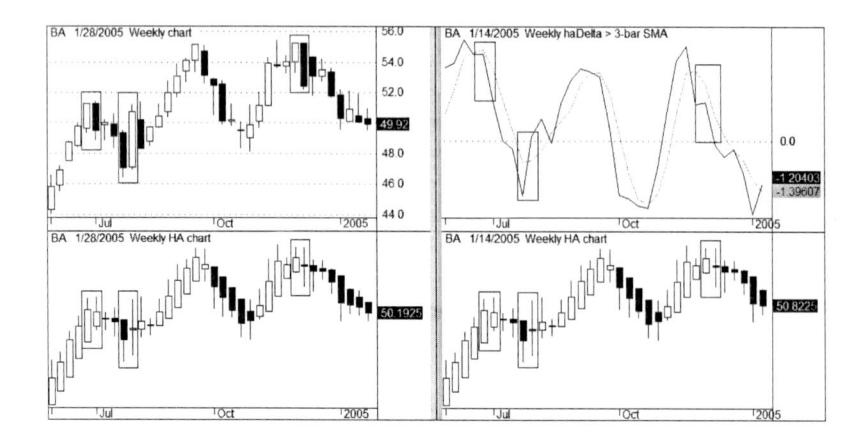

FIGURE 10.5: *Boeing (BA) weekly chart with Japanese and modified candles for June 2004 through January 2005. Note the three different candles patterns indicated by boxes. Two follow the rules; one is a rebel.*

The first bearish engulfing pattern has C1 = $51.30 and O2 = $51.30, where C1 is the close of the first candle and O2 is the open of the second candle. With these values, the pattern tells that a weaker downtrend is expected. This is what happened, and the assumption worked fine. We go one step further and check how things are from a heikin-ashi perspective:

- 6/25/04: A white candle emerges in the uptrend. The modified candle shows a superb uptrend; there is no reason to worry. However, haDelta is below its average, and this is a matter of concern. Handle this situation with care.

- 7/2/04: The week opens at the close of the previous one and ends with a black candle with a body that overlaps the previous body. A bearish engulfing pattern is now in place. The equivalent heikin-ashi candle has a body inside the preceding body, a sign that the uptrend is slowing down. haDelta is deeper below its average and adds negative bias to the picture.

- 7/9/04: There is still no confirmation of the bearish engulfing pattern. The modified candle suggests a trend reversal (doji-like candle). haDelta is deeper below the average. The pattern has a bearish bias.

- 7/16/04: A short downtrend starts.

The second engulfing pattern in Figure 10.5 has C1 = $47.06 and O2 = $47.10, where C1 is the close of the first candle and O2 is the open of the second candle. Based on accepted engulfing pattern rules, any automated pattern recognition process would skip this formation as a valid bearish engulfing pattern. It would be sad because the subsequent trend proves to be healthy. We do not look at rules and instead proceed with our heikin-ashi analysis. Here is a bar replay for this *engulfing-like* pattern:

- 7/23/04: The short downtrend extends with a long black candle. The heikin-ashi chart shows no sign of reversal or slowdown. haDelta is deep below its average. These signs point to a bearish picture.

- 7/30/04: A long white candle looks like it is completing a bullish engulfing pattern. A careful measurement shows O2 > C1; this is not a bullish engulfing pattern. Do *four cents* really matter? Not for us, and heikin-ashi wins again: The modified candle is a doji-like candle suggesting a trend reversal. haDelta is above its average. There is no doubt that modified candles offer positive indications, despite the fact that we did *not* deal with a bullish engulfing pattern. A solid weekly uptrend follows.

This example proves again that rigid rules for Japanese candlestick patterns are not useful and eliminate good trading setups. On the other hand, more flexible definitions introduce a higher degree of subjectivity which is not desired. How can we find some middle ground?

One solution is to use Japanese candlesticks as price information and confirm patterns with numerical tools, such as haDelta. This approach requires some changes but is worth the effort.

We now move on to the next pattern. The third bearish engulfing pattern, which developed between December 3 and 10, has C1 = $55.26 and O2 = $55.26. Measurements, colors, and trend qualify it as a valid pattern with weaker expectations ahead. What do heikin-ashi candles say? A look at these candles reveals the following:

- 12/3/04: A white candle emerges. The heikin-ashi chart shows no sign of reversal or slowdown. We have another pleasant surprise: haDelta is below its average with a cautious message about the current uptrend.

- 12/10/04: A long black candle completes a bearish engulfing pattern. The modified candle is suggesting a bearish trend reversal. haDelta is now deeper below its average.

- The trend that follows is strong. This is definitely not the weak downtrend we expected.

In general, the bullish engulfing pattern is a black/white pair while the bearish engulfing pattern starts with a white body and ends with a black body (white/black). When colors switch and all other rules are kept, the new patterns become the last bullish engulfing pattern (white/black) and last bearish engulfing pattern (black/white), respectively.

Figure 10.6 illustrates a last engulfing bullish pattern, also known as a last engulfing bottom. Its black candle body overlaps the previous white body. It is presented as a potential reversal formation, similar to the bullish engulfing pattern. Can we reach similar findings using heikin-ashi but with earlier indications? A look at AGCO Corporation (AGCO) helps answer this question.

HEIKIN-ASHI AND ENGULFING PATTERNS

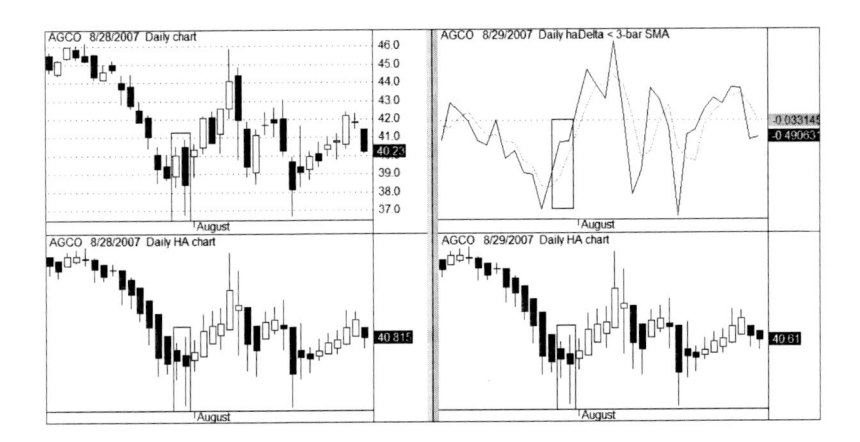

FIGURE 10.6: *AGCO Corporation (AGCO) daily charts with Japanese and modified candles for July through August 2007. The boxed area indicates a bullish last engulfing bottom.*

Here is how events develop on this chart:

- 7/30/07: A white candle emerges late in a downtrend. The modified candle chart shows a downtrend with a possible slowdown/reversal. Again, haDelta is early to flag a possible bullish reversal (the indicator is above its average).

- 7/31/07: A black candle has a range engulfing previous day's range. The body engulfs that of the previous day. On the heikin-ashi chart, there is another black heikin-ashi candle with longer shadows, indicating possible consolidation after the downtrend. haDelta is higher above its average. The pattern is showing a positive bias.

- 8/1/07: There is positive price action, although the close is not above the previous close (warning). The heikin-ashi chart prints a third candle with upper and lower shadows, this time with a white body. These signs point to a still undecided consolidation with a positive bias. haDelta is higher above its average. The uptrend hits a high of almost $46. Even here, heikin-ashi helps with early signals.

Figure 10.7 shows another last engulfing pattern—this time a last engulfing top with its white candle body overlapping the previous black body in an uptrend. It is considered a potential reversal formation similar with the traditional bearish engulfing pattern.

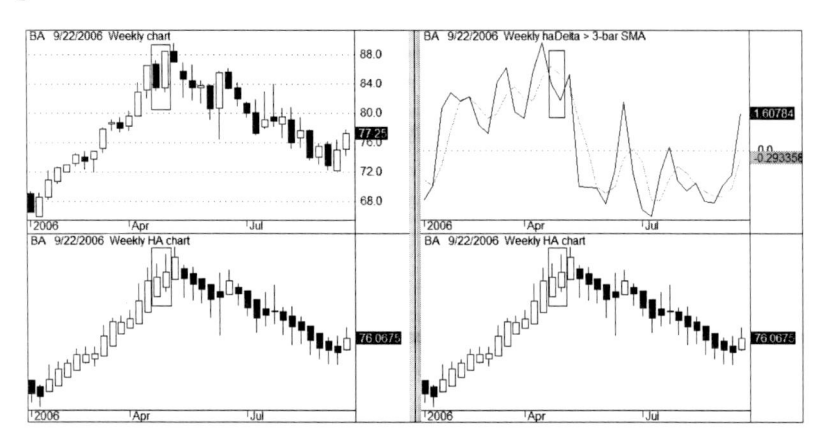

FIGURE 10.7: *Boeing (BA) weekly chart with Japanese and modified candles for January through September 2006. The boxed areas show a last engulfing top in April-May (bearish).*

As in previous examples, we examine how the heikin-ashi technique translates this pattern on the chart:

- 4/28/06: A black candle emerges in a long uptrend. The heikin-ashi chart shows an uptrend with no sign of slowdown/ reversal. Again, haDelta is early to indicate a possible bearish reversal (the indicator is below its average).

- 5/5/06: A white candle appears with O2 = C1 = $83.45. Its body overlaps previous day's body. The modified candle shows the uptrend is unchanged. haDelta is lower below its average; the pattern shows more negative bias.

HEIKIN-ASHI AND ENGULFING PATTERNS

- 5/12/06: This is a negative week. The heikin-ashi chart still shows an uptrend. haDelta is confusing.

- 5/19/06: This is another negative week. The modified candle chart prints the first black candle. haDelta is below the average. A downtrend follows.

Even in this example, haDelta helped by issuing early negative warnings at the end of April.

30-Second Summary

- The bullish and bearish engulfing patterns are two-candle patterns considered reversal formations.

- The second body of the pattern must engulf the first body.

- The heikin-ashi technique, both in visual and quantifiable formats, ignores Japanese patterns and their orthodox or flexible definitions, and reveals earlier price action indication.

- Although typical patterns are black/white (bullish) and white/black (bearish) pairs, other combinations are also possible. The heikin-ashi technique ignores these subtleties, saving time and money.

- Heikin-ashi candles and especially their quantification (haDelta and average) help remove much of the subjectivity introduced by nuances, exceptions, and personal experience.

- Heikin-ashi quantification helps translate engulfing patterns that do not follow definitions but still *look* like valid formations.

CHAPTER 11

HEIKIN-ASHI, PIERCING LINE, AND DARK-CLOUD COVER

This chapter discusses piercing line and dark-cloud cover on both traditional candlestick and heikin-ashi charts. The discussion will touch upon basic and more nuanced features of these patterns.

Facts

- Both patterns must appear in a trend.
- The patterns are two-candle formations and considered reversal patterns.
- For a piercing line:
    - The trend must be down.
    - Candle 1 is black.
    - Candle 2 is white.
    - Candle 2 opens below the low of candle 1 and closes above the midpoint of the body of candle 1.

- For a dark-cloud cover:
    - The trend must be up.
    - Candle 1 is white.
    - Candle 2 is black.
    - Candle 2 opens above the high of candle 1 and closes below the midpoint of the body of candle 1.

Questions to Consider

- How many bars should define an uptrend or downtrend?
- For a dark-cloud cover, can candle 2 open below the high, but above the close of candle 1? Can candle 2 close above the midpoint of the body of candle 1?
- In the case of a piercing line, can candle 2 open above the low, but below the close of candle 1? Can candle 2 close below the midpoint of the body of candle 1?
- How relevant are the heights of the two bodies for the quality of the anticipated reversal?
- Can these patterns have other color combinations? What are the consequences for the quality of the anticipated reversal?

Piercing Line

Figure 11.1 shows a daily chart of Agilent Technologies (A) with a piercing line in January 2002. It follows the rules to the letter and is considered a stronger reversal pattern. How does the heikin-ashi technique translate it?

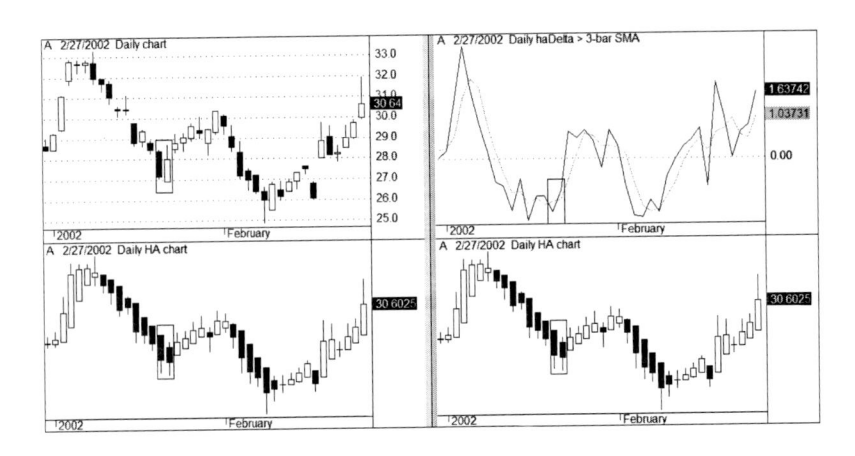

FIGURE 11.1: *Agilent Technologies (AT) daily charts with Japanese and modified candles for January through February 2002. A piercing pattern emerges in January 2002. It is expected to be strong, but it is not. haDelta shows positive signs already on the second day of the pattern.*

As in all other cases, we look at each day of the pattern and see what both techniques indicate:

- 1/22/02: A long black body emerges in an established downtrend. The heikin-ashi candle also points to a negative trend. haDelta is below its average but tries to make a bottom, with a short positive divergence.

- 1/23/02: A white candle emerges, as Agilent closes above the midpoint of the previous body. The end of the day completes a bullish piercing line. The modified candle on this day is still black, but its upper and lower shadows *suggest* a trend slowdown. When in doubt, haDelta saves us again; it crosses above its average with positive indication. At this time, heikin-ashi offers already good indications that favor a bullish trend reversal.

- 1/24/02: Agilent closes above the high of the pattern and confirms the piercing pattern. The heikin-ashi chart shows a trend (color) shift from bearish to bullish. haDelta is higher above the average. An uptrend in the works.

This example shows that heikin-ashi helped with positive signs even on January 23, one day before the pattern was confirmed with a close above its high.

On the other hand, Figure 11.2 shows a similar pattern with the second candle closing higher from the midpoint of the previous body. Theoretically it is supposed to generate a stronger uptrend. We leave the reader to translate it quickly with heikin-ashi but not before making a short observation: haDelta went above its average at the close of the second day. This is an advantage that cannot be ignored.

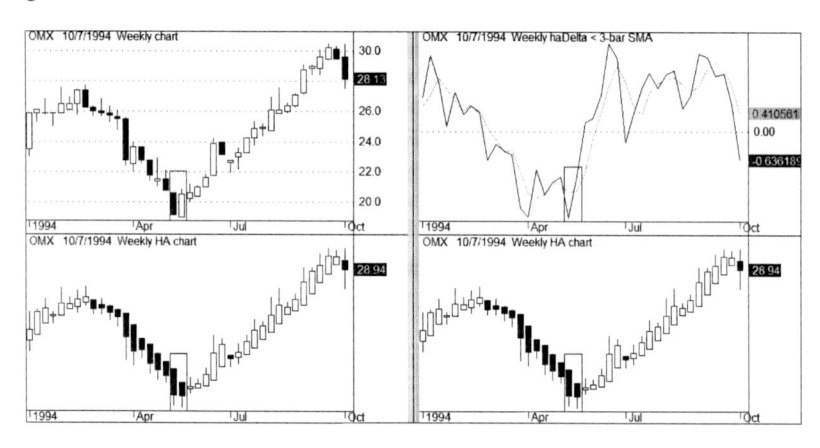

FIGURE 11.2: *OfficeMax (OMX) weekly charts with Japanese and modified candles for January through September 1994. This time, the bullish piercing pattern is followed by a strong uptrend. Even here, haDelta excels with a positive indication on the second day of the pattern.*

The Japanese candlestick conventional wisdom says that if the second candle of the pattern does not push with its close beyond the midpoint of the previous body, the pattern is expected to be

HEIKIN-ASHI, PIERCING LINE, AND DARK-CLOUD COVER

weak. Figure 11.3 shows such piercing pattern on a daily chart of Lowe's (LOW).

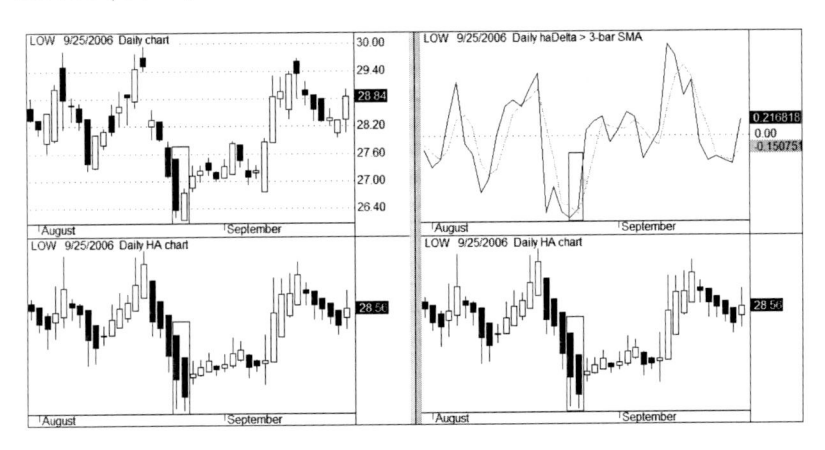

FIGURE 11.3: *Lowe's Companies, Inc. (LOW) daily charts with Japanese and modified candles for August through September 2006. The piercing pattern is expected to be weak. Heikin-ashi offers reversal indications on the second day of this formation, before the price confirmation.*

Here is a replay of the behavior of this pattern:

- 8/24/06: A long black body appears in a downtrend. The heikin-ashi candle shows also a negative trend. haDelta is below the average. Everything points to a downtrend.

- 8/25/06: A white candle closes below the midpoint of the previous body; the bullish piercing line has weak expectations. The modified candle on this day is still black with no sign of slowdown. haDelta again comes to the rescue, rising above its average (positive bias). Odds favor a bullish reversal with no indication about weakness or strength of the expected trend.

- 8/28/06: Although the day did not close above the high of the pattern, the heikin-ashi candle gave a reversal/consolidation sign. haDelta is higher above the average. An uptrend is just starting.

- Lowe's is in consolidation for the next nine days. The piercing line pattern was weaker.

This example shows again a heikin-ashi reversal sign on August 25 before the price confirmed the bullish pattern. Although any candlestick pattern may announce strong or weak trends, it is far safer to rely on trend using heikin-ashi.

Figure 11.4 displays another piercing pattern, this time on a daily chart of Agilent Technologies (A). Looking at where the second candle of the pattern closed, we should have expected a weak trend ahead. This turns out to be a false assumption.

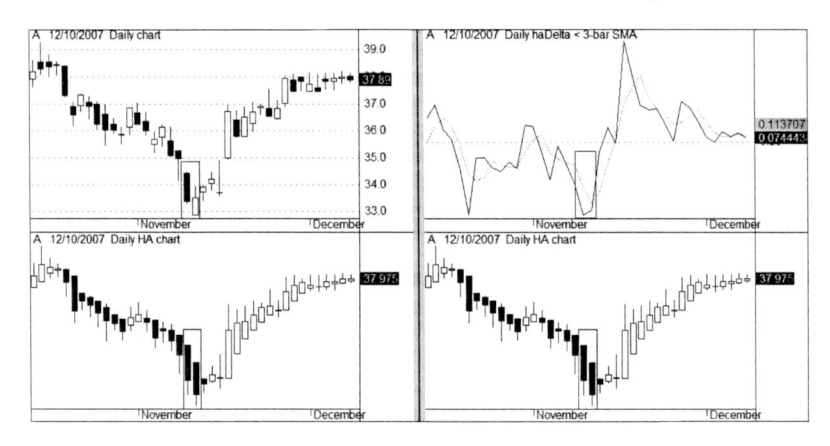

FIGURE 11.4: *Agilent Technologies (A) daily charts with Japanese and modified candles for October through December 2007. The folklore says that the piercing pattern in November is expected to be weak, but it is not. Heikin-ashi offers reversal indications on the second day of this formation prior to price confirmation.*

To see why, we look at the following activity in November:

- 11/9/07: A long black body appears in a downtrend. The heikin-ashi candle shows no sign of weakness. haDelta is below the average. Everything is bearish.

- 11/12/07: The white candle opens below the previous low and closes far below the midpoint of the previous body. This is a sign of a weak piercing pattern. The modified candle is black on this day with no upper shadow. haDelta is minimally below its average. There is no clear picture of a bullish reversal at this time.

- 11/13/07: A positive day with a close way below the high of the pattern. The modified candle is still black, but it is small and inside the previous body. This is a sign of a slowdown. haDelta is higher above the average, indicating an uptrend that brings the price from below $33 to over $38.

In theory, the weak piercing line setup announced a weak trend ahead. However, the price action offered a nice surprise for the buyers. Again, heikin-ashi helped with early reversal signals.

The lesson learned from this example is the same: Follow the trend, set your stops, look for trend reversals, and do not get anxious about how strong or weak the trend might be.

Dark-Cloud Cover

The second pattern in this chapter is the dark-cloud cover, governed by the basic rules and doubts outlined in the beginning of the chapter. Figure 11.5 shows a daily chart of LDK Solar (LDK) with a dark-cloud cover in May 2008. It follows all basic rules and is considered a stronger reversal pattern.

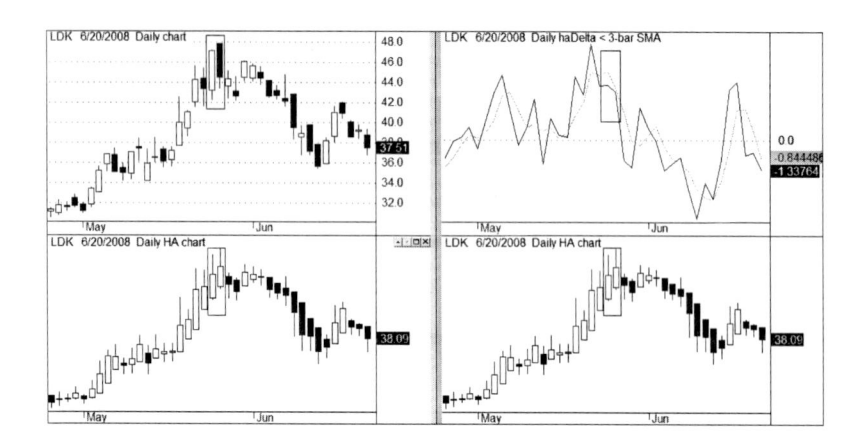

FIGURE 11.5: *LDK Solar Co. Ltd. (LDK) daily charts with Japanese and modified candles for May and June 2008. Although the pattern in late May was a valid dark-cloud cover, the immediate results were weak.*

The following activity confirms the downtrend:

- 5/23/08: A long white body appears in an established uptrend. The heikin-ashi candle reinforces the idea of a strong uptrend. To the contrary, haDelta is already below its average and offers a negative bias worth consideration.

- 5/27/08: A black candle closes below the midpoint of the previous day's body. The end of the day establishes a textbook example of a bearish dark-cloud cover. The modified candle is still white with a negligible lower shadow. haDelta is deeper below its average, indicating a prolonged negative bias. The odds favor a bearish reversal.

- 5/28/08: The closing price is between the close and the low of the previous day. The modified candle turns black and is still unconvincing. The situation is not clear because of the small size of the candle body and the two shadows. A more conclusive indication is haDelta, which is deeper below the average. For the next four days, price is up and down with a reversal heikin-ashi candle on June 3. The downtrend becomes fact the day after.

This is an example that involves a pattern like textbook examples, with strong expectations. In real life, it was followed by hesitation; only later was it followed by a downtrend as expected. It shows again that the fragility brought about by pattern expectations can be removed with quantifiable tools such as haDelta and its short average.

Figure 11.6 shows a formation that may bear resemblance to a dark-cloud cover in January 2000. Why the doubt? Visually it can be a valid pattern, but there is one problem: The second candle does not open above the high of the first one; it opens *exactly* at the close of $4.84. How will heikin-ashi translate this pattern?

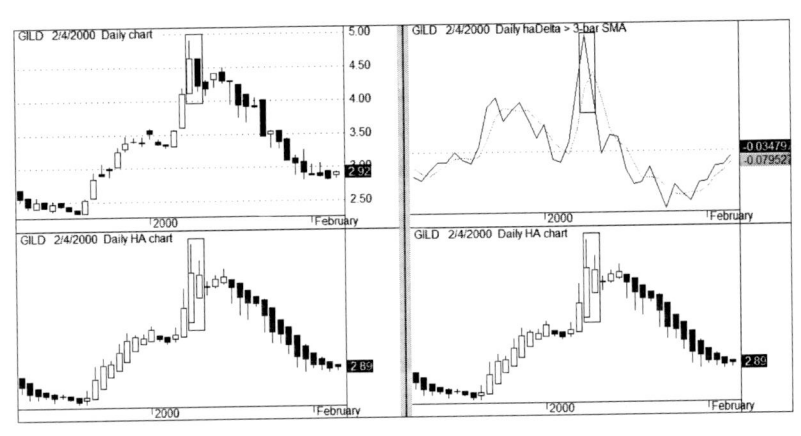

FIGURE 11.6: *Gilead Sciences Inc. (GILD) daily charts with Japanese and modified candles for December 1999 through February 2000. A candle pattern similar to a dark-cloud cover appears in January 2000. Some ignore it; some accept it. It is a reversal pattern when examined with heikin-ashi.*

Here is how the pattern translates with heikin-ashi:

- 1/10/00: A long white body appears in an uptrend. The heikin-ashi candle reinforces the idea of a strong uptrend. haDelta is high above its average. The picture is bullish.

- 1/11/00: A black candle opens exactly at the close of the previous day ($4.84). The end of the day completes the two-candle pattern as a formation *similar* to a bearish dark-cloud cover. The modified candle is still white but with a smaller body inside the previous one (a sign of trend slowdown). haDelta is below its average, indicating a negative bias. The odds favor a bearish reversal.

- 1/12/00: The day closes below the close of the previous day but not below the low of the pattern. The heikin-ashi chart shows a doji-like candle, indicating a trend reversal or even consolidation. Things are not yet clear, although the reversal is in the works with haDelta deep below the average. The decisive move comes when the modified candle turns black. Note that another confirmation of the downtrend comes when haDelta average enters the negative territory in January.

This is an example of a pattern different from textbook examples. Its behavior was one we would expect from a typical bearish cloud cover but with a short hesitation before the decisive move down.

Names, definitions, and expectations are all ignored by the heikin-ashi technique. Each price candle is analyzed as it appears on the chart. This is a huge advantage for everyone who runs away from subjectivity in trading.

Dark-cloud cover patterns with the second candle closing above the midpoint of the first body are *considered* weak. Figure 11.7 shows such dark-cloud cover for LDK Solar (LDK) in June 2009. Adding insult to injury, the second candle opens between the high and the open of the first candle. As a result, we now have a special situation that defies the rules of pattern classification. As always, we want to see how heikin-ashi translates it.

HEIKIN-ASHI, PIERCING LINE, AND DARK-CLOUD COVER

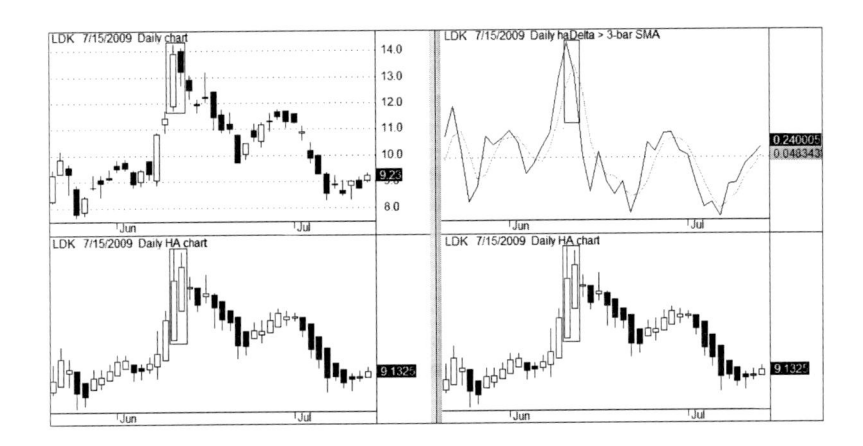

FIGURE 11.7: *LDK Solar Co. Ltd. (LDK) daily charts with Japanese and modified candles for mid-May through mid-July 2009.*

Here is how the pattern translates with heikin-ashi:

- 6/10/09: A long white body emerges in an uptrend. The heikin-ashi candle confirms the strong uptrend. haDelta is high above its average. The overall picture is positive.

- 6/11/09: A black candle opens above the previous close but below the high; it closes above the midpoint of the prior body. It looks like a weak reversal pattern. The modified candle is long and white with no lower shadow, a sign of continued uptrend despite the negative day. haDelta is slightly below the average; this is a warning of a top and pullback, nothing more. *Even if* the pattern looks weak, haDelta suggests a bearish signal worth considering.

At the risk of repetition, this is another example of a pattern (dark-cloud cover) subject to interpretations. From a heikin-ashi perspective, things are already clear: Definitions and subjective interpretations do not count. They are ignored. More important are the signals generated by haDelta and its short average on a candle-by-candle basis.

30-Second Summary

- The piercing line and the dark-cloud cover are two-candle patterns.

- They are generally *considered* stronger reversal formations.

- The strength of these patterns depends on where the second candle closes relative to the midpoint of the previous body.

- haDelta and its average are tools of great help for indicating at an early stage if the pattern shows negative or positive bias. Signals issued on the second day of the pattern prove to be reliable.

- The heikin-ashi chart does not act well as a warning signal. The reason is the one-bar delay between reversals on this chart and price chart.

- Heikin-ashi quantification helps translate patterns that do not follow definitions but still *look* like ones.

- Do not anticipate the strength of the trend since in many cases efforts will fail; heikin-ashi helps to anticipate and analyze the trend as it develops.

CHAPTER 12

HEIKIN-ASHI AND THE MORNING STAR

This chapter examines the morning star pattern on both traditional candlestick and heikin-ashi charts. The discussion focuses on how the morning star pattern can sometimes be ambiguous and how haDelta can help eliminate that ambiguity.

Facts

- The morning star pattern must appear in a downtrend.
- The pattern is a three-candle formation and considered a stronger reversal pattern.
- Candle 1 has a long black body.
- Candle 2 has a very short body with irrelevant color.
- If candle 2 is a doji, the pattern is a morning doji star.
- Candle 3 has a long and white body and closes well into the body of candle 1, above its midpoint.
- The body of candle 2 must be below the bodies of candles 1 and 3.

Questions to Consider

- How many bars should define a downtrend?
- What is a *long* or *short* body in this context? How is it measured?
- If candle 3 closes *well into* the body of candle 1, can "well into" also cover a close above the first body?
- Can other color combinations occur? What is the impact?

Figure 12.1 shows a daily chart of Ciena (CIEN) with a questionable morning star in February 2007. The pattern can be seen as uncertain for two reasons: The first candle is not long enough, and the third candle does not have a long body. Is this a handicap? Does the pattern have the strength to reverse the trend? How does heikin-ashi translate it?

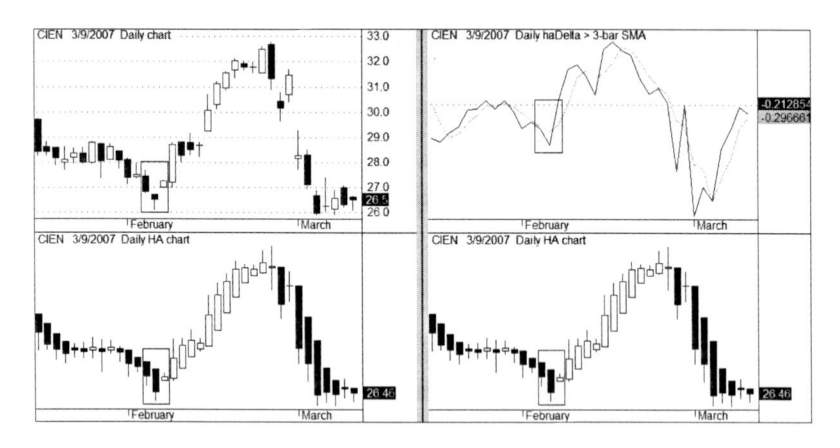

FIGURE 12.1: *Ciena Corporation (CIEN) daily charts with Japanese and modified candles for January through March 2007. A doubtful morning star is still followed by a strong trend. Does the candlestick pattern definition count? Think twice.*

As in all other cases we look at each day of the pattern:

- 2/5/07: A black candle appears in an established downtrend. The body may or may not be considered long, depending on subjective factors. The heikin-ashi candle points also to a negative trend. haDelta is below its average, and both are in negative territory.

- 2/6/07: We see a gap down day, with the emergence of a candle with a small black body. The modified candle is still black and long because of the gap that is incorporated into it. haDelta is below its average, and both are in negative territory.

- 2/7/07: We see a gap up day, with a small white candle that closes above the midpoint of the first candle body. The heikin-ashi chart shows a doji-like white candle, suggesting a trend change from bearish to bullish. haDelta is higher above the average. A timid uptrend is in place.

The subsequent strong trend ends with a superb bearish engulfing pattern. Fortunately, with heikin-ashi and haDelta, we could see positive reversal signals on the last day of the morning star before the price confirmed it.

The following example in Figure 12.2 illustrates an exception from the rules: There is no gap between the bodies of the second and third candles. As a result, pattern scanning software does not pick up this pattern, and a trading opportunity is missed.

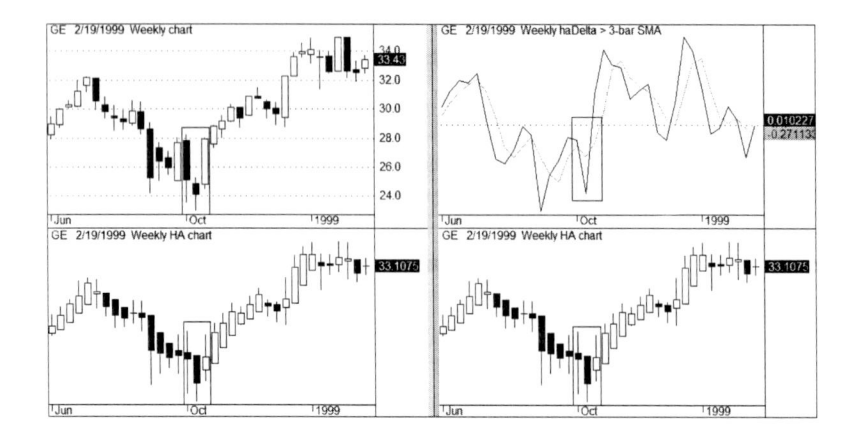

FIGURE 12.2: *General Electric Co. (GE) weekly charts with Japanese and modified candles for the second half of 1998. A strong trend follows after an unconventional morning star in October, although the third body overlaps slightly the body of the second candle.*

Here is the summary of events during the three weeks of this pattern:

- 10/2/98: A black long body appears in a clear downtrend. The heikin-ashi chart shows a possible bullish reversal. haDelta is above its average, but both are in negative territory. The picture is uncertain and not as bearish as the price chart would suggest.

- 10/9/98: A small black body emerges. The modified candle is still black and long with no upper shadow; this is a sign of a strong downtrend. haDelta is below the average, and both are in negative territory. The picture is negative.

- 10/16/98: The week opens inside the body of the previous week, but it closes well into the body the first candle (in fact, *above* the body of the first week). The heikin-ashi chart shows a white candle with both upper and lower shadows, suggesting a trend change from bearish to bullish. haDelta is higher above the average. An uptrend is in place.

The conclusion remains unchanged: A candlestick pattern *may look* valid but is rejected *if* the trader follows the rules. Despite this, the pattern works as initially thought. Heikin-ashi helps to look beyond candlestick patterns and filter out the noise; it offers advance indications about the upcoming trend.

Figure 12.3 shows another example that breaks one of the rules mentioned earlier in this chapter. The three-day pattern looks like a morning doji star, but with one element of doubt: The third candle closes *above* the first candle, *not inside it*. Can heikin-ashi help and offer indications about a reversal?

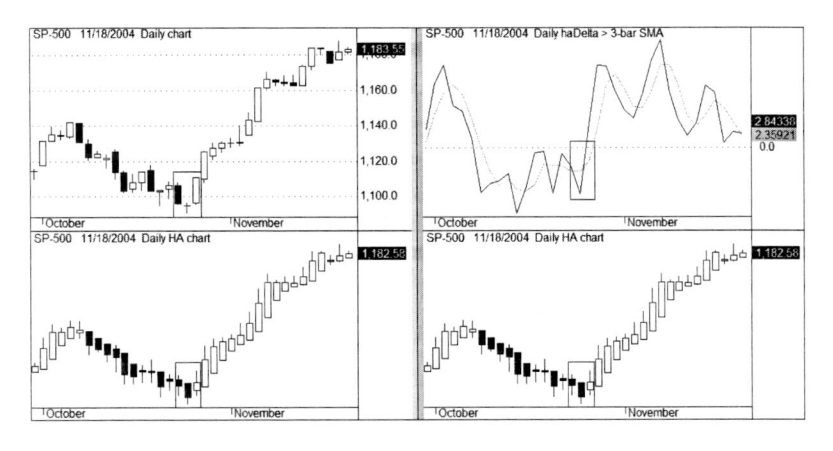

FIGURE 12.3: *S&P 500 Index (SP-500) daily charts with Japanese and modified candles for October and November 2004. A pattern similar to a morning doji star identifies the potential for an uptrend in November 2004.*

A step-by-step review of this pattern helps demonstrate how the two techniques apply in this case:

- 10/22/04: A long black body appears in a downtrend. The heikin-ashi chart shows possible slowdown/reversal with the emergence of a doji-like candle with upper and lower shadows. For the past few days, haDelta fluctuated above and below its average, both being in negative territory. The picture is uncertain with a negative bias. On the other hand, we notice a positive divergence between haDelta and the index, indicating better odds for a reversal.

- 10/25/04: A doji emerges. The modified candle is still black with no upper shadow; this is a sign of a strong downtrend. haDelta is below the average, and both are in negative territory. The picture remains negative.

- 10/26/04: We see a strong positive day. The heikin-ashi candle is white with upper and lower shadows, sending a message of a trend change from bearish to bullish. haDelta is higher above the average. An uptrend is in place.

The conclusion again may be boring, but it remains the same: Ignore pattern rules since they can be deceptive. Look at how the heikin-ashi technique (visual and quantifiable) takes apart each price formation and offers indications for immediate price action.

Figure 12.4 shows Broadcom Corp. (BRCM) on a daily chart with another out-of-the-box morning star in November 2008. The pattern follows all rules but fails to meet the condition that the third candle should have a long body.

HEIKIN-ASHI AND THE MORNING STAR

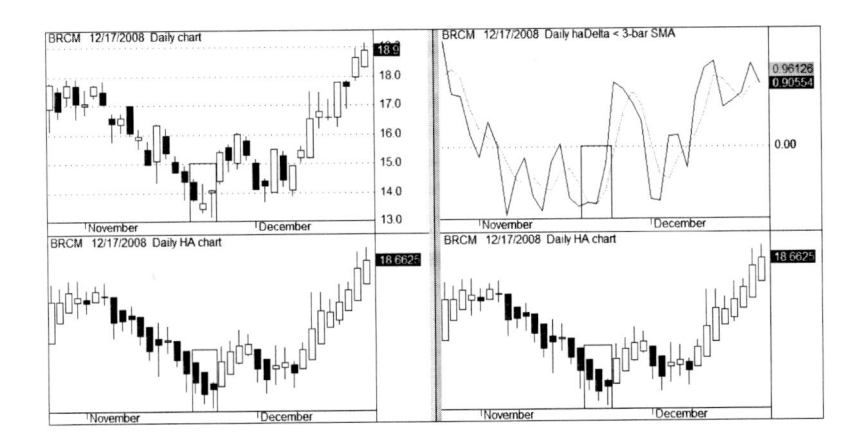

FIGURE 12.4: *Broadcom Corp. (BRCM) daily charts with Japanese and modified candles for November and December 2008. We see another debatable bullish morning star with a small-body as the last candle of the pattern.*

Here is how heikin-ashi works for this particular setting:

- 11/19/08: A black candle appears in an established downtrend. The heikin-ashi candle is black. haDelta turns up and is very close to its average, though below it. These are some positive signs, but no big indications for a reversal. The picture is still negative. A sharp eye will notice the positive divergence between haDelta and the price during the past two weeks; this is definitely something to watch closely.

- 11/20/08: A white candle similar to an inverted hammer brings hopes for a reversal. The modified candle is still black and long with no upper shadow; this indicates a strong downtrend. haDelta is now slightly above the average; both are still in negative territory. The picture is still negative with a weak sign for a bullish reversal.

- 11/21/08: This is a positive day with an open far from the previous close. The heikin-ashi chart shows still a black candle with upper and lower shadows and a body inside the previous one. It is a sign that the downtrend is getting tired and will possibly shift from bearish to bullish. haDelta is higher above the average. An uptrend may start here.

A very bullish day on November 24 brings a confirmation by changing the color on the heikin-ashi chart; we have a new uptrend.

This example highlights again the high level of subjectivity used to translate Japanese candlestick patterns. The only solution to improve pattern reading is to use a numerical method to remove the dangerous ambiguity allowed in many cases by the Japanese candlestick theory. Heikin-ashi is a great technique to eliminate this ambiguity.

30-Second Summary

- The morning star is a bullish three-candle pattern and is generally considered a stronger reversal formation.

- This pattern is considered weak or strong depending on where the third candle closes relative to the midpoint of the first body.

- The morning star is also considered weak if the third body is short.

- haDelta and its average are very helpful tools for indicating at an early stage if the pattern shows a positive bias.

- The heikin-ashi charting component does not act well as a warning signal due to its known one-bar delay.

- A best practice is to ignore pattern definitions and rules and to use the heikin-ashi technique in both formats to remove the "ifs."

- Quantification of the modified candles helps translate patterns that do not follow definitions but still *look* like valid patterns.

- Do not anticipate the strength of the trend as in many cases efforts will fail; heikin-ashi helps anticipate and analyze the trend as it develops.

CHAPTER 13

HEIKIN-ASHI AND THE EVENING STAR

This chapter discusses the three-candle evening star pattern on both traditional candlestick and heikin-ashi charts. Particular attention is focused on situations in which the third candle violates evening star rule definitions and how heikin-ashi can see through "pseudo" evening star patterns to validate trend bias.

Facts

- The evening star pattern must appear in an uptrend.
- The pattern is a three-candle formation and considered a stronger reversal pattern.
- Candle 1 has a long white body.
- Candle 2 has a very short body with irrelevant color.
- If candle 2 is a doji, the pattern is an evening doji star.
- Candle 3 has a long and black body and closes well into the body of candle 1, below its midpoint.
- The body of candle 2 must be above the bodies of candles 1 and 3.

Questions to Consider

- How many bars should define an uptrend?
- What is a *long* or *short* body in this context? How is it measured?
- If candle 3 closes *well into* the body of candle 1, can "well into" also cover a close below the first body?
- Can other color combinations occur? What is the impact?

Figure 13.1 shows a daily chart of World Platinum Index (XPLT) with a questionable evening star in December 2004. It follows definition rules but fails having a third candle with a long body closing well into the body of the first day, below its midpoint. Moreover, the second day is also subject to discussion. Is this a handicap? Obviously this formation is a variation of a classic strong reversal pattern. Will heikin-ashi show earlier signs of a reversal? Does the weak pattern have the strength to reverse the trend?

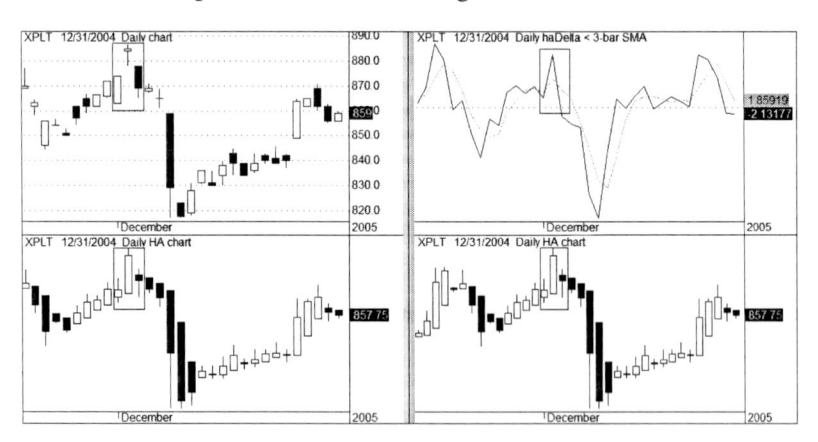

FIGURE 13.1: *World Platinum Index (XPLT) daily charts with Japanese and modified candles for November and December 2004. A strong trend follows this evening star pattern, although the third candle lacks energy and closes above the midpoint of the first candle body.*

HEIKIN-ASHI AND THE EVENING STAR

As in all other cases we look at each day of the pattern and see what heikin-ashi shows:

- 12/1/04: A long white body appears in an uptrend. The heikin-ashi candle is part of an uptrend, but it points to a trend slowdown with the emergence of a small body inside the previous one. In addition, the modified candle has upper and lower shadows. haDelta is slightly below its average, and both are in positive territory.

- 12/2/04: The day opens with a massive gap up from the previous close and finally takes the shape of a hanging man. The modified candle is white and very long because of the gap that is hidden inside it. haDelta is higher above its average.

- 12/3/04: A black candle closes above the midpoint of the first candle body (a weak evening star pattern). The heikin-ashi chart shows a black candle with upper and lower shadows, suggesting a trend change from bullish to bearish. haDelta is now lower below the average. All signs point to a top and reversal.

- The next four days show that although the pattern was considered arguable due to its construction, the price action was strong. Even in a weak format, the pattern worked and could be monitored successfully with a heikin-ashi chart and haDelta.

Figure 13.2 shows a pattern that *resembles* an evening star in November 2005 on the Genzyme (GENZ) weekly chart. It looks like an evening star, but it is not because the gap between the second and third body is missing. In addition, the third candle closes far above the midpoint of the first body. Are these variations sufficient to ignore the pattern? Are they a handicap? Does the altered pattern have the strength to reverse the trend? How will heikin-ashi see through this pseudo pattern?

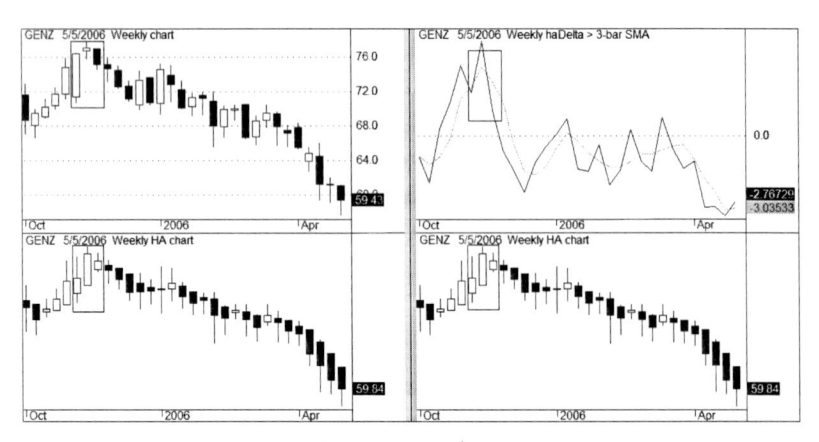

FIGURE 13.2: *Genzyme Corp. (GENZ) weekly charts with Japanese and modified candles for October 2005 through April 2006. Although the evening star is questionable, the pattern in November 2005 is strong enough to trigger a rollover.*

Here is how heikin-ashi helps evaluate the pattern:

- 11/11/05: A long white body appears in an uptrend. The heikin-ashi candle remains white but indicates a possible reversal/slowdown with the emergence of upper and lower shadows. Even in this bullish setup, haDelta is below its average.

- 11/18/05: A candle with a small black body with upper and lower shadows emerges. Up to this point, two thirds of a possible evening star pattern have developed. The modified candle is white and long, pointing to a continuation of the uptrend. haDelta is higher above its average.

- 11/25/05: The week opens inside the body of the previous candle, violating the evening star rule definition. The week closes above the midpoint of the first body, indicating a weak pattern. The heikin-ashi candle indicates a slowdown with a body inside the previous body. haDelta is lower below the average. These are signs of a top and reversal.

- The next weeks show that although the pattern was a variation of an evening star, the trend favored the negative expectations with a loss of over $20. The pseudo pattern, even in its weak format, worked as an evening star and could be monitored successfully with heikin-ashi and haDelta (as its moving average remained negative during the downtrend).

Figure 13.3 shows an evening doji star for Newmont Mining (NEM) in August 2005. The third candle completes a weak pattern, with the close above the midpoint of the body. The purists may also argue that the doji is invalid because the close is different from the open. However, we are allowed to be flexible, so we consider the tiny body a doji.

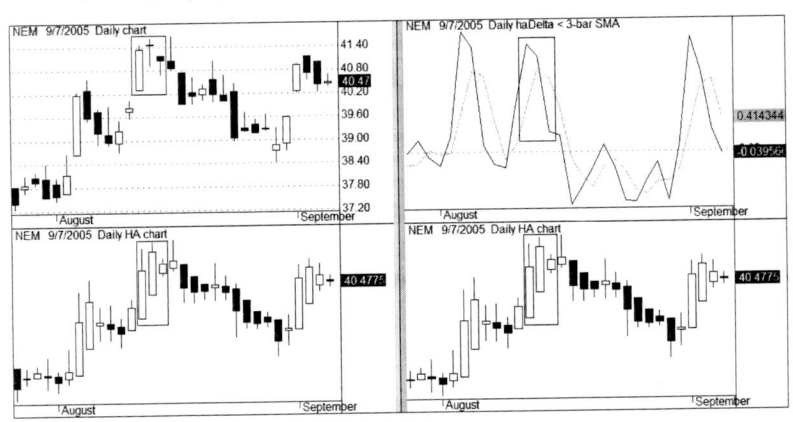

FIGURE 13.3: *Newmont Mining Corp. (NEM) daily charts with Japanese and modified candles for August 2005. A weak evening doji star pattern is strong enough to start a downtrend.*

Here is how heikin-ashi can help us evaluate the evening doji star in this example:

- 8/11/05: A long white body appears in a young uptrend. The heikin-ashi chart shows an uptrend. haDelta is above its average. There are no doubts about the positive trend.

- 8/12/05: We see the possible rise of a doji (see remarks above). The modified candle is white and long, indicating an uptrend. haDelta is still above its average.

- 8/15/05: We see a black candle with a close well above the midpoint of the first body (weak evening doji star). The heikin-ashi candle shows a slowdown (body inside body and small shadows) but still an uptrend (white candle). haDelta is below the average. These are signs of a tired uptrend in preparation for a reversal.

In this case, the pseudo pattern worked as an evening star and could be monitored successfully using heikin-ashi and haDelta. Note that the average remained negative during the downtrend.

Figure 13.4 shows New Germany Fund Inc. (GF) with a three-candle pattern that looks *like* an evening doji star, but may not be. Why the doubt? Generally, the first and third candles are white and black, respectively. Rules are quite specific in this regard, leaving no room for any other combination. In our case, we got a black/black pair. Is this still seen as an evening star? Can heikin-ashi ignore the pattern and look at it from a pragmatic and objective perspective?

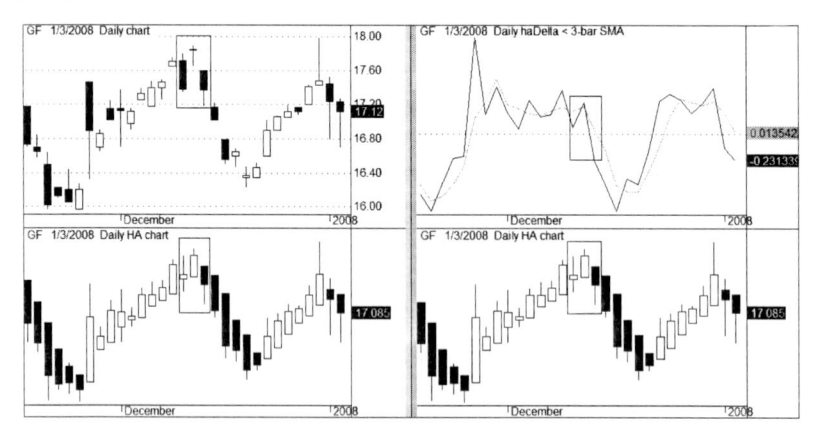

FIGURE 13.4: *New Germany Fund Inc. (GF) daily charts with Japanese and modified candles for late November 2007 through early January 2008. Is the pattern developed in December 2007 still a reversal formation?*

- 12/11/07: A long black body appears in an established uptrend. At this point, the last two candles are a bearish engulfing pattern. The heikin-ashi chart shows a possible reversal due to the emergence of a small body with upper and lower shadows. haDelta is below its average. Negative bias is building up.

- 12/12/07: A doji (or something similar to one) emerges. The modified candle is longer with no lower shadow. haDelta crosses above its average. We see some positive bias.

- 12/13/07: We see a black candle with a close well below the midpoint of the first body. The heikin-ashi candle shows a decisive trend reversal. haDelta is below the average. We again see negative bias.

Even with this black/black color combination, the pattern acted as a valid evening doji star. In this example, heikin-ashi and haDelta have been ambiguous.

The last example is another pseudo evening star as shown in Figure 13.5. Comparing it with the rules, there are three problems with this pattern:

1. Candle 2 does not have a small body.

2. Candle 3 is neither long nor black.

3. Candle 3 does not close below the midpoint of the body of candle 1.

However, heikin-ashi offers a solution as it does not process candlestick patterns, but rather only individual candles.

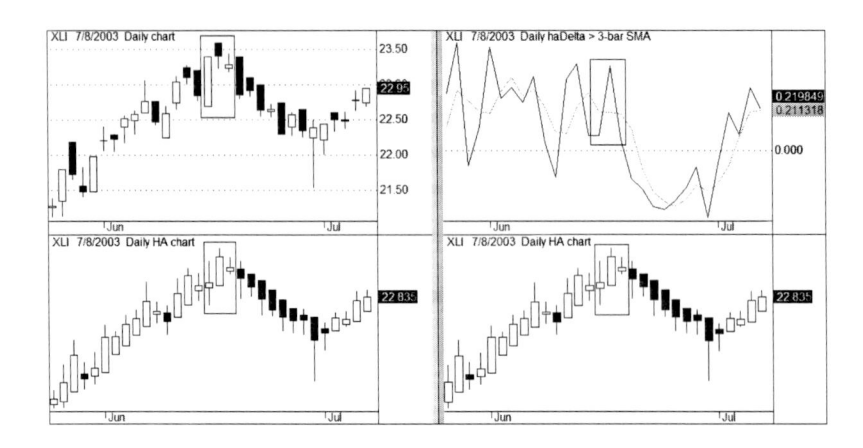

FIGURE 13.5: *Industrial Select Sector SPDR ETF (XLI) daily charts with Japanese and modified candles for May through July 2003. An unorthodox three-candle pattern emerges in June 2003.*

Here is how heikin-ashi translates the individual candles in this example:

- 6/16/03: A long white body appears in an established uptrend. The heikin-ashi chart shows a possible reversal due to the emergence of a second small body with upper and lower shadows. haDelta is below its average. We see some negative bias.

- 6/17/03: A black candle with a significant body emerges. The modified candle is white and longer with no lower shadow, indicating an uptrend. haDelta is above its average. Heikin-ashi offers a positive bias.

- 6/18/03: The third candle of the pattern emerges as a small body with shadows. It is far from closing well into the body of the first candle. The heikin-ashi candle again shows a typical trend reversal candle. haDelta is below the average. We again see negative bias.

Although the three-candle pattern was far from being a classic bearish evening star, it acted like a reversal pattern. Heikin-ashi and haDelta were sending conflicting signals during the first two days, but haDelta gave a signal for bearish trend reversal at the end of the third day.

30-Second Summary

- The evening star is a bearish three-candle pattern and is generally considered a stronger reversal formation.

- This pattern is considered weak or strong depending on where the third candle closes relative to the midpoint of the first body.

- It is also considered weak if the third body is short.

- The examples discussed in this chapter show that subjectivity is very common in judging the evening star pattern. A best practice is to ignore definitions and rules and use the heikin-ashi technique in both formats to remove the "ifs."

- haDelta and its average are very helpful tools for indicating at an early stage if the pattern shows a negative bias.

- The heikin-ashi charting component does not act well as a warning signal due to its known one-bar delay.

- Quantification helps translate patterns that do not follow definitions, but still *look* like valid patterns.

- Do not anticipate the strength of the trend as in many cases efforts will fail; heikin-ashi helps anticipate and analyze the trend as it develops.

CHAPTER 14

HEIKIN-ASHI AND HAMMERS

This chapter discusses single-candle patterns such as the hammer and its variations—hanging man, inverted hammer, and shooting star—on both traditional candlestick and heikin-ashi charts. They are all *considered* reversal patterns and look like hammers. Existent trends, body size-to-shadows ratio, and gaps are elements taken into account in defining and translating hammer patterns.

For each pattern, we outline basic rules and discuss several examples. The discussion will touch upon basic and more nuanced features of hammer patterns. The objective, as with any other candlestick pattern, is to see how the heikin-ashi technique translates these patterns.

Hammer

Facts

- The pattern must appear in a downtrend.
- The hammer pattern covers a single candle and is considered a reversal pattern.

- The candle has a small body at the upper end of the range.
- The pattern has a long lower shadow with a very small or no upper shadow.
- The length of the lower shadow should be two or three times the height of the body.
- Candle color is irrelevant.

Questions to Consider

- How many bars should define a downtrend?
- What is a *small* upper shadow in this context? How is it measured?
- Can we accept a candle with no upper shadow, or even with a very small shadow, as a hammer pattern?
- Does a very small upper shadow make the difference?
- Is the pattern really a hammer or takuri line? Is the difference *really* important for the trader?
- Is the color really irrelevant? Does a white hammer make a difference?
- Is the size of the body (small) really so important?
- What happens when the hammer's body overlaps the previous body?
- Is a gap from the prior candle considered an advantage?

Figure 14.1 shows a daily chart of Akamai Technologies (AKAM) with a hammer emerging in the downtrend between mid-December 2007 and the beginning of January 2008. This pattern follows all the basic rules, but it is not followed by a reversal as expected. Readers may argue here that the next day did not offer a reversal confirmation. This is true. However, the main objective remains to see whether heikin-ashi may have helped to warn about a reversal from bearish to bullish.

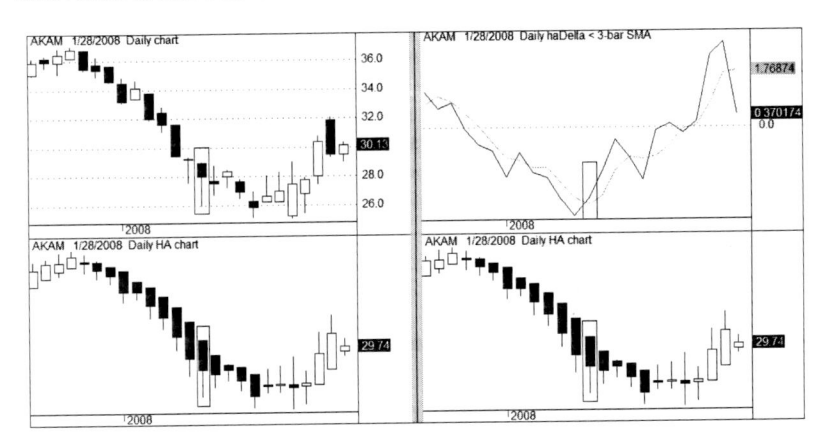

FIGURE 14.1: *Akamai Technologies (AKAM) daily charts with Japanese and modified candles for December 2007 through January 2008, showing a hammer in a downtrend.*

The following activity confirms the downtrend:

- 1/10/08: A hammer emerges in a strong downtrend. The corresponding modified candle offers no hint about a slowdown or reversal. Fortunately, as in many other cases, haDelta being above the short average offers a bullish indication.

- The downtrend continues on the following days, but the haDelta average makes a low then turns up. We also notice a positive divergence of haDelta with the price.

This example shows the positive signs brought about by using modified candles, in particular haDelta and its average. Although the hammer was not confirmed the following day and the downtrend continued, haDelta offered positive indications about the upcoming trend reversal at $26.

Figure 14.2 shows another example of a hammer in a downtrend with a more traditional interpretation from the perspective of Japanese candlestick theory. In fact, this hammer is a takuri with a lower shadow of over three times the height of its body.

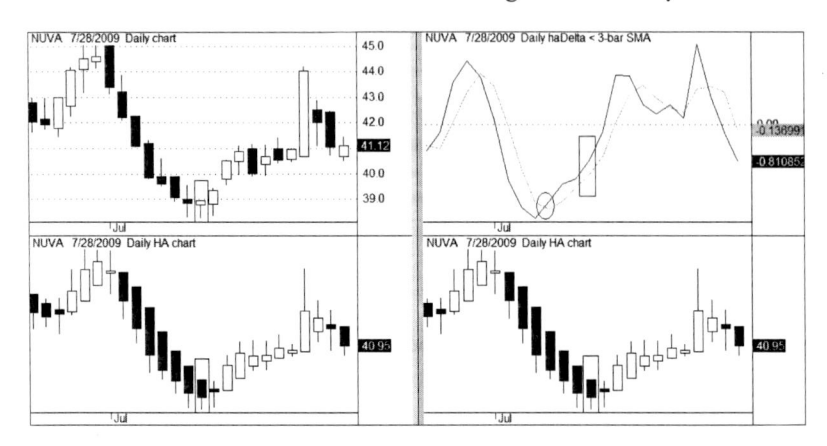

FIGURE 14.2: *NuVasive Inc. (NUVA) daily charts with Japanese and modified candles for June through July 2009. A takuri line emerges in a downtrend in mid-July. haDelta already warned about the trend reversal.*

Here is how the action can be interpreted through heikin-ashi:

- 7/13/09: A takuri appears in a strong downtrend. The corresponding heikin-ashi candle offers a very weak indication for a slowdown (smaller body than the previous day). haDelta again comes to the rescue, being above its average since July 8. Coincidence or not, the downtrend recorded an inverted hammer with a message of a possible trend reversal on July 8. It has not been confirmed the next day, but haDelta was above its short average.

- 7/14/09: The modified candle is typical for a trend reversal (small body with long upper and lower shadows). haDelta is higher above its average. We see the start of an uptrend.

This example in Figure 14.2 shows two candle patterns that, in theory, indicate a message of trend change. haDelta and its position relative to the average helps prepare in advance for the change. Note the timid positive signal from the inverted hammer and a stronger one later for the takuri. The positive divergence between haDelta and price improves odds for an end to the existing downtrend. We benefit again by using the quantification of heikin-ashi candles.

Figure 14.3 shows the daily price of Akamai Technologies (AKAM) with a candle that resembles a hammer because of the higher shadow; however, the shadow is not small as required by the rules. In fact, *small* and *long* remain vague concepts unresolved by the definitions. In other words, the chart is showing a hammer-like candle (that is not necessarily recognized as a valid hammer candle) has emerged in a downtrend. Can heikin-ashi help again?

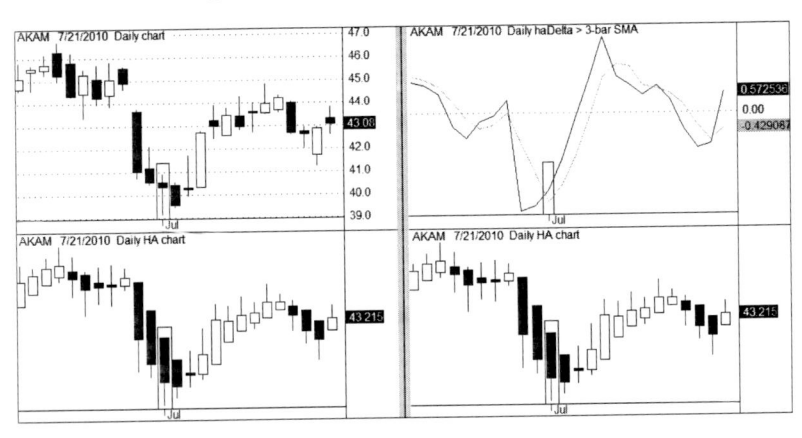

FIGURE 14.3: *Akamai Technologies (AKAM) daily charts with Japanese and modified candles for June and July 2010. Can heikin-ashi help with the hammer-like pattern in the beginning of July 2010?*

Using heikin-ashi, we can interpret the candles as follows:

- 7/1/10: A candle *similar* to a hammer emerges in a strong downtrend. The corresponding modified candle offers no indication of a slowdown or reversal. Fortunately, haDelta is already above the average (reversal indication) and suggests an upward bias for the price.

This example shows the behavior of a hammer-like candle in a downtrend. Although it is not a hammer by orthodox candlestick rules, it behaves like one and heikin-ashi helps prepare *in advance* for the reversal.

Hanging Man

Facts

- The hanging man pattern must appear in an uptrend.
- The pattern contains a single candle and is considered a reversal pattern.
- The candle has a small body at the upper end of the range.
- The pattern has a long lower shadow with a very small or no upper shadow.
- Candle color is irrelevant.

Questions to Consider

- How many bars should define an uptrend?
- What is a *small* upper shadow in this context? How is it measured?

- Can we accept a candle with no upper shadow, or with even a very small upper wick, as a hanging man pattern?
- Does a very small upper shadow make the difference?
- Is the color really irrelevant? Does a black body make a difference?
- Is size of the body (small) really so important?
- What happens when the hanging man's body overlaps the previous body?
- Is a gap from the prior candle considered an advantage?

Figure 14.4 shows a hanging man in an uptrend during October 2009 for Citigroup (C). The immediate thought is to bet on a reversal, especially looking at the gap up.

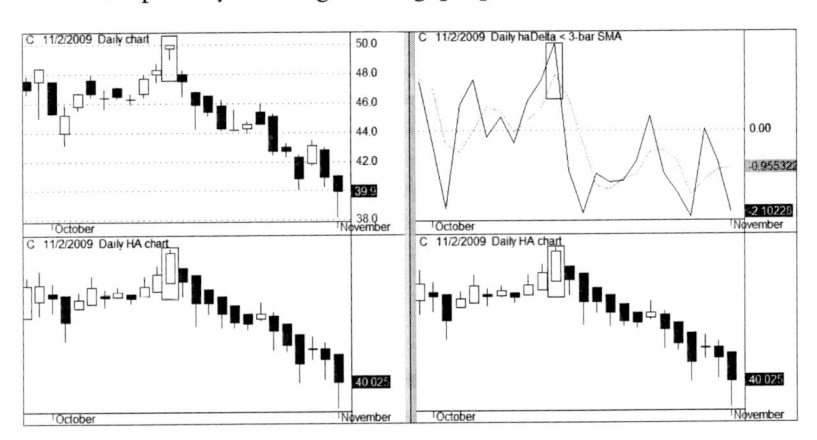

FIGURE 14.4: *Citigroup Inc. (C) daily charts with Japanese and modified candles for October 2009. A hanging man points to a trend reversal.*

Here is how Japanese and heikin-ashi candles perform in this context:

- 10/14/09: A hanging man appears in an uptrend. The heikin-ashi chart shows a long white candle with no sign of slowdown. Note that gaps are not visible on the heikin-ashi charts since they are hidden inside the modified candle. Our last hope for a reversal sign lies with haDelta. Even this indicator looks very bullish, so we must wait for the next day's action.

- 10/15/09: The day opens with a gap down and closes with a black candle. This is a bearish sign by conventional wisdom. The modified candle is black with no upper shadow (trend reversal). haDelta moves below its average. The picture is bearish and points to a trend reversal.

In this case, the hanging man acts as expected. Heikin-ashi does not bring advance signals for this example; rather, it confirms the next day.

Figure 14.5 displays a hanging man emerging in a shorter uptrend on a daily chart for Under Armour Inc. (UA) in July 2010.

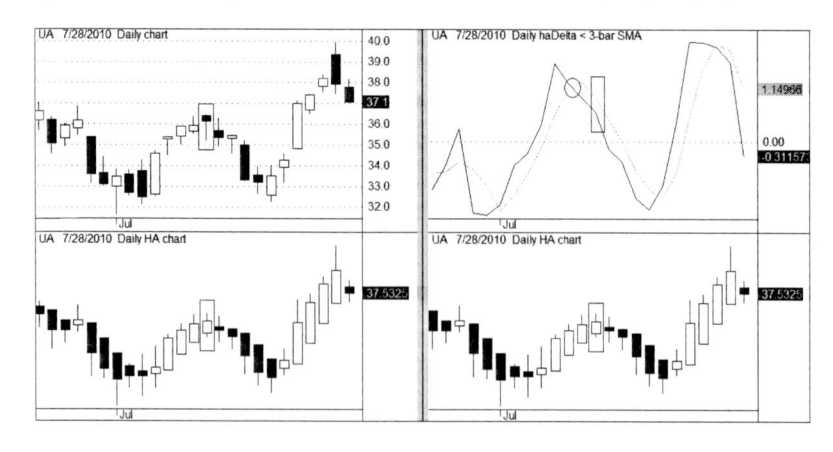

FIGURE 14.5: *Under Armour Inc. (UA) daily charts with Japanese and modified candles for July 2010. A hanging man emerges mid-month in a shorter uptrend.*

Can we see earlier signs for a reversal? Here is how the candlestick and heikin-ashi charts play out in this example:

- 7/13/10: A valid hanging man appears in a shorter uptrend. The modified candle is still white but shows a possible slowdown/reversal because of its two shadows. The indication is weak (the body is not small and the shadows are short) but still worth taking into account. Hope is not lost, however, because haDelta moved below the average one day *before* the emergence of the hanging man. The odds favor a slowdown/reversal.

- 7/14/10: The day opens with a gap down from the previous close and displays a black candle, which is a bearish sign. The modified candle is small with long upper and lower shadows, indicating possible trend reversal. haDelta is lower below the average. The sentiment changed to bearish.

Neither Japanese candlestick theory nor heikin-ashi charting is infallible. However, an indication one bar ahead of the pack, as demonstrated in this example, is worth the attention and money. It is better to use quantifiable and more objective ways to filter out the noise and get earlier indications about reversals and continuations.

The heikin-ashi technique helps either when used with candlestick patterns or by itself on a chart. Although the hanging man in this example worked as anticipated, heikin-ashi offered a negative signal one day *before* price action turned bearish on the candlestick chart.

Inverted Hammer

Facts

- The inverted hammer pattern must appear in a downtrend.

- The pattern contains a single candle and is considered a reversal pattern.
- The candle has a small body at the lower end of the range.
- The candle has a long upper shadow with a very small or no lower shadow.
- Candle color is irrelevant.

Questions to Consider

- How many bars should define a downtrend?
- What is a *small/long* shadow in this context? How is it measured?
- Should we define the inverted hammer as a two-pattern candle, requiring a long black candle to precede the small body?
- Can we accept a candle with no lower shadow, or even with a very small lower shadow, as an inverted hammer pattern?
- Does a very small lower shadow make the difference?
- Is the size of the body (small) really so important?
- What happens when the inverted hammer's body overlaps the previous body?
- Is a gap from the prior candle considered an advantage?

Figure 14.6 exhibits an inverted hammer on a daily chart for Randgold Resources (GOLD) at the end of July 2004.

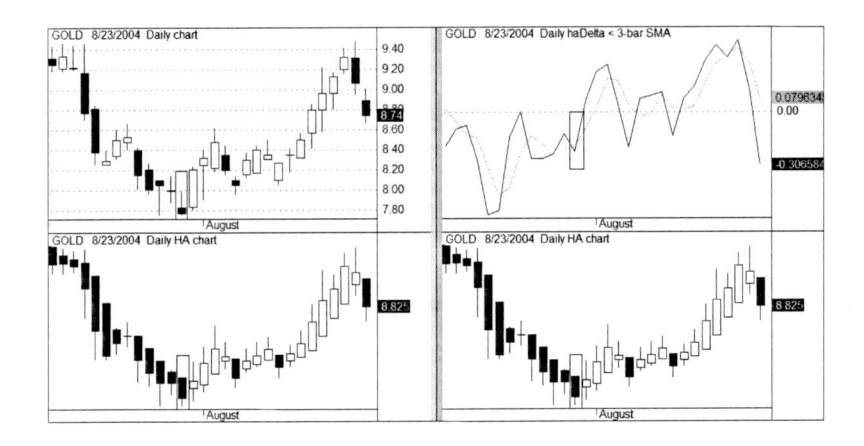

FIGURE 14.6: *Randgold Resources Ltd. (GOLD) daily charts with Japanese and modified candles for July and August 2004. The inverted hammer in late July 2004 works as expected.*

- 7/29/04: An inverted hammer emerges in a downtrend. The heikin-ashi chart shows a black candle with no upper shadow (downtrend). haDelta is below its average, and both are in negative territory. The picture is bearish.

- 7/30/04: The end of the day confirms the reversal character of the inverted hammer. The modified candle is white with a small body but with long upper and lower shadows, indicating a possible trend reversal. haDelta is higher above its average. The bias has changed from bearish to bullish.

The application of heikin-ashi candles and haDelta in this case does not lead to radical findings, with one exception for the sharper eye: A positive divergence developed between haDelta (its average) and the price during the last ten days of July.

In Figure 14.7, an inverted hammer emerges in early February 2004 on a daily chart for Citigroup (C). The example is worth discussing because of the way modified candles quantification comes into the picture.

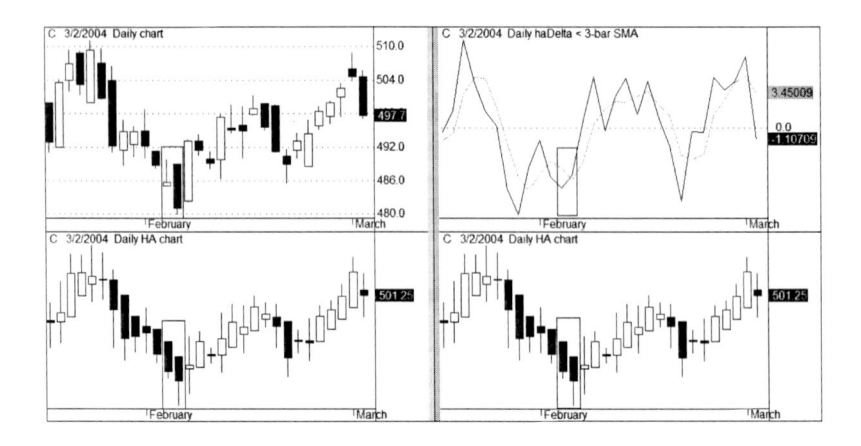

FIGURE 14.7: *Citigroup Inc. (C) daily charts with Japanese and modified candles for January and February 2004. The inverted hammer in early February is followed by a bearish day, but heikin-ashi offers a hint at what will happen.*

- 2/4/04: An inverted hammer appears in a downtrend. The corresponding heikin-ashi candle is black with no upper shadow (downtrend). haDelta is below the average, and both are in negative territory. The picture is bearish.

- 2/5/04: A long black candle emerges. The modified candle is still black with no upper shadow; there is no indication of a possible reversal. haDelta is slightly above its average. Add the positive divergence with the price since the end of January, and you get a positive bias for a trend reversal ahead.

- 2/6/04: This is a very bullish day. The heikin-ashi chart shows a white reversal candle. haDelta is now higher above its average. The positive indications of the previous day are now confirmed.

In this case, the inverted hammer has not been confirmed on the following day (February 5); this is a sign of a very bearish performance. Regardless, the use of heikin-ashi quantification brought positive signals and prepared the trader to take smaller long positions. Advantage heikin-ashi!

Shooting Star

Facts

- The shooting star pattern must appear in an uptrend.
- The pattern contains a single candle and is considered a reversal pattern.
- The candle has a small body at the lower end of the range.
- The candle has a long upper shadow with a very small or no lower shadow.
- The length of the higher shadow should be at least two times the height of the body.
- Candle color is irrelevant.

Questions to Consider

- How many bars should define an uptrend?
- What is a *small/long* shadow in this context? How is it measured?
- Can shooting stars be two-candle patterns?
- Can we accept a candle with no lower shadow, or even with a very small lower shadow, as a shooting star pattern?
- Does a very small lower shadow make the difference?
- Is the ratio of upper shadow to body height important?

- Is the size of the body (small) really so important?
- What happens when the shooting star's body overlaps the previous body?
- Is a gap from the prior candle considered an advantage?

Figure 14.8 shows a daily chart of Finish Line (FINL) with a perfect shooting star in the beginning of January 2010.

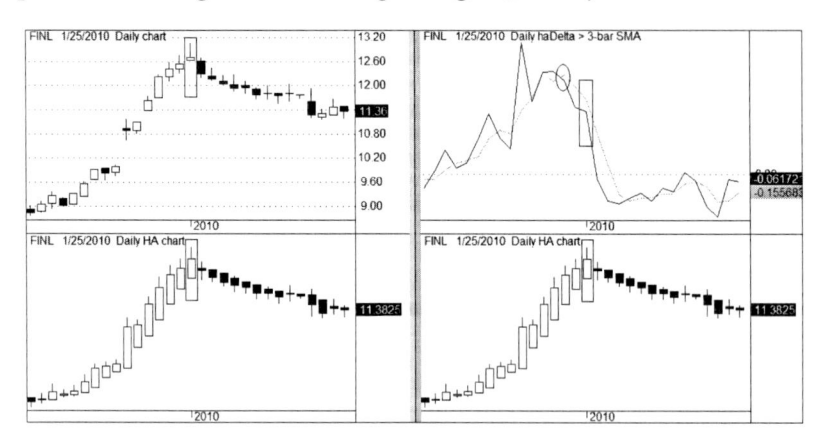

FIGURE 14.8: *Finish Line Inc. (FINL) daily charts with Japanese and modified candles for December 2009 and January 2010. A shooting star emerges in an uptrend in early January. The heikin-ashi technique performs well again, giving early reversal signals.*

Let us review the events on and around the date when the pattern occurred:

- 1/4/10: A shooting star emerges in a long uptrend. The heikin-ashi chart shows an uptrend, too. However, haDelta displays a totally different picture: It is below its average and both have negative slopes. These are signs that the uptrend will reverse soon.

- 1/5/10: This turns out to be a negative day. The modified candle points to a trend reversal. haDelta is deeper below its average.

- 1/6/10: We see another negative day. The heikin-ashi candle is black with a lower shadow, suggesting a trend change from bullish to bearish. haDelta is deeper below the average, which is ready to cross into negative territory.

This example shows once again that the combination of heikin-ashi charting and haDelta helps detect weakness *before* trend reversals.

Figure 14.9 illustrates two shooting stars in May and June 2002, respectively, for Arch Coal (ACI). The first pattern develops after a *short* uptrend. This may be a deviation from the rules. The second shooting star looks fine, as it has an upper shadow over three times the size of the body ($0.52 vs. $0.17). We again ignore classifications and rules and proceed with an analysis of the two patterns using heikin-ashi. Are the candles really shooting stars or are they some other candlestick specimen?

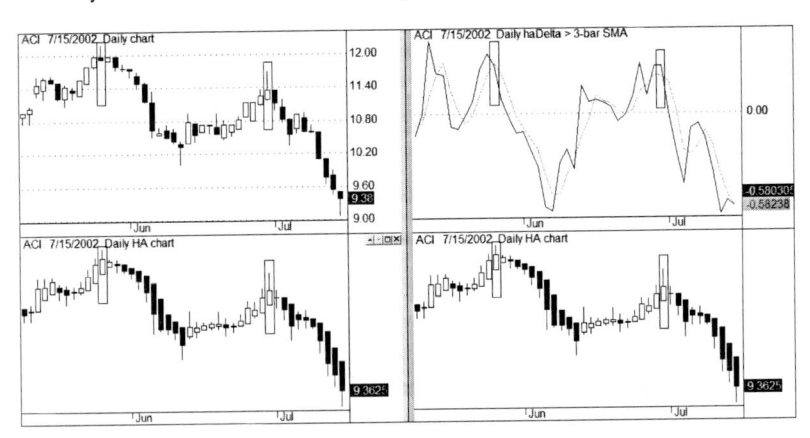

FIGURE 14.9: *Arch Coal Inc. (ACI) daily charts with Japanese and modified candles for May through June 2002. Two candlestick patterns believed to be shooting stars confirm expected bearish behavior.*

A look at the first shooting star pattern reveals the following:

- 5/28/02: A shooting star emerges in a short uptrend. The heikin-ashi candle shows an uptrend, too. haDelta turns below its average, and both are positive. The overall bullish bias has some cracks.

- 5/29/02: The day is modest in terms of price action, with an open below the previous close and a close above it. The heikin-ashi candle is white, with a small body inside the previous one (a sign of a slowdown, at least). haDelta is deeper below its average and offers a bearish sign.

- 5/30/02: This is a negative day from tip to toe. The heikin-ashi chart displays a reversal candle. haDelta is still below the short average. All signs point to a clear bearish message.

Although the uptrend preceding this shooting star pattern was short, the result was a downtrend from over $12.00 to almost $10.00. On the day of the shooting star, haDelta worked well and offered a bearish indication.

We move now to the second shooting star in June. Will heikin-ashi act as an early warning signal again? Heikin-ashi helps us assess the candles:

- 6/28/02: A shooting star emerges in an uptrend. The heikin-ashi chart shows an uptrend. haDelta is still above its average. The overall picture remains positive.

- 7/1/02: A black candle marks the second candle of a bearish engulfing pattern, giving us further reason to believe that a reversal is imminent. The heikin-ashi candle is a typical doji-like candle, indicating a reversal. haDelta is deeper below its average. The bias is negative.

- 7/2/02: We see a negative day. The modified candle confirms the start of the expected downtrend. haDelta is below the short average, and both are negative. We have a clear bearish message.

In this particular example, we are not sure whether the shooting star or the bearish engulfing pattern triggered the reversal. One thing is certain and fast: Heikin-ashi candles, together with haDelta, provide early warning signs of a trend change.

The NVIDIA (NVDA) chart in Figure 14.10 illustrates a shooting star, this time as a continuation candle. How does heikin-ashi work here?

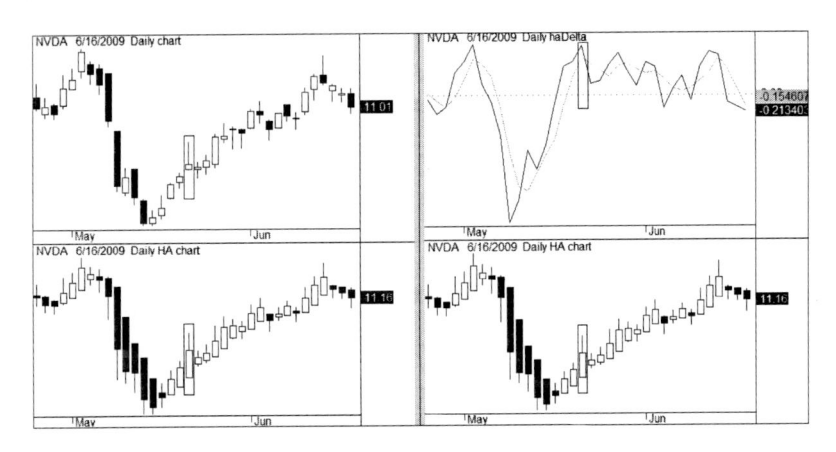

FIGURE 14.10: *NVIDIA Corp. (NVDA) daily charts with Japanese and modified candles for May and June 2009. The shooting star in mid-May works fine as a continuation candle.*

- 5/20/09: A shooting star emerges after a short consolidation in an uptrend. Japanese candlestick theory says that the gap from the previous close *suggests* a continuation of the uptrend and not a reversal as is normally expected with a shooting star. The heikin-ashi chart shows a stronger uptrend. haDelta is above its average, and both are positive. The picture is bullish.

- 5/21/09: This is an undecided day. The modified candle is white, has a small body with both shadows, and is inside the previous body (all signs of a slowdown). haDelta turns down below its average. This is a bearish sign but also a move toward a consolidation. It is *not* a sign of advance.

- 5/22/09: We see another positive day. The heikin-ashi candle is white with small shadows, a sign of consolidation. haDelta is still below the average. We see confusing messages.
- 5/26/09: A very bullish candle emerges. The modified candle is white with no lower shadow (uptrend). An uptrend follows.

One interesting element to observe and take into account every time is the polarity of the moving average. We know that haDelta is, in many cases, very rough or nervous. However, its short average improves the odds that a winning trend will continue.

A similar example is illustrated in Figure 14.11 for AmerisourceBergen (ABC). The price candle that emerges on December 16, 2009 can be translated either as a shooting star or a gravestone doji. The relaxed rules of each pattern allows for this freedom of judgement. For the purpose of this analysis, we interpret the candle as a shooting star. It gaps up, and although the black candle that follows brings bearish vibes, the uptrend continues. Note that the uptrend that ends in early February has several modified black candles that point to pullbacks. haDelta and its average are accurate in showing both trends and pullbacks.

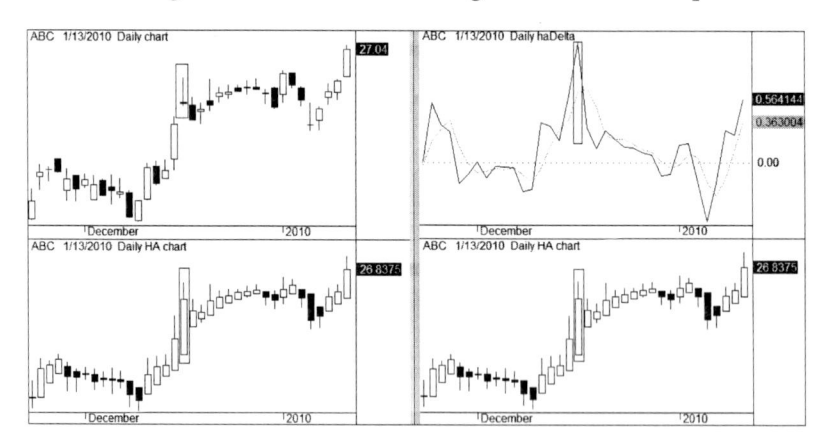

FIGURE 14.11: *AmerisourceBergen Corp. (ABC) daily charts with Japanese and modified candles for November 2009 through early January 2010. A (questionable) shooting star emerges in mid-December, acting as a continuation pattern.*

Here is how heikin-ashi helps confirm the uptrend:

- 12/16/09: A shooting star emerges in an uptrend. Japanese candlestick theory says that the gap from the prior close *suggests* a continuation of the trend and not a reversal as is normally expected from a shooting star. The heikin-ashi chart shows a stronger uptrend with haDelta above its average, and both are above zero. The picture has a positive bias.

- 12/17/09: We see a negative day. The modified candle is white, has a small body with upper shadow, and is inside the previous body (signs of a slowdown). Anything may follow. haDelta turns below its average. This is a bearish sign but also a move toward a consolidation. It is *not* a sign of advance.

- 12/18/09: This is a non-event day. The heikin-ashi chart shows another white candle with small shadows as sign of slowdown/consolidation. haDelta is still below the average. We receive confusing messages.

Although haDelta remains below its average for several days, the heikin-ashi candles are white and confirm the uptrend. The fact that the haDelta average remains positive adds to the confirmation of the uptrend following the gapping shooting star.

30-Second Summary

- The hammer family consists of one-candle patterns which are generally considered reversal formations.

- haDelta and its short average are very helpful tools for identifying reversal signs at an early stage.

- The heikin-ashi chart does not always act as a warning signal because the well-known one-bar delay.

- Heikin-ashi quantification helps translate patterns that do not comply with definitions but still *look* like valid patterns.

CHAPTER 15

HEIKIN-ASHI AND DOJI

In this chapter we discuss doji, a single-candle pattern that appears very frequently in any time frame and with any financial instrument. From the perspective of Japanese candlestick theory, a doji is a moment of reflection: What will price do next? Rise, fall, or wait? We will analyze a common doji and some of its variations: long-legged doji, dragonfly, and gravestone doji. Each type of doji has specific features and is expected to act in different ways *if* certain events precede and follow it.

Some doji are considered continuation patterns, but all require price confirmation. This single-candle pattern has the closing price equal, or almost equal, with the open. Its character (whether a reversal or continuation) depends on the position in the existing trend, the preceding candle, and the confirmation offered by the next candle(s).

Our objective, as with each other candlestick pattern, is to translate doji behavior using the heikin-ashi technique in both formats, visual and quantifiable.

Doji

Facts

- An ideal doji has no body; that is, the opening and closing price are equal.
- A *very small* body is also considered a doji.
- A doji may or may not have shadows.
- Doji emerge everywhere in trends and consolidations.
- A doji is considered a reversal pattern if it emerges after a long trend.
- A doji is considered a continuation pattern if it emerges after a short trend and is linked to the previous candle body size and color.

Questions to Consider

- How many bars are required to assess a trend as being long or short?
- What is considered a very small body? How is it measured?
- What is considered a long or short shadow? How is it measured?
- Is a gap from the prior candle considered an advantage?
- What is considered to be a confirmation for a doji? A next close above/below the high/low of the doji or above/below the body of the doji?

Figure 15.1 shows a daily chart of Briggs & Stratton (BGG). There are several doji here depending on how you look at them, but we focus on the first two. Since a doji means indecision, it would be a great advantage if heikin-ashi could pick up earlier indications.

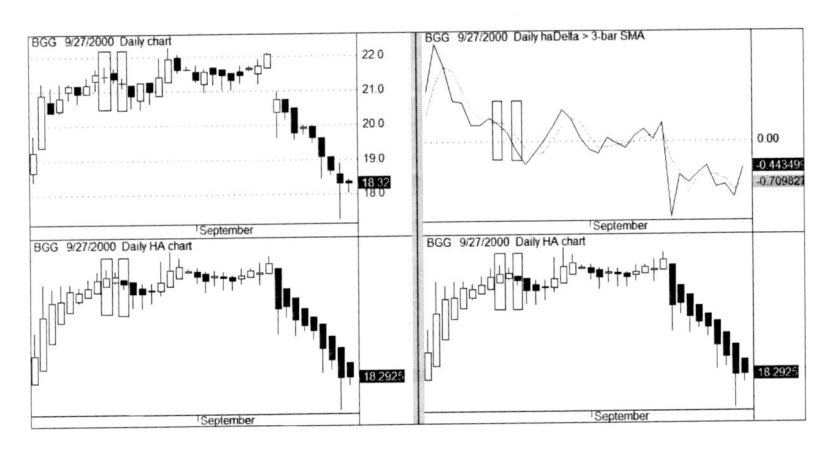

FIGURE 15.1: *Briggs & Stratton (BGG) daily charts with Japanese and modified candles for August and September 2000. Can heikin-ashi help find earlier price indications?*

Here is how heikin-ashi can be applied in this case:

- 8/18/00: A doji emerges in a strong uptrend. Is this time to digest the gains and pull back? The corresponding modified candle is white with a smaller body (a sign of trend slowdown). Fortunately, haDelta helps and offers a bearish indication with its position slightly below the average. Note that the bearish crossing occurred *five days earlier.* Although the price went up, haDelta hinted at the deterioration of the uptrend.

- 8/21/00: The day closed below the previous close but not below the low. The confirmation requirements vary among proponents of Japanese candlestick practice and theory. The biggest advantage of using modified candles—and especially their quantification—is that you can ignore Japanese pattern names, rules, and configurations. The modified candle indicates a slowdown (smaller body and the emergence of timid shadows). haDelta is deeper below the average, and both have negative short-term slopes. While we do not know the future, we are prepared for it with heikin-ashi.

- 8/22/00: Another doji emerges, this time in a lateral consolidation. A downtrend starts on the heikin-ashi chart. There is no change with haDelta, which is deeper below the average. This offers a negative bias.

- This short downtrend reversed two days later when haDelta moved above its average. Note that the two Japanese candles that follow the second doji on August 22 *look like* a bullish engulfing pattern with positive expectations.

Figure 15.2 shows a doji for Coach (COH) in the beginning of July 2002 that is particularly interesting because all four prices are equal.

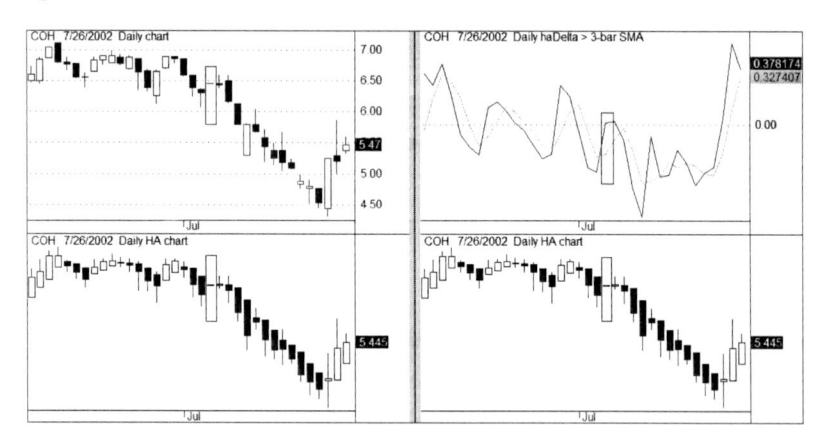

FIGURE 15.2: *Coach (COH) daily charts with Japanese and modified candles for June and July 2002. A doji reflecting identical four prices is a non-event day.*

We again use heikin-ashi to detect possible earlier indications of bullish or bearish character.

- 7/5/02: A rare doji emerges in a weak downtrend. The corresponding heikin-ashi candle is also unique, with no shadows and a very thin white body; you cannot ask for more indecision. haDelta is slightly above its average. However, the average is negative, and the pressure is more negative than positive.

- 7/8/02: The candle shows a lack of conviction. The modified candle points to a reversal or consolidation. haDelta is above the average. This reflects more uncertainty with minimal positive bias.

- 7/9/02: The candle shows a strong negative day. Signs of a downtrend appear on the heikin-ashi chart. haDelta offers a better indication for the continuation of the downtrend by turning back below the average. Both are in negative territory. All signs indicate a negative bias.

- 7/10/02: The downtrend is now reality.

This example shows no clear signs of reversal or continuation when the doji emerges on July 5. The negative bias builds up during the next days. The only heikin-ashi element that should be seriously looked at is the negative average, which does not invite traders to buy.

Long-Legged Doji

Facts

- A long-legged doji is a single-candle pattern with equal opening and closing prices (no body).
- A *very small* body is also acceptable.
- The shadows are long.

- Long-legged doji may emerge everywhere in trends and consolidations.

- A long-legged doji is considered a reversal pattern if it emerges after a long trend.

- A long-legged doji is considered a continuation pattern if it emerges after a short trend and is linked to the previous candle's body size and color.

Questions to Consider

- How many bars are required to define a trend as being long or short?

- What is considered a very small body? How is it measured?

- What is considered a (very) long shadow? How is it measured?

- Is there an acceptable ratio between the upper and lower shadows?

- Is a gap from the prior candle considered an advantage?

- What is considered to be a confirmation of a doji? A next close above/below the high/low of the doji? A next close above or below the candle preceding the doji?

The long-legged doji shows a high degree of indecision. It is considered a reversal or a continuation candle depending on the position in the existing trend, the preceding candle, and the confirmation offered.

In Figure 15.3 we see a long-legged doji for Coach (COH) in November and a second long-legged doji in December 2009. The length of the shadows is subject to discussion, but this is a result when rules applicable to all patterns lack precise measurement. We ignore names and configurations for our analysis as we apply the heikin-ashi technique.

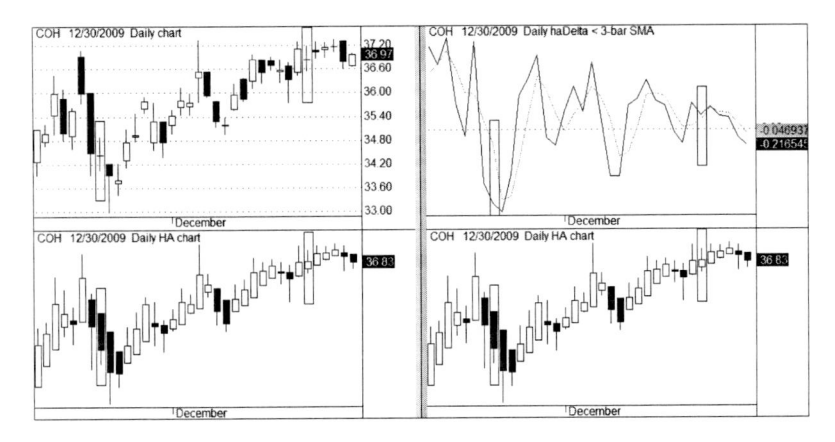

FIGURE 15.3: *Coach (COH) daily charts with Japanese and modified candles for November and December 2009. The two long-legged doji show high indecision.*

We start with the first doji in November 2009:

- 11/18/09: A long-legged doji appears in a short but powerful downtrend. Buyers and sellers are waiting for the next move. The corresponding modified candle indicates a strong downward. To nobody's surprise, haDelta is below the average, and both are negative. This paints a very bearish picture, and the next day will be interesting.

- 11/19/09: The candle shows a negative day. The modified candle is black, with no change from yesterday. haDelta is still below, but closer to the average, indicating a slowdown of the descent.

- 11/20/09: The candle reveals that a positive but undecided day follows in this decline. The heikin-ashi candle has a smaller body but still shows a downtrend. haDelta moves above the average, and both are rising. This is a sign of an imminent reversal.

- 11/23/09: The day is bullish and confirms a price reversal. A white modified candle shows a trend change. haDelta is higher above the average. The picture is positive.

Let us look at the second doji in December 2009:

- 12/22/09: A long-legged doji appears in a longer uptrend dominated by many candles with upper and lower shadows. The modified candle shows a weak uptrend (small body with timid shadows). haDelta is above the average, and both are positive.

- 12/23/09: A doji with a very thin body emerges. This is indecision with a higher close than yesterday. The heikin-ashi chart shows a stronger trend. haDelta is still above the average but near it; this is a sign of a fading uptrend. The following two days are unconvincing (doji) and although their closings are higher, the heikin-ashi chart shows weaker white candles. haDelta adds a sharper image of the trend when it crosses below the average and warns about a negative bias.

- 12/29/09: The candle shows a negative day. The modified candle points to a possible trend reversal. Notice again that haDelta had an earlier negative crossing.

Dragonfly Doji

Facts

- The opening and closing prices are equal.
- The dragonfly doji closes at the top of the range.

- It has no upper shadow.
- The lower shadow is long.
- Dragonfly doji emerge everywhere in trends and consolidations.
- In general, the dragonfly doji is seen as a bullish candle in a downtrend.

Questions to Consider

- Although a dragonfly doji looks like a bullish candle, will it reverse if it emerges after a long uptrend?
- How many bars should be considered for a trend to be long?
- Is a *very small* body also acceptable?
- What is considered to be a very small body or a long lower shadow? How are these measured?
- Does a very small upper shadow, or a very long lower shadow, alter its character at the end of trends or in consolidations?
- Is a dragonfly doji a particular case (with similar behavior) of a hammer or hanging man?

Like any other doji, the dragonfly doji displays indecision, though it has a positive bias (the close is at/near the high). It is considered a reversal candle if it appears in a downtrend; otherwise, it may signal a continuation of the trend.

A daily chart of Anooraq Resources (ANO) with a dragonfly doji in late July 2010 is shown in Figure 15.4. The doji successfully passes the test to qualify as a dragonfly doji.

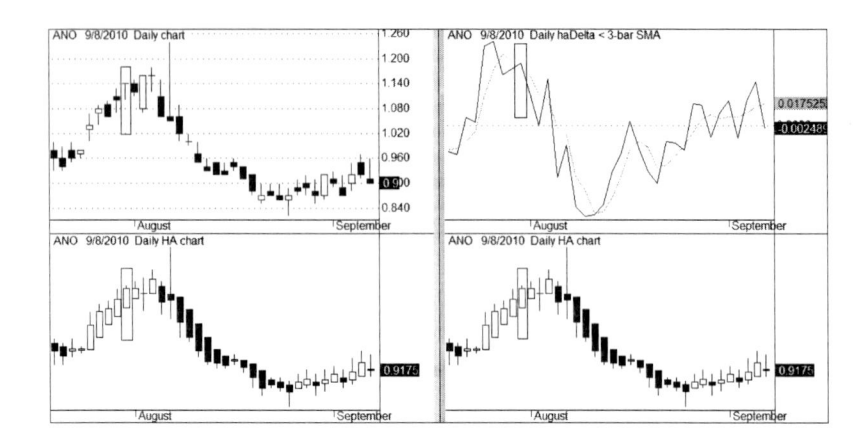

FIGURE 15.4: *Anooraq Resources (ANO) daily charts with Japanese and modified candles for July through September 2010. The emergence of the dragonfly doji in an uptrend is considered a sign of continuation.*

We again use heikin-ashi to see whether there are earlier reversal signs:

- 7/30/10: A dragonfly doji appears in an uptrend. The corresponding modified candle offers no hint of a slowdown or reversal. haDelta shows a bullish indication being above its average. However, there is a serious negative flavor here with the average turning down.

- 8/2/10: The candle shows a negative day. The heikin-ashi candle has a white body inside the previous body (slowdown of the uptrend). haDelta is below the average. These are indications of negative bias.

- 8/3/10: The candle indicates a very strong bullish day, but the open is way below the previous close. It translates as a modified candle pointing to a trend reversal. haDelta is further below the average. The tone is still bearish.

- 8/4/10: Buyers try to push prices up, but the day ends with a doji with longer shadows and the same close as the previous day ($1.16). The modified candle shows an uptrend. A clearer picture comes from haDelta average: While the indicator jumps again above the average, the smoothed average is still pointing down. haDelta had two whipsaws while its average had a steady path downwards. We know that haDelta is very nervous and may cause false signals; however, the short average carries more weight and confirms the bearish background.

- 8/5/10: The Japanese candlestick shows a negative day, confirmed with a black modified candle. The safest indication of a downtrend is the presence of the average in negative territory.

This example shows that despite its positive connotation, a dragonfly doji can be a reversal candle in a longer uptrend, but not with immediate action. haDelta and particularly its average are used to analyze each candle and to warn about and confirm the downtrend.

Gravestone Doji

Facts

- The opening and closing prices are equal.
- A gravestone doji closes at the bottom of the range.
- A gravestone doji has no lower shadow.
- The upper shadow is long.
- Gravestone doji emerge everywhere in trends and consolidations.
- After a long uptrend, this candle is considered bearish and points to a trend reversal.

Questions to Consider

- How many bars should be considered for a trend to be long?
- Are a *very small* body, or a long upper shadow, also acceptable?
- What is considered to be a very small body or a long upper shadow? How are these measured?
- Does a very small lower shadow alter a gravestone doji's character at the end of trends or in consolidations?
- Could a gravestone doji be construed as a particular case of a shooting star or inverted hammer?

A gravestone doji is considered a reversal candle in an uptrend but may also signal a continuation of the trend if it is short.

Figure 15.5 shows a daily chart of Lowe's Companies, Inc. (LOW) with a gravestone doji emerging in a long uptrend in late April 2010. Some experts in Japanese candlesticks and some pattern recognition software may reject this pattern. The doubt rises from the very thin body (four cents) and the extremely small lower shadow (two cents). On the other hand, other people may accept the pattern as a gravestone doji.

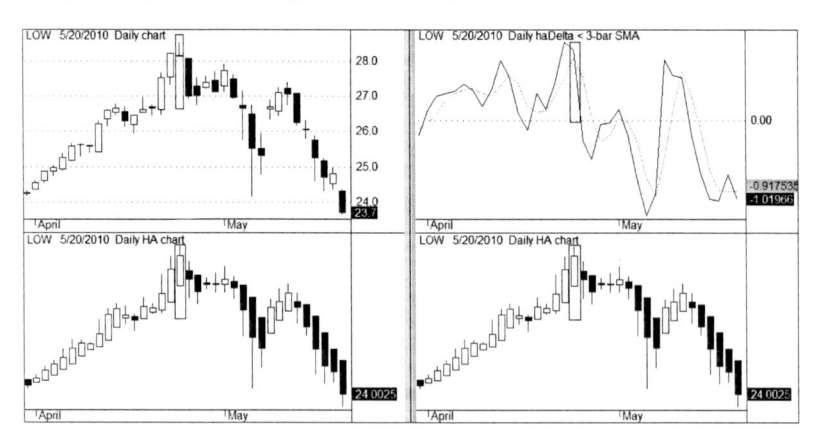

FIGURE 15.5: *Lowe's Companies, Inc. (LOW) daily charts with Japanese and modified candles for April and May 2010. An imperfect gravestone doji behaves as expected, bringing a reversal after a long uptrend.*

To remove doubts, we will be using heikin-ashi to look at each price candle as it emerges on the chart.

- 4/26/10: A gravestone doji emerges in a strong uptrend. The corresponding modified candle is white and offers no hint of a slowdown or reversal. Even haDelta stops short from a bearish indication, staying above its moving average. The only warning we get is the smaller distance between haDelta and the average.

- 4/27/10: A very bearish candle confirms the gravestone doji. The modified candle is black, with the shadows pointing to a reversal. haDelta crosses below its average. There are no doubts about the negative reversal taking place.

This example confirms the bearish expectations of the gravestone doji in general, although here it is not in its purest and widely accepted form. The only warning heikin-ashi brought was the smaller distance between haDelta and its average on the day when the doji emerged.

Figure 15.6 shows an example similar to that discussed in Figure 15.5. This gravestone doji has a thin body (one cent) and a very small lower shadow (two cents). Will this unconventional gravestone doji show bearish signs, too?

Here is how heikin-ashi helps interpret this gravestone doji:

- 6/22/05: A gravestone doji emerges in an uptrend. The corresponding modified candle is white and offers no hint of a slowdown or reversal. Even haDelta stops short of a bearish indication; it remains above its average. The only warning we get on this chart is the smaller distance between haDelta and the average.

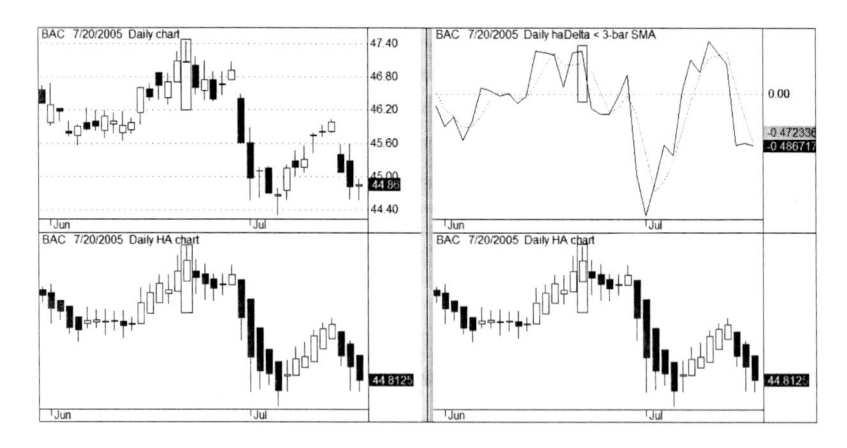

FIGURE 15.6: *Bank of America (BAC) daily charts with Japanese and modified candles for June and July 2005. Another imperfect gravestone doji behaves as expected after a long uptrend.*

- 6/23/05: A bearish candle confirms the gravestone doji. The modified candle shows a negative bias, and the shadows point to a reversal from uptrend to downtrend. haDelta is below its average. There are no doubts about the reversal.

This gravestone doji has a bearish outcome although it is not an orthodox pattern. Heikin-ashi did not bring any more warnings than the smaller distance between haDelta and the average on the day when the doji emerged.

30-Second Summary

- Doji in its several variations is a one-candle pattern indicating uncertainty. A price confirmation is required to determine the next action.

- haDelta and its short average are simple instruments for finding earlier indications of reversals or continuations.

- The heikin-ashi technique provides a particular advantage in the case of doji when uncertainty is removed by sequential price bar analysis.
- This charting technique does not serve well as a warning signal because of its known one-bar delay.
- Quantification helps translate patterns that are outside definitions but still *look* like valid ones.
- Doji are further evidence that the heikin-ashi technique can look beyond candlestick pattern names, definitions, and structure by analyzing each price bar as it emerges.

CHAPTER 16

HEIKIN-ASHI AND TWEEZERS

Tweezers are candlestick patterns that provide indications about support (tweezers bottom) and resistance (tweezers top). They suggest a reversal; however, to confirm a reversal, the prices must be in an uptrend or downtrend. When this pattern is seen after a longer trend, the idea of reversal should be seriously taken into consideration.

Japanese candlestick theory and practice are, in many cases, grounds for subjective judgement. We have seen this already and will continue to do so. The tweezers patterns are no exception: Rule definitions regarding the number of candles in the pattern and the values of the highs and lows vary from author to author.

In their more complex format, tweezers may include additional reversal patterns like dark-cloud cover, piercing line, shooting star, inverted hammer, hanging man, and hammer, to name just a few. As a result, the bullish or bearish reversal character becomes more convincing.

Our objective, as with each candlestick pattern, is to look at tweezers using the heikin-ashi technique and to establish a method to reduce subjectivity in assessing this pattern.

Tweezers Bottom

Some sources describe the tweezers bottom as a two-candle pattern with equal lows. Other people extend the number from two to several candles. The number of candles composing the pattern is determined by the subsequent candle that has a low equal to the first candle in the pattern.

Facts

- Tweezers bottom is a two-candle pattern that appears in a downtrend.
- The lows of both candles are equal.
- Shapes and colors do not matter.

Questions to Consider

- How many bars should be considered for a downtrend?
- Can a tweezers bottom pattern consist of more than two candles (see comments above)?
- Should we accept unequal but similar lows?
- Is the first candle more relevant if it is long and black?

Figure 16.1 exhibits a daily chart of EarthLink (ELNK) in which a tweezers bottom emerges in the beginning of November, with both days recording identical lows at $7.92. Normally, this value is expected to work as support for the future, and a reversal should be in the cards.

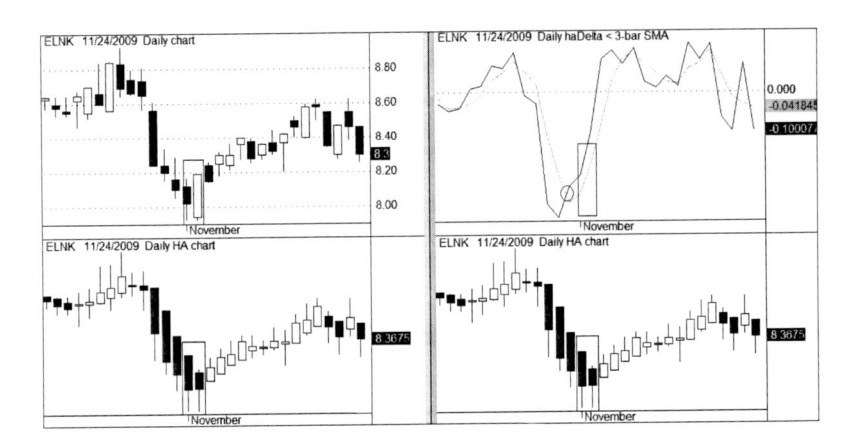

FIGURE 16.1: *EarthLink (ELNK) daily charts with Japanese and modified candles for October and November 2009. A perfect tweezers bottom points to a support and trend reversal. Heikin-ashi quantification is better, showing positive signs days in advance.*

Heikin-ashi is extremely useful for analyzing trends and reversals, so we focus on indications, if any, of a turning point:

- 11/2/09: A negative day appears in a downtrend. The corresponding modified candle is black with no sign of slowdown or reversal. Fortunately, haDelta helps and offers a bullish indication already at the end of the previous day when haDelta closed above its average. Advantage heikin-ashi!

- 11/3/09: A very positive day translates into an extremely bullish candle. Looking only from the perspective of the Japanese patterns, the last two days generate a bullish engulfing pattern with expectation of a trend reversal. We go our way and implement the same analysis using heikin-ashi. The modified candle shows a slowdown of the existing trend (body inside the previous one and emergence of both shadows). haDelta has a more positive action and is higher above its intersection with the average. The bullish reversal is confirmed.

- 11/4/09: Although the day closed below the open price, the modified candle is white, with no lower shadow. This is a clear indication of an uptrend. As always, haDelta is telling the story in real time: It is higher up and more distanced from its average, offering a very bullish picture.

We have seen on this chart a perfect tweezers bottom that is also a bullish engulfing pattern. The reversal character of the tweezers bottom is reinforced by association with another pattern considered bullish. From another perspective, heikin-ashi (haDelta and its average) offers leading bullish signals *two days before* the completion of the pattern.

Figure 16.2 shows a daily chart for the chip maker Rambus (RMBS) with a tweezers bottom in December 2010. Visually, the two candles are different from the pattern shown in Figure 16.1. Playing by the rules, this is a tweezers bottom that is *expected* to create a support level at the low of the pattern ($19.84) and reverse after such long and vicious downtrend. The events unfolding after the tweezers bottom show the opposite; the trend goes on.

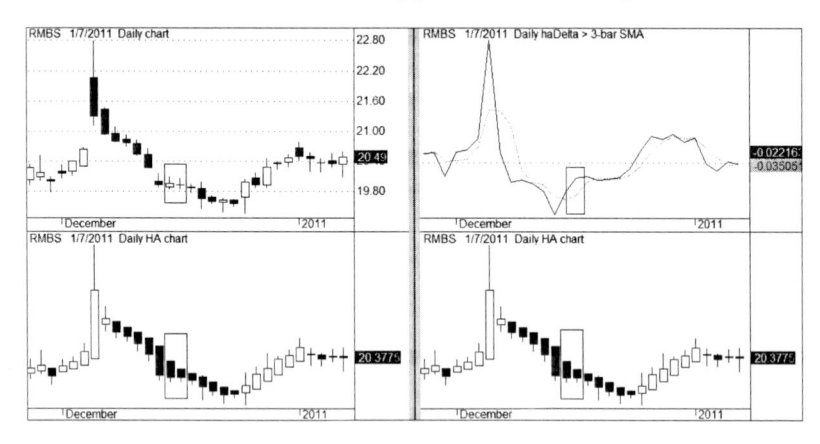

FIGURE 16.2: *Rambus (RMBS) daily charts with Japanese and modified candles for late November 2010 through early January 2011. A strong downtrend is followed by a tweezers bottom that points to a support and trend reversal. The expectations were not met, and heikin-ashi helped again.*

HEIKIN-ASHI AND TWEEZERS

We again use heikin-ashi to see if we can get advance signals in this case.

- 12/15/10: A timid positive day emerges in a strong downtrend. The modified candle is black with no sign of slowdown or reversal. haDelta helps with a bullish indication when it crosses above the short average.

- 12/16/10: A doji-like candle shows more indecision regarding the character of the trend. The tweezers bottom is in place with a low of $19.84 and is seen as support for future price action. The modified candle has a smaller body inside the previous one (slowdown of the trend). haDelta advances above the average. These are positive signs for a reversal.

- 12/17/10: A doji adds to indecision. The modified candle has a small body and indicates a continuation of the downtrend. Support for future price action is broken. haDelta is still above the average. All indications tell us to wait and see.

- 12/20/10: The downtrend resumes with a bearish day that decisively penetrates the support. The modified candle develops a small upper shadow as a sign of a *possible* bottom and reversal. haDelta moves below the average, bringing back the negative bias. We have a confusing picture.

- 12/21/10: The candlestick and heikin-ashi charts show nothing of real importance.

- 12/22/10: A hammer emerges after a downtrend, sending a reversal message. The heikin-ashi chart shows a continued downtrend. haDelta is again above the average with positive bias. The next days are part of a trend reversal.

This example shows a tweezers bottom with support and reversal expectations attached. Contrary to expectations, this tweezers bottom does not act as expected. The support is broken and the change of trend is delayed for several days when a three-candle tweezers bottom precedes the reversal.

Even in this example, heikin-ashi helps remove a certain degree of guessing. The heikin-ashi chart shows a clear negative conviction before and after the first pattern. On the other hand, haDelta offers advance bullish indications after the support broke.

The most important observation here is that the haDelta average keeps an upward slope throughout the period immediately after the pattern failure, translating to a positive divergence with the price followed by a trend change.

Tweezers Top

The tweezers top pattern is the opposite of the tweezers bottom pattern. Some sources describe the tweezers top as a two-candle pattern with equal highs. Other people extend the number from two to *several* candles. The number of candles composing the pattern is determined by the subsequent candle a high equal to that of the first candle in the pattern.

Facts

- Tweezers top is a two-candle pattern that appears in an uptrend.
- The highs of both candles are equal.
- Shapes and colors do not matter.

Questions to Consider

- How many bars should be considered for an uptrend?
- Can a tweezers top pattern have more than two candles (see comments above)?

- Should we accept unequal but similar highs?
- Is the first candle more relevant if it is long and white?

Figure 16.3 shows the daily price of Elan (ELN) with a tweezers top in November 2006. The pattern emerges in an uptrend, and two days hit the same high at $15.27. Conventional wisdom says that resistance is expected at the high and a reversal may follow soon.

This chart shows a pattern that works as expected with a trend change. Can heikin-ashi bring earlier reversal indications?

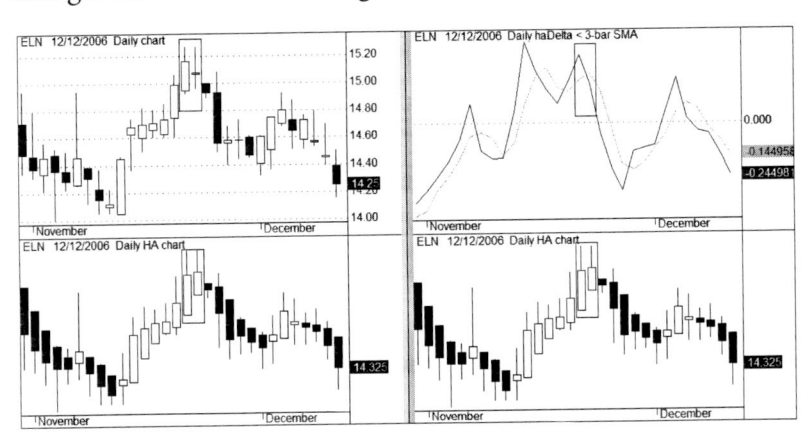

FIGURE 16.3: *Elan (ELN) daily charts with Japanese and modified candles for November and December 2006. A perfect tweezers top defines a resistance and prepares for a trend reversal. Heikin-ashi quantification helps us catch the top, with haDelta below the average on the day when the pattern was finalized.*

Here is how heikin-ashi helps in analyzing the situation:

- 11/21/06: A very bullish candle appears in an uptrend. The corresponding modified candle is white. haDelta is above the average, reinforcing the positive outlook. There is no sign of slowdown.

- 11/22/06: The candle with long shadows can be interpreted as a long-legged doji and indicates a clear fight between the bulls and bears at these heights. The top of the day hits resistance at the previous high. The modified candle is white with a body almost inside the previous one. This is a sign of a slowdown, confirming the character of indecision of the long-legged doji. haDelta is below its average, reinforcing the bearish character of the day. Interesting days will follow.

- 11/24/06: A negative day closes slightly above the low of the pattern. This is not an acceptable confirmation of the tweezers top. The modified candle is black with no upper shadow, a sign that the downtrend is about to begin. haDelta is still below its average, pointing to a confident downtrend.

This example shows a perfect tweezers top acting as expected. Any advance sign of reversal remains in our focus. haDelta again offers advance warning on the last day of the pattern.

FIGURE 16.4: *EarthLink (ELNK) daily charts with Japanese and modified candles for November and December 2009. A stretched tweezers top marks a resistance at $8.63 and warns about a reversal. With heikin-ashi, the warning comes sooner when the haDelta average turns negative before the completion of the pattern.*

An extended tweezers top with a span over several days is illustrated for EarthLink (ELNK) in Figure 16.4.

Here is how heikin-ashi provides indication of the reversal:

- 11/18/09: A candle with a small body and long lower shadow appears in a strong uptrend after a very bullish day. The corresponding modified candle remains white and long with no lower shadow (uptrend). haDelta is above, but near, its average and unstable.

- 11/19/09: The candlestick chart shows a very bearish candle. The heikin-ashi chart changes color from white to black, and the emergence of shadows indicates an undecided moment. haDelta turns below the average. All signs point to a negative trend.

- 11/20/09: Another extreme day, this time bullish, closes above the midpoint of the previous body. The modified candle shows a downtrend. haDelta is below its average, but the distance between the two is very wide (time to return to the mean). It is worth observing that the average is negative.

- 11/23/09: This is a negative day, with a high equal to that on November 18. This candle completes a tweezers top extended over four days. It marks a resistance at $8.63 and warns about a reversal of the uptrend. The white modified candle is confusing. Are green shoots sprouting ahead? The presence of both shadows introduces more uncertainty. haDelta moves above the average, bringing back the positive bias. The picture is confusing.

- 11/24/09: A negative day pushes the modified candle to a decisive bearish character and haDelta below the average. Everything points to a downtrend here.

This example shows an extended tweezers top stretching over several days. The resistance on the chart has been tested unsuccessfully once in January 2010. There are two important findings here. First, the average had already turned negative on November 20 at a time when haDelta was undecided. Second, heikin-ashi correctly translated the consolidation in December as a sequence of doji-like candles.

30-Second Summary

- In general, the tweezers bottom and tweezers top are patterns consisting of two consecutive candles of equal lows and highs, respectively.

- Tweezers bottom points to support; its opposite pattern, tweezers top, identifies resistance.

- The patterns may extend over several candles as long as the "same high/low" requirement is met.

- For these patterns, heikin-ashi works better in detecting advance indications for reversals.

- The extended tweezers may cause false signals even with the use of the heikin-ashi technique. A price confirmation of the extended pattern is recommended.

CHAPTER 17

HEIKIN-ASHI AND SPINNING TOPS

Spinning tops are single candles with a small body. Since their main feature is the small body, spinning tops show that buyers and sellers lack commitment. Their role becomes more important when they are part of a multi-candle pattern such as evening star, morning star, bullish harami, or bearish harami. As we have seen with other candlestick patterns, subjective interpretation may occur even in the case of a spinning top.

For example, this chapter examines the high-wave candle as a special case of a spinning top. Both these single-candle patterns have small bodies, but what sets apart a high-wave candle is that it has long upper and lower shadows attached. The question to consider, though, is just how long or short do the shadows have to be to differentiate a high-wave candle from a spinning top?

Our objective, as with each candlestick pattern, is to look at spinning tops using the heikin-ashi technique.

Facts

- Spinning top is a single-candle pattern.
- It has a small body and small shadows.

- The size of the upper and lower shadows is not important.
- This pattern comes in two flavors—spinning top white and spinning top black—depending on the color of the body.
- It is considered a warning after a trend, showing indecision in a lateral move.

Questions to Consider

- Should we require that the body be *very* small (more restrictive)?
- What is considered to be a (*very*) small body? How is it measured and which reference is used?
- How relevant is the size of the shadows? Some define a spinning top as a small body *with* shadows at least the size of the body. For others, size of the shadows is irrelevant.
- According to the Japanese candlestick rules regarding irrelevant shadow length for spinning tops, could we consider the high-wave candle to also be a spinning top?
- Is a small body with no shadows also a spinning top?

Spinning Tops

Figure 17.1 shows a daily chart of EPIQ Systems Inc. (EPIQ) with a black spinning top candidate emerging on November 12, 2010. If we decide to validate a spinning top as a small body with shadows at least the height of the body, this candle falls short of passing the test. We choose instead the flexible definition where the size of the shadow does not matter.

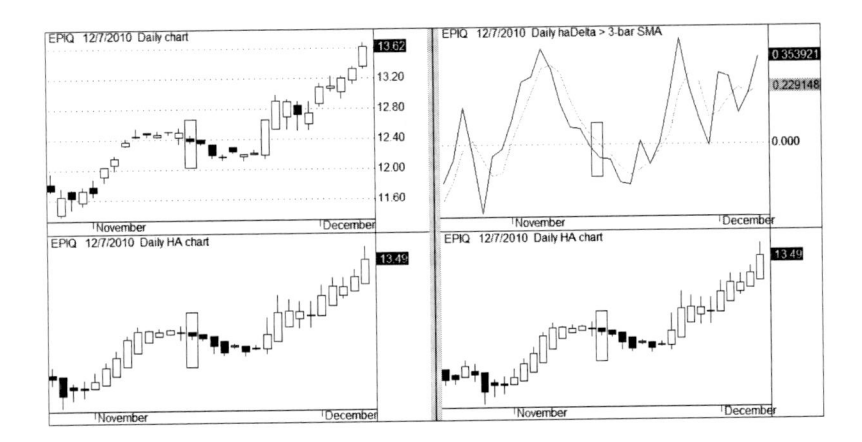

FIGURE 17.1: *EPIQ Systems Inc. (EPIQ) daily charts with Japanese and modified candles for November and December 2010. A black spinning top shows indecision. Heikin-ashi helps again, pointing to a top and reversal.*

We then proceed with the heikin-ashi analysis to see if it offers any advantage when looking at this pattern:

- 11/12/10: A black candle with a small body and shadows (black spinning top) emerges in consolidation. There is a slight negative bias but nothing evident. The corresponding modified candle is black with no upper shadow – a sign that a downtrend is starting, *especially* after the doji-like modified candle that emerged the previous day. In heikin-ashi analysis, haDelta removes many twists. We see that haDelta crossed below its average five days ago. Again, advantage heikin-ashi!

Figure 17.2 exhibits a white spinning top candidate for JPMorgan Chase & Co. (JPM) on May 26, 2006. We choose to validate this candle as a genuine white spinning top, taking into account that its shadows are bigger than the height of the body.

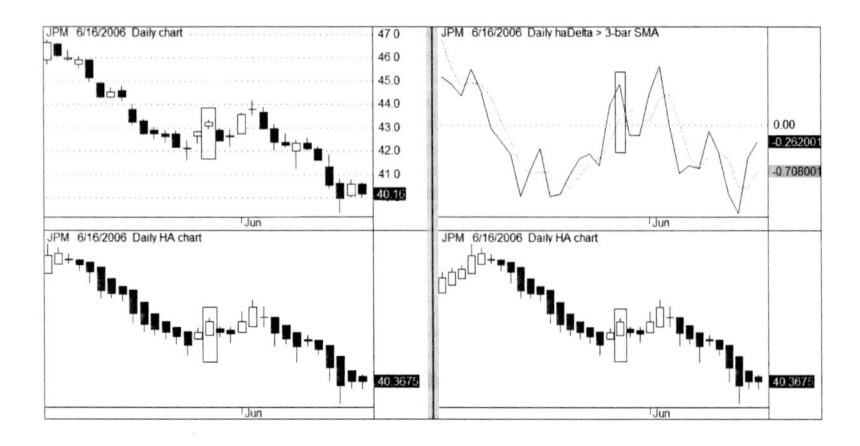

FIGURE 17.2: *JPMorgan Chase & Co. (JMM) daily charts with Japanese and modified candles for May and June 2006. A white spinning top shows indecision. Heikin-ashi helps by indicating an immediate positive bias.*

What does heikin-ashi find? A look at the chart shows the following:

- 5/26/06: A spinning top emerges with a gap up in a timid reaction. The corresponding modified candle is white with no lower shadow as sign of ongoing uptrend. haDelta is well above it average. The picture is very positive.

- 5/30/06: This is a negative gap down day. In a reaction like this, this is usually a bearish sign. The heikin-ashi candle shows possible reversal/consolidation (small body with long shadows). We need a black modified candle with no upper shadow to be sure the downtrend starts. haDelta turns below the positive average. The picture is still undecided.

- 5/31/06: A long-legged doji emerges as a sign of indecision. The modified candle is similar to the previous one, indicating the start of a consolidation. There is no change as far as haDelta is concerned. The important thing to watch here is the polarity of the average—positive or negative.

HEIKIN-ASHI AND SPINNING TOPS

- 6/1/06: This is a very bullish day. There are signs of continued uptrend confirmed by the modified candle. haDelta adds more confidence to this positive character.

- Two days later on June 5, the negative day generates a heikin-ashi candle with a stronger indication for a bearish reversal. Both the modified candle chart and haDelta show the downtrend is resuming. Note again the relationship between the trend and polarity of the average.

High-Wave Candle

We conclude this chapter with a discussion about the high-wave candle and the heikin-ashi technique. Figure 17.3 shows a daily chart of Bank of America (BAC) with a high-wave candle in late January 2010.

FIGURE 17.3: *Bank of America Corp. (BAC) daily charts with Japanese and modified candles for January and February 2010. The high-wave candle in late January shows indecision. Its value in this context is better assessed using the heikin-ashi technique.*

Here is how this situation plays out on the charts:

- 1/28/10: A high-wave candle appears in a reaction. After the very bullish stance of the previous day, the long shadows are testimony of the fierce battle between bulls and bears. The modified candle is white, pointing to an uptrend, while haDelta is above its negative average. The setting is slightly bullish.

- 1/29/10: This is a negative day. The modified candle remains white, but its body is now inside the previous body and adds shadows (a sign of slowdown leading to reversal or consolidation). haDelta is positive and above the average. There are no black clouds at this time, although the day was dangerously bearish.

- 2/1/10: The inside day suggests indecision. This is translated into a doji-like modified candle with a message for consolidation, possibly reversal. However, the small shadows indicate consolidation rather than reversal. haDelta turns again below the average that remains positive.

- 2/2/10: This is a positive day. The modified candle shows decisiveness. haDelta is again above the average. The picture looks bullish.

- 2/3/10: A shooting star appears in an uptrend. Can this be a top? Heikin-ashi shows a sustained uptrend, but the only indication about a possible deterioration of the trend is the small distance between haDelta and its average. We need one more day for confirmation.

In all these examples the heikin-ashi analysis again ignores the character of spinning tops or high-wave candles as indecision patterns. **Heikin-ashi translates these candles more objectively according to their position on the chart at the moment they emerge.**

30-Second Summary

- The spinning top shows indecision with its very small body.
- It works as a warning when it emerges in an established trend.
- Flexible definitions allow a high-wave candle to be seen as a spinning top.
- Heikin-ashi charting neither looks at nor recognizes Japanese candlestick patterns. Instead, it looks at each individual candle as a component of the price sequence.
- Modified candles, haDelta, and its average are all tools for significantly reducing a subjective definition and interpretation of any candle pattern, including spinning tops and high-wave candles.

CHAPTER 18

HEIKIN-ASHI AND BELT HOLD LINES

Belt hold lines are single-candle patterns with a very long body and with minimal or no shadows. With their long bodies, they show strength and suggest reversals after trends. Belt hold lines can be part of reversal formations such as bullish and bearish engulfing, piercing line and dark-cloud cover, morning star, and evening star.

When they are part of multi-candle reversal formations, belt hold lines are more credible in predicting future price action. Even with this pattern, subjective interpretation is possible.

Our objective here is to look at belt hold candles, both bullish and bearish, using heikin-ashi charting to see how this technique reduces subjectivity in translation.

Bullish Belt Hold

Facts

- The bullish belt hold is a single-candle pattern.
- It is expected to act as a reversal candle when it emerges in a downtrend.

- The bullish belt hold candle has a very long white body, with the open at the low and the close near its high.

Questions to Consider

- How many bars should be used to define a downtrend?
- Should we accept this pattern with a very small lower shadow?
- What is considered to be a very long white body? How it is measured and which reference is used?
- Could a white marubozu candle in a downtrend be considered a bullish belt hold candle?

Figure 18.1 shows a weekly chart of International Paper (IP) with two bullish belt hold *candidates* occurring in December 2003 and May 2004, respectively. Why are they candidates? Because both have tiny lower shadows, with the first one exhibiting a longer upper shadow.

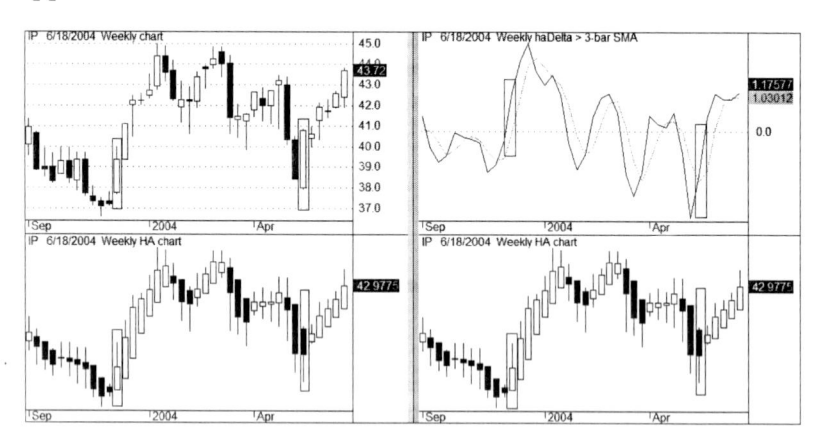

FIGURE 18.1: *International Paper Co. (IP) weekly charts with Japanese and modified candles for September 2003 through June 2004. Heikin-ashi ignores candlestick patterns; it makes a better assessment based on haDelta and its moving average.*

HEIKIN-ASHI AND BELT HOLD LINES

Candidates or not, we will use the heikin-ashi technique to see if it offers any advantage in judging this type of candle:

- 12/05/03: A tall white candle with a minimal lower shadow and a close relatively distant from the high emerges in a downtrend. As said, people may or may not interpret this candle as a bullish belt hold. We ignore definitions and look further using heikin-ashi. The corresponding modified candle is white with no lower shadow; this is a sign of the start of an uptrend, especially as it changes color. haDelta crossed above its average one week earlier, but the average is still slightly negative (-0.0324). The overall bullish indications overcome this deficiency.

- 12/12/03: This bullish candle *can be seen as* a bullish belt hold; however, there is a problem as it does not emerge in a downtrend. Heikin-ashi confirms once more the uptrend that started last week.

- 5/14/04: A second bullish belt hold candidate appears after a fall from $45 to almost $38. The corresponding modified candle is black with a timid indication of a slowdown (the emergence of a very small upper shadow). haDelta is slightly above the average, pointing to a possible trend reversal. Small long positions may be taken with a stop-loss below the previous low in November 2003.

- You may observe that the long white body engulfs the previous black one. It looks like a bullish engulfing pattern, but its translation depends on the length of the existing downtrend (very short in this case). Fortunately, heikin-ashi does not look at patterns and definitions, only at modified candles and body quantification.

Figure 18.2 is a daily chart of Home Properties Inc. (HME) with a white marubozu after a downtrend in late October 2003.

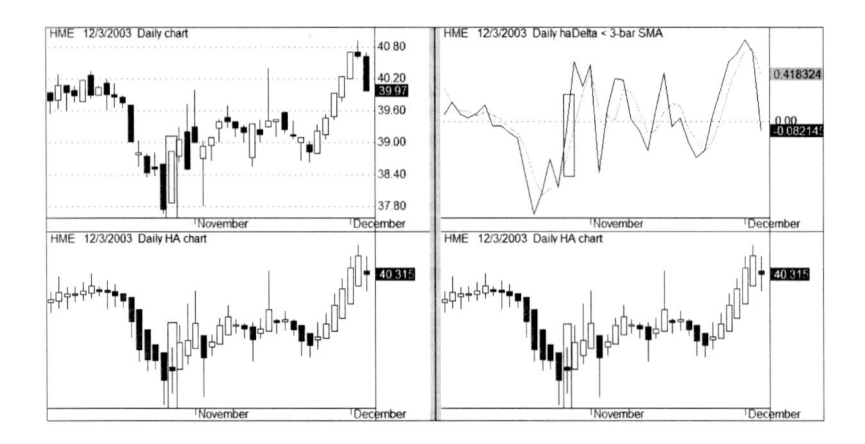

FIGURE 18.2: *Home Properties Inc. (HME) daily charts with Japanese and modified candles for October and November 2003. Heikin-ashi charting identifies the white marubozu as a reversal candle.*

The bullish expectancy is confirmed by applying the heikin-ashi technique:

- 10/29/03: A tall white candle with no shadows emerges in a downtrend. Is this a reversal candle? Is it similar, in terms of behavior, to a bullish belt hold? We ignore definitions and use heikin-ashi. The corresponding modified candle is still black but with long shadows (a sign of a possible trend reversal). haDelta adds positive energy, with the crossing above its average. There are reliable indications for a trend reversal.

- The next three days are part of an uptrend illustrated clearly by the sequence of white heikin-ashi candles.

- Subsequent price action is a sequence of higher highs and higher lows going as far as mid-December.

Bearish Belt Hold

Facts

- The bearish belt hold is a single-candle pattern.
- It is expected to act as a reversal candle when it emerges in an uptrend.
- The bearish belt hold candle has a very long black body, with the open at the high and the close near its low.

Questions to Consider

- How many bars should be used to define an uptrend?
- Should we accept this pattern with a very small upper shadow?
- What is considered to be a very long black body? How it is measured and which reference is used?
- Could a black marubozu candle in an uptrend be considered a bearish belt hold candle?

Figure 18.3 shows a daily chart of Schlumberger NV (SLB) with a bearish belt hold candle in an extended uptrend in May 2009.

FIGURE 18.3: *Schlumberger NV (SLB) daily charts with Japanese and modified candles for April through June 2009. Heikin-ashi totally ignores candlestick patterns and makes a more accurate assessment based on haDelta and its moving average.*

Here is how the candle analysis plays out when applying heikin-ashi:

- 5/7/09: A long black candle with an open at the high of the day and a small lower shadow emerges in an uptrend. It is a bearish belt hold with an indication for a reversal. The corresponding modified candle remains white with two shadows (a sign of slowdown and even of a possible reversal). haDelta already turned below its average one day earlier. Heikin-ashi is sending a bearish signal.

- Note that a bearish engulfing pattern during the past two days reinforces the character of the bearish belt hold. Again, heikin-ashi does not look at patterns and definitions, only at modified candles and body quantifications. And we can see again how this is an advantage.

We raised the question whether a black marubozu in an uptrend can be considered a bearish belt hold. Figure 18.4 shows a daily chart of Winthrop Realty Trust (FUR) with a black marubozu in an uptrend in July 2007. On this chart, common sense makes us anticipate the bearish character of this candle.

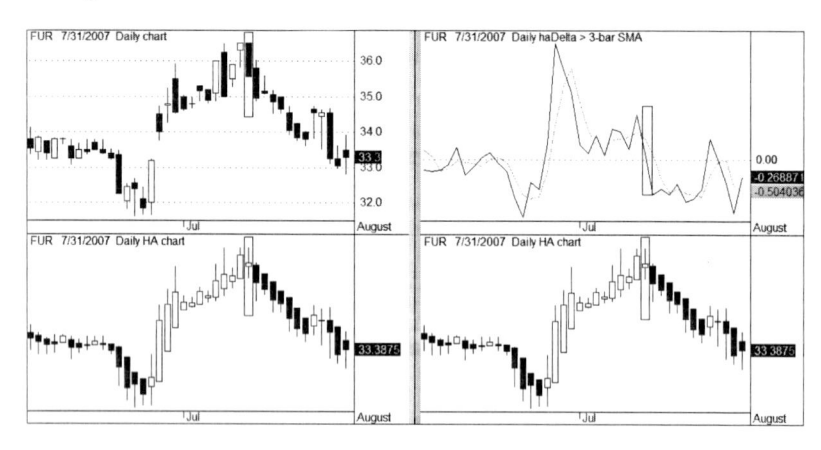

FIGURE 18.4: *Winthrop Realty Trust (FUR) daily charts with Japanese and modified candles for June and July 2007. A reversal is expected after the emergence of the black marubozu, and heikin-ashi confirms it.*

Let us see what heikin-ashi says about the black marubozu in this context:

- 7/13/07: A long black candle with no shadows (black marubozu) appears in an uptrend. Since the only difference between this candle and a bearish belt hold is the absence of the lower shadow, can its behavior be similar to that of a bearish belt hold? The corresponding modified candle on the heikin-ashi chart is a classic reversal candle: a small body with long upper and lower shadows. haDelta is below its average and signals price top. The following days are further evidence that heikin-ashi cannot be ignored. (Or it can be ignored, at your own risk.)

- Note the presence of a bearish engulfing pattern at the top where the black marubozu appears. Although this pattern supports the bearish picture, heikin-ashi disregards patterns and definitions, replacing them with a quantifiable format.

30-Second Summary

- A belt hold candle shows the likelihood of a trend reversal when it emerges in a trend.

- In terms of behaviors, a marubozu candle in a trend could be considered a belt hold candle.

- While Japanese candlestick study leaves plenty of room for interpretation, the heikin-ashi technique ignores candlestick patterns. It looks at each individual candle as a component of the price sequence.

- The modified candles, haDelta, and its average are tools used to significantly reduce subjective definitions and interpretations of any candle pattern, including belt hold lines and marubozu.

CHAPTER 19

HEIKIN-ASHI WITH ON-NECK, IN-NECK, AND THRUSTING PATTERNS

On-neck, in-neck, and thrusting patterns are variations of the piercing line. Although a piercing line pattern is considered a sign of price reversal, these three configurations have a bearish connotation in an existing downtrend. In other words, they are seen as continuation patterns.

Speaking of on-neck, in-neck, and thrusting patterns, the difference comes from the extent to which the second candle penetrates into the territory of the first one. Since the strongest push (thrusting candle) goes only near and below the midpoint of the first body, theoretically, there is insufficient force to reverse the downtrend.

Even these patterns are examples of subjective interpretation of Japanese candlesticks. We need something simple and readily available to everyone to reduce the degree of personal translation in the context in which the candlesticks appear: the heikin-ashi technique.

On-neck

Facts

- On-neck is a two-candle pattern.
- This pattern is expected to act as continuation when it emerges in a downtrend.
- Candle 1 has a long black body.
- Candle 2 is white with a smaller body. It opens below the low of the first candle and closes at or near the low of the first candle.

Questions to Consider

- What is considered to be a *long* body? How it is measured and which reference is used?
- How many bars should be used to define a downtrend?
- How restrictive should we be about the close? Some are strict about the close *at* the low of the prior candle. Others are more flexible and accept a close *near* the low of the first candle.

Figure 19.1 shows a daily chart of Olympic Steel Inc. (ZEUS) with an on-neck pattern in the last week of September 2004. The size of the second body may be subject to discussion, but as long as it follows the main rules we accept the pattern as valid.

Here is how the on-neck pattern can be translated through heikin-ashi:

- 9/22/04: A black candle with a long body appears in an established downtrend. The corresponding modified candle is black with no upper shadow (a sign of ongoing downtrend). haDelta is used to go one level deeper into the analysis and is seen crossing above its average with a positive bias.

HEIKIN-ASHI WITH ON-NECK, IN-NECK, AND THRUSTING PATTERNS

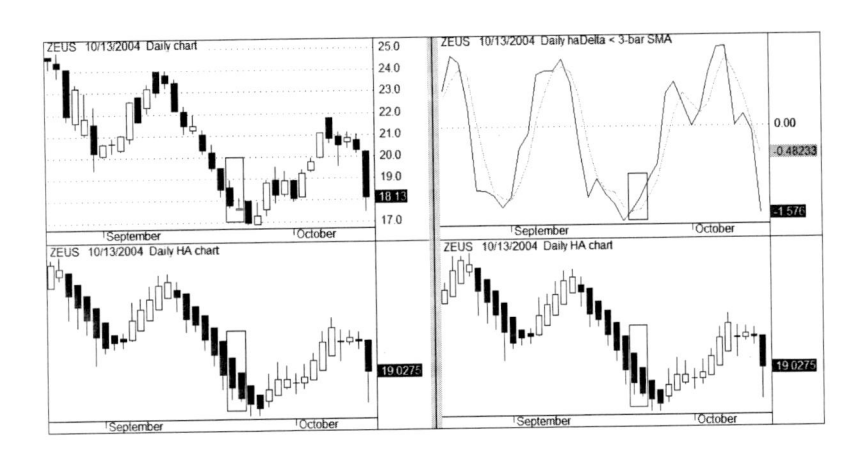

FIGURE 19.1: *Olympic Steel Inc. (ZEUS) daily charts with Japanese and modified candles for September and October 2004. In theory, an on-neck pattern provides a confirmation message for a continuation of the downtrend. In contrast, haDelta tells a bullish story.*

- 9/23/04: A small white candle of questionable body size closes *near* the low of the previous day. It may be also associated with an inverted hammer in a downtrend with potential for a reversal. However, names and definitions do not count for heikin-ashi which seeks, as objectively as possible, early signs of continuation or reversal. The modified candle on the heikin-ashi chart shows a continuation of the downtrend. haDelta goes above its average, which is now advancing. In the absence of haDelta, the trader would see a continued price decline, but by applying haDelta and its average, the results improve.

- The trend reversal confirmation comes three days later when the modified candle changes color. At that time, haDelta is far away from its initial bullish indication.

This is another example where the heikin-ashi technique (visual and quantifiable) disregards patterns and definitions and looks *only* at modified candles and body quantification in the specific context on the chart.

In-neck

Facts

- In-neck is a two-candle pattern.
- It is expected to act as continuation when it emerges in a downtrend.
- Candle 1 has a long black body.
- Candle 2 is white with a smaller body. It opens below the low of the first candle and closes slightly into the body of the first candle.

Questions to Consider

- What is considered to be a long black body? How it is measured and which reference is used?
- How many bars should be used to define a downtrend?
- In terms of candle 2's close, what does "slightly" mean? How is this penetration measured?

Figure 19.2 shows a daily chart of Google Inc. (GOOG) with an in-neck pattern in the beginning of May 2010. Conventional wisdom calls for a continuation of the downtrend. As with all other patterns, we use the heikin-ashi technique to see if it offers advantages in judging the pattern on this chart.

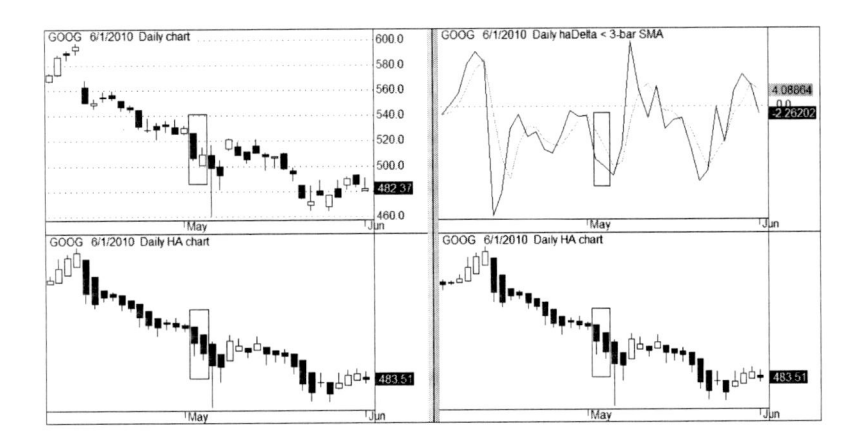

HEIKIN-ASHI WITH ON-NECK, IN-NECK, AND THRUSTING PATTERNS

FIGURE 19.2: *Google Inc. (GOOG) daily charts with Japanese and modified candles for May and June 2010. As long as haDelta average is negative, the downtrend continues.*

Here is how heikin-ashi confirms the expected downtrend:

- 5/4/10: A black candle with a long body appears in an established downtrend. There are no doubts about the character of the trend as the modified candle is bearish, and haDelta is positioned below its average. Both indicators are negative.

- 5/5/10: An in-neck pattern emerges at the end of the day with a close slightly into the body of the previous day. As far as heikin-ashi features are concerned, there is no change. The downtrend is alive.

- 5/6/10 and 5/7/10: The decline continues for two more days and includes the flash-crash on May 6. The gap up that followed brought some positive energy, but it was not sufficient in keeping haDelta average positive for more time. Soon after, the downtrend returns with a negative haDelta average. This setting shows a whipsaw that occurred when price gapped up on May 7 as the white the heikin-ashi candle indicated a trend change, later invalidated.

On a side note, haDelta provided a weak buy signal when it crossed its average one day before the gap up. These indications are in very many cases (though not in this case) leading and lasting indications. Again, heikin-ashi in any format does not look at candle patterns and definitions; it only looks at modified candles and body quantification.

The duration of the downtrend discussed in Figure 19.2 is more evident in Figure 19.3, showing Google in a weekly time frame. The price hit the bottom in early July when a tweezers bottom emerged. The pattern is again correctly identified using heikin-ashi: haDelta is slightly above the average (a weak buy signal because both the indicator and average are still negative), and the following week starts with a bullish white modified candle.

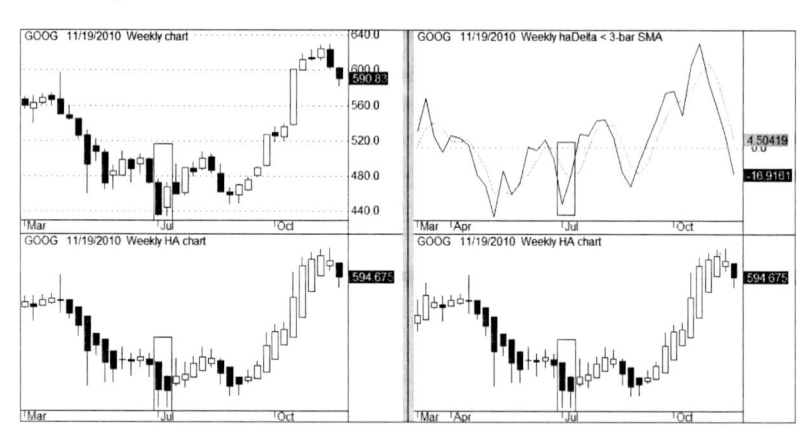

FIGURE 19.3: *Google Inc. (GOOG) weekly charts with Japanese and modified candles for March through November 2010. This weekly chart shows the extended downtrend from the moment the in-neck pattern emerges on the daily chart.*

Thrusting

Facts

- Thrusting is a two-candle pattern.
- This pattern is expected to act as continuation when it emerges in a downtrend.
- Candle 1 has a long black body.
- Candle 2 is white with a tall body. It opens below the low of the first candle and closes below the midpoint of the first candle body.
- It is similar to a piercing line pattern, only the close is below the midpoint of the previous body.

Questions to Consider

- What is considered to be a long black body? How it is measured and which reference is used?
- How many bars should be used to define a downtrend?
- Does this pattern really show a continuation, or does it indicate a reversal? Some statistics show that in more than 50% of cases, this formation is a reversal pattern and not a continuation as expected.

Figure 19.4 shows a daily price chart of Home Properties Inc. (HME) with a thrusting pattern in the first week of June 2007. It is a scenario similar to that displayed in Figure 19.2, where the downtrend continued for a longer period of time.

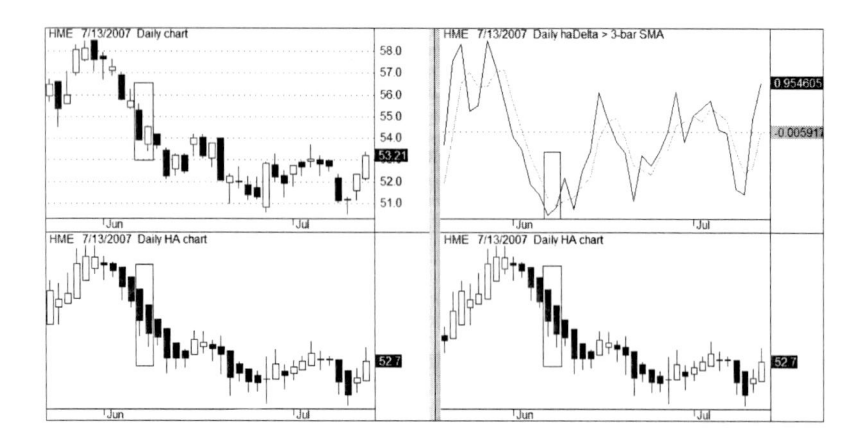

FIGURE 19.4: *Home Properties Inc. (HME) daily charts with Japanese and modified candles for June and July 2007. As long as haDelta average remains negative, the downtrend continues.*

Here is how heikin-ashi tracks the downtrend:

- 6/7/07: A candle with a long black body emerges in a downtrend. The heikin-ashi chart shows a negative candle in a downtrend. haDelta is below its average, and both are negative. There is no doubt about the falling trend.

- 6/8/07: The day closes just below the midpoint of the prior body, and the last two days represent a thrusting pattern. The candlestick theory calls for a continuation of the downtrend. The corresponding modified candle is still black with no indication of a slowdown. haDelta is ready to go above its negative average. The picture is still negative.

- The downtrend is clearly visible on the heikin-ashi chart and continues for four more days. It is followed by a gap up (open vs. prior close). The energy is not sufficient to change the downtrend; the price starts falling again with a bottom reached in July.

The reader may interpret the white candles on the heikin-ashi chart as price reactions because these candles are short and with tight ranges. However, one very important element to consider is the moving average that is negative (downtrend) but with higher lows. This is a positive divergence with the price and announces an uptrend that becomes fact after the low in July.

30-Second Summary

- On-neck, in-neck, and thrusting formations are considered continuation patterns.

- The weak reversal character leads to trend continuation and is due to a lack of strength to close above the midpoint of the body of the previous candle.

- Heikin-ashi charting and modified candle quantification help assess each candle in the context in which it emerges. Heikin-ashi totally ignores Japanese candlestick rules and definitions.

CHAPTER 20

HEIKIN-ASHI, THREE WHITE SOLDIERS, AND THREE BLACK CROWS

As their names imply, the three-candle patterns of three white soldiers and three black crows have a positive or negative connotation depending on the color of the candles. Color aside, the pattern's position in the trend is also important.

Even with these formations, expert opinions vary; some require long candle bodies, others look only for the same color. Some validate the pattern if the opening of a candle is inside the body of the previous one. For others, it is sufficient if the open price of each candle is near the top/bottom of the previous white/black candle. Rules are fluid, and translations may be different. Every trader and investor needs simplicity to reduce the degree of personal interpretation in the context in which the patterns appear.

In this chapter, the objective is again to minimize this personal interpretation by applying the heikin-ashi technique.

Three White Soldiers

Facts

- Three white soldiers is a three-candle pattern.
- This pattern is expected to act as a reversal when it emerges in a downtrend.
- Each candle has a (long) white body with a close near the high.
- The consecutive closings should be higher.
- Each candle opens inside the previous body.

Questions to Consider

- What is considered to be a long white body? How it is measured and which reference is used?
- How many bars should be used to define a downtrend?
- How flexible or restrictive should we be in assessing the open of each candle? Some experts are strict about the open of each candle. Others are more flexible, requiring the candle to open *near* the top of the previous candle body.
- How stringent should we be about the height of the candle bodies, as there are different interpretations and rules about body height?
- How is "near" measured to reduce subjectivity?
- How is "inside" measured to reduce subjectivity?
- What happens when three white soldiers emerge in an existing uptrend?

HEIKIN-ASHI, THREE WHITE SOLDIERS, AND THREE BLACK CROWS

With these flexible rules, we focus on groups of consecutive white candle bodies, such as those for Olympic Steel in January 2007. (See the series of candles numbered 1 through 4 in the candlestick chart in Figure 20.1). In this figure, there are two occurrences with good chances to pass the validity test for the three white soldiers pattern: the candles marked 1-2-3 and the candles marked 2-3-4.

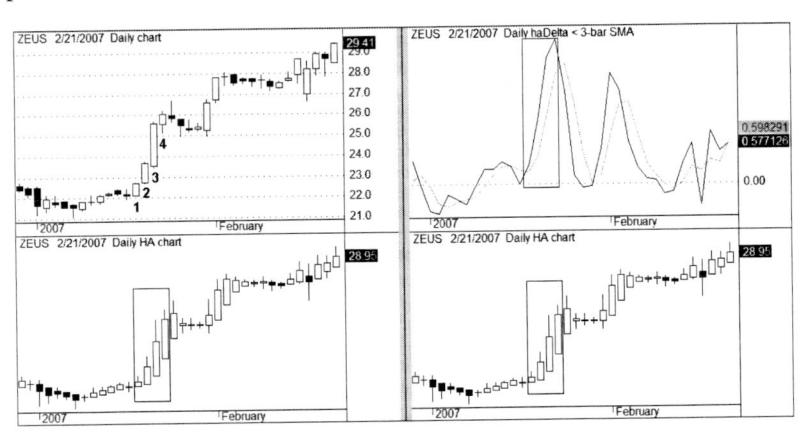

FIGURE 20.1: *Olympic Steel Inc. (ZEUS) daily charts with Japanese and modified candles for January and February 2007. Two candidates for three white soldiers status emerge in mid-January 2007.*

We will again apply heikin-ashi charts and modified candlestick quantification:

- 1/19/07: A white candle (1) appears in a timid uptrend shown on the heikin-ashi chart, indicated by a series of small body candles with no lower shadows. haDelta crosses above the average, which is already in positive territory. Note that the polarity of the average is a very good trend indication.

- 1/22/07: A white candle (2) opens one cent above the close of the previous day. Since rules are not strict, the open falls into the "near the previous close" category. Heikin-ashi shows a stronger trend with a taller white candle while haDelta continues to confirm price bullishness.

- 1/23/07: A white candle (3) opens inside the body of previous candle (2), near the top. Everything is bullish. At this point, candles 1 through 3 complete the three white soldiers pattern, and we are looking for an uptrend from here.

- 1/24/07: A white candle (4) opens inside the body of candle (3), near the top. This candle has a smaller body and may complete a stalled pattern (candles 2-3-4) with limited immediate upside. This actually is what happened. On the heikin-ashi chart, we see a continuation of the uptrend (long white body with missing lower shadow). We already know that heikin-ashi charts have a one-bar delay, and this is why we choose candle quantification, haDelta. The excessive value of haDelta—proof of an overbought condition—raises some concern about the immediate future. Even with a very long white candle today, haDelta would have been higher with limited upside in the very short term.

- A bullish flag develops over the next few days. Over the next three and a half months, a strong uptrend develops and brings the price to a high of $33.62.

Figure 20.2 shows Olympic Steel in a weekly time frame for an extended period of 2007, with clear trends on the heikin-ashi chart. Candle patterns 1-2-3 and 2-3-4 from Figure 20.1 are now inside the boxed area. Although haDelta looks tired from $28 to the top, its average remains positive for the duration of the uptrend.

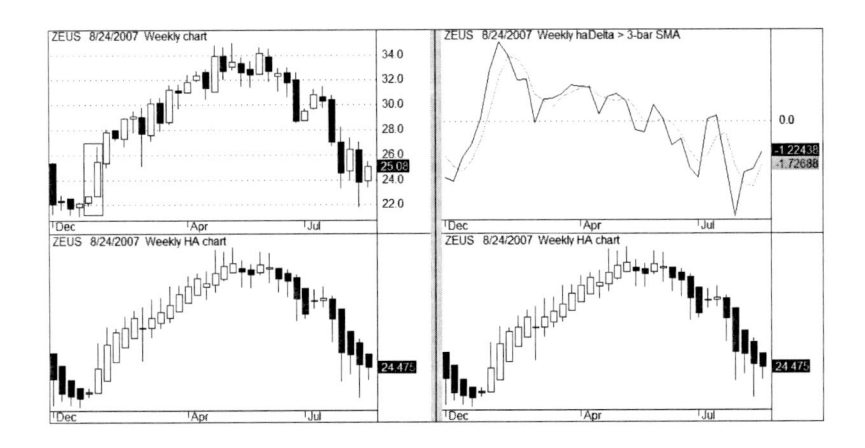

FIGURE 20.2: *Olympic Steel Inc. (ZEUS) weekly charts with Japanese and modified candles for December 2006 through August 2007. A longer time frame displays an improved picture on a heikin-ashi chart.*

Figure 20.3 shows the Commodity Research Bureau Index (CRY0) on a daily chart with a three white soldiers pattern in August 1991 that resembles a stalled pattern.

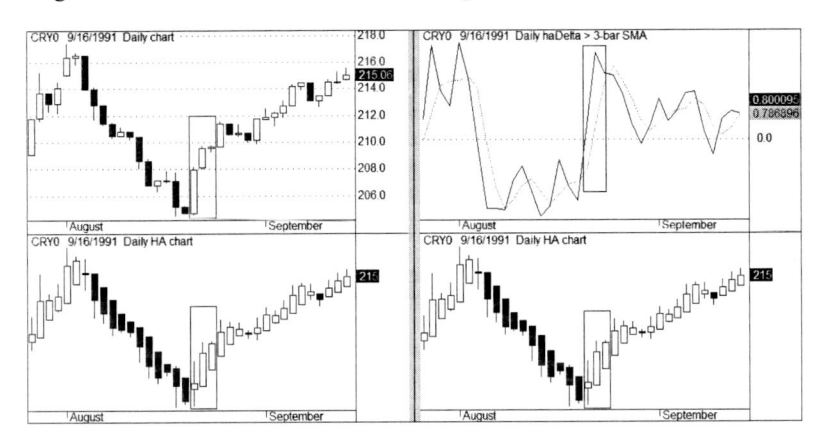

FIGURE 20.3: *Commodity Research Bureau Index (CRY0) daily charts with Japanese and modified candles for August and September 1991. To be or not to be a stalled pattern? haDelta helps with the answer.*

Normally, one would expect a loss of strength immediately after this pattern, but another very bullish candle emerges the next day, August 26. Although the day is bullish, haDelta crosses below the average, indicating a loss of momentum. It is exactly what followed during the next three days when the price went into a short pullback. During this time, the heikin-ashi candles became smaller with bodies inside previous ones (a sign of a slowdown). The bullish candle on August 30 completes a bullish rising three methods pattern. It is worth observing that when this last pattern developed, the heikin-ashi chart never showed a bearish sign; rather, it showed only possible reversal signs with small bodies and upper and lower shadows.

A last example of a three white soldiers pattern is seen in Figure 20.4 for Microsoft Corp. (MSFT) when the formation emerges in an uptrend. The heikin-ashi chart remains bullish for the duration of this pattern, but haDelta reveals a tired uptrend with a negative divergence between the indicator and price. The bearish day on October 31 confirms a dark-cloud pattern with haDelta pointing to a possible reversal. The rest is history.

FIGURE 20.4: *Microsoft Corp (MSFT) daily charts with Japanese and modified candles for October and November 1995. An energized three white soldiers pattern emerges in an uptrend. haDelta takes a closer look and reveals a tired uptrend.*

All these examples show *again* that even if an outcome is expected using Japanese candlestick conventional wisdom, it is more reliable to use modified candles and their quantification to evaluate each candle as it emerges. A more objective analysis improves decisions and results.

Three Black Crows

Facts

- Three black crows is a three-candle pattern.
- This pattern is expected to act as a reversal when it emerges in an uptrend.
- Each candle has a long black body with a close near the low.
- Consecutive closings should be lower.
- Each candle opens inside the previous body.

Questions to Consider

- What is considered to be a long black body? How it is measured and which reference is used?
- How many bars should be used to define an uptrend?
- How restrictive should we be about the open? Some experts are strict about the open of each candle. Others are more flexible, requiring the open to be *near* the bottom of the previous candle body.
- Why are there different views and requirements concerning the heights of the bodies?
- How is "near" measured to reduce subjectivity?

- How is "inside" measured to reduce subjectivity?
- What happens when three black crows emerge in an existing downtrend?

Figure 20.5 shows a three black crows pattern (see boxed candles) preceded by an uptrend in late March 2008 for Financial Select Sector SPDR (XLF). Theoretically, its negative force is expected to push prices lower. Practically, this figure shows that the pattern reverses quickly and prices are pushed to a higher high of over $25. A period of consolidation follows for the next four weeks. The anticipated decline does not become reality. Was the pattern a failure? Could heikin-ashi have made better judgements than the indications of the candlestick pattern?

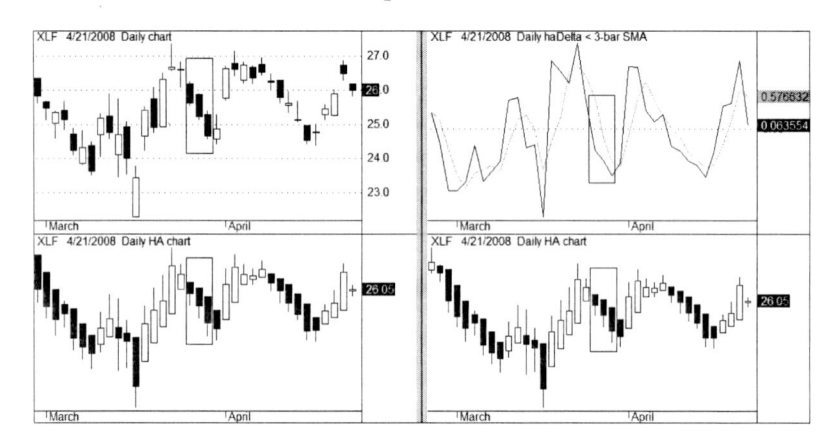

FIGURE 20.5: *Financial Select Sector SPDR (XLF) daily charts with Japanese and modified candles for March and April 2008. The three black crows pattern is preceded by an uptrend. Contrary to conventional wisdom, it does not have the immediate anticipated result.*

Although it was a valid pattern, expectations were not met. We will analyze three black crows using heikin-ashi charts and modified candlestick quantification:

- 3/26/08: A black candle with an acceptable long body appears at the top of an uptrend. The heikin-ashi chart shows the start of a downtrend. haDelta is below the average. A downtrend is starting.

- 3/27/08: A long black candle opens inside the previous body at its lower range. This may be a second black candle of a *potential* three black crows pattern. Heikin-ashi shows the same bearish conviction with another black candle without an upper shadow. haDelta is still below its average. More negative bias is added. At this stage, the three black crows pattern is not complete, and the negative bias is caused *only* by the actions of two bearish candles.

- 3/28/08: A third black long-body candle appears and completes the bearish (in theory) formation. The heikin-ashi chart shows a continuation of the downtrend, and haDelta goes deeper below the short average with an excessive value, indicating an oversold condition. Everything looks bearish with the exception of an extreme haDelta.

- 3/31/08: The white candle completes a new formation on this chart—an in-neck pattern—with reversal potential. Although the second candle of the pattern opens at, and not below, the low of the first candle, we accept it as an in-neck pattern. The modified candle is still black, but a closer look at haDelta (which is slightly above the average) reveals a sign of a *possible* reversal.

This example again reinforces the core of the heikin-ashi technique: While the 100-plus Japanese candlestick patterns require rules, definitions, and *inevitable* subjectivity, the heikin-ashi technique is simple and looks only at each price bar as it appears on the chart. Heikin-ashi does not solely rely upon candlestick patterns.

Figure 20.6 shows AT&T Inc. (T) on a daily chart with a three black crows pattern in an existing downtrend in mid-January 2010. Should we expect continuation or reversal upon the completion of this formation?

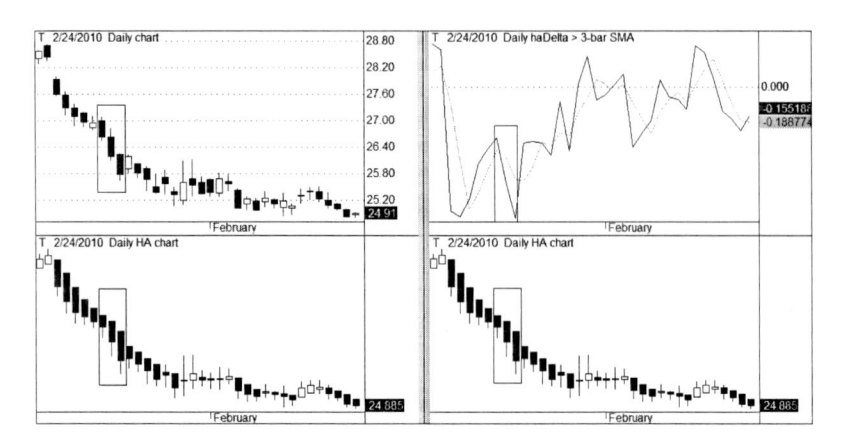

FIGURE 20.6: *AT&T Inc. (T) daily charts with Japanese and modified candles for January and February 2010. The three black crows pattern (see the boxes) is bearish even in an existing downtrend. On the other hand, haDelta points to a slowdown of the trend.*

The answer is *irrelevant* as we use heikin-ashi charting and supporting quantification:

- 1/13/10: A black candle emerges in a price decline. The heikin-ashi chart shows a clean downtrend with one doubt raising from haDelta, which is above the average.

- 1/14/10: Another black candle appears. At the end of the day, the last two black candles may be part of a three black crows formation *if* the next day will fit the pattern definition.

- 1/15/10: A black candle opens inside the prior body but near the bottom. The end of the day visually validates the pattern. The corresponding modified candle shows a more powerful downtrend with haDelta below its average. These signs point to a bearish picture.

After January 15, things look bearish in the absence of haDelta. Bringing the indicator on the chart, we see the combination of higher lows for haDelta and its average as a sign of a positive divergence with the price. The positive reversal and the reaction come later in March.

This example shows that heikin-ashi is able to remove a great deal of the subjectivity about the interpretation of this pattern. Its position is not important for the heikin-ashi trader; more important is the quantification applied to each candle in the sequence.

30-Second Summary

- The three white soldiers and three black crows patterns are expected to add positive or negative energy.

- They emerge anywhere on the chart.

- Heikin-ashi charting and quantification help analyze the components of these patterns in the context in which they emerge. Japanese candlestick rules and definitions are totally ignored.

CONCLUSIONS

Japanese candlestick theory, the knowledge accumulated during time, and the service industry developed around it cover over 100 candlestick patterns—some simple and some more complex.

It is practically impossible for anyone to remember a majority, if not all, of the pattern definitions and locate them on charts of interest. This is a tedious process and, in the end, traders, investors, and analysts focus on a limited number of patterns with higher probability of success. Or worse, they abandon Japanese patterns altogether, missing great trading opportunities.

This is why it would be financially rewarding for traders to use a form of candlestick analysis that ignores names, definitions, and expectations. As discussed *at length* in this book, heikin-ashi is one such form of simplified analysis. The current Japanese theory does not provide a similar instrument.

Some traders not aware of the heikin-ashi technique combine Japanese candles with indicators as confirmations. Others remove candlestick patterns completely from their trading and replace them with old-fashioned bars or quantifiable techniques.

In discussing the examples presented in Part Two of this book, we found over and over again that certain aspects of Japanese candlestick theory can be improved:

- Each Japanese candlestick pattern has flexible definitions and lacks strict measurement criteria.

- Interpretation of Japanese candlestick patterns in their visual format is subjective and very much artistic, and it requires extensive experience to translate each nuance.

- Good proficiency is reached after considerable time and financial investment in education.

- Many candlestick patterns do not act as expected, and this is very normal. They can emerge anywhere on charts and may have a short life span. Moreover, recent statistical studies invalidate some facts that, up to now, were considered conventional wisdom.

Is heikin-ashi a solution to improve analysis and decisions with Japanese candlestick patterns?

It may sound dramatic and, for many deeply involved in their study and practice, even a heresy. At a closer look, **heikin-ashi is not a bad suggestion at all; in fact, it makes your life easier.**

We have seen that heikin-ashi charting and modified candle quantification dissect each pattern in the context in which it emerges. Japanese patterns rules and definitions can *totally* be ignored. Traders have limited time to analyze, decide, and execute in environments full of information and especially price noise. They need some tools to improve decisions.

Heikin-ashi is here and worth applying tomorrow.

PART THREE

MARRYING HEIKIN-ASHI WITH OTHER TECHNIQUES AND INDICATORS

"There is no such thing as absolute value in this world. You can only estimate what a thing is worth to you."

Charles Dudley Warner, American writer (1829-1900)

We looked first at what heikin-ashi is and how the modified candles are built. Then, it was show time to see how popular Japanese candlestick patterns are used with the heikin-ashi technique and how they are translated. Now it is time to see how heikin-ashi works with several trading techniques widely used by traders and investors. The list of techniques we discuss here is far from exhaustive; actually, Part Three is just the beginning of the exploration.

Heikin-ashi, both as a visual and quantifiable instrument, can be used with your choice of trading strategies, either your own or someone else's. If you can initiate a trade one bar before most of the people or if you can avoid a false signal, the value of using heikin-ashi is immense. Moreover, you are free to focus the attention on issues other than studying, reading, and translating candlestick patterns.

Before going deeper into its use, remember that **the heikin-ashi technique is not a mechanical system; it is a component of your discretionary trading system.**

CHAPTER 21

HEIKIN-ASHI AND MOVING AVERAGES

The idea behind the original heikin-ashi charting technique was to remove much of the price noise and clearly identify trends. The quantification introduced recently adds more value by the advance entry and exit signals it can generate.

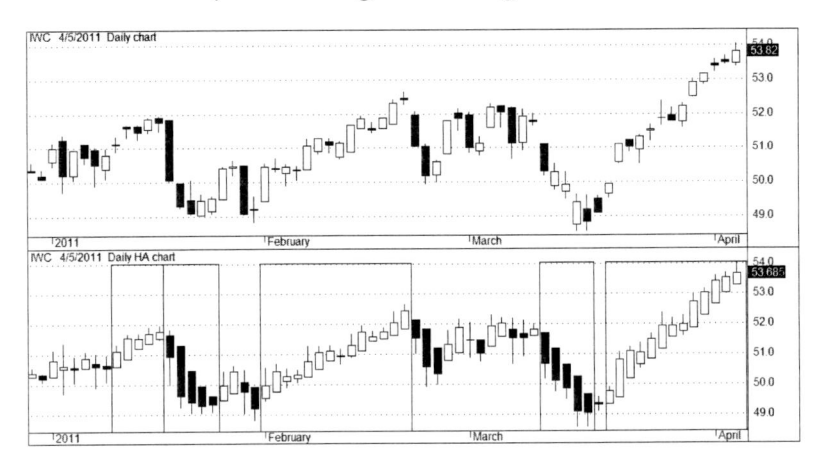

FIGURE 21.1: *iShares Russell Microcap Index Fund ETF (IWC) daily charts with Japanese and modified candles for January through March 2011. Trends and consolidations are more visible on the heikin-ashi chart, but whipsaws are still present during consolidations.*

The visual advantage is evident in Figure 21.1 which exhibits a daily chart of iShares Russell Microcap Index Fund ETF (IWC).

In the top pane of this figure we see uptrends, downtrends, reversals, and consolidations. There are many gaps, doji, and stars. The color, shape, and patterns of traditional Japanese candlesticks help determine the dynamics of each bar and pattern and, to a certain extent, an expected outcome. Although things look and are fine, they can be improved if pattern trading can join forces with other indicators or strategies.

In the lower pane of Figure 21.1, even an inexperienced eye rapidly identifies trends and consolidations. White candles are associated with bullish trends while black candles are associated with downtrends.

Trends and their strength are visible with white candles with upper shadows. Black candles with only lower shadows point to decisive negative trends.

Consolidations always introduce uncertainty and false signals. White or black candles with both upper and lower shadows identify these moments. One method used to remove some whipsaws is to apply moving averages.

In the lower pane of Figure 21.2, a seven-bar simple moving average of the closing price C is displayed on the daily heikin-ashi chart of iShares Russell Microcap Index Fund ETF (IWC).

The rules are simple but not mechanical:

- **Buy (exit short)** at the close of the price bar when haClose crosses above the average.

- **Sell (enter short)** at the close of the price bar when haClose crosses below its average.

HEIKIN-ASHI AND MOVING AVERAGES

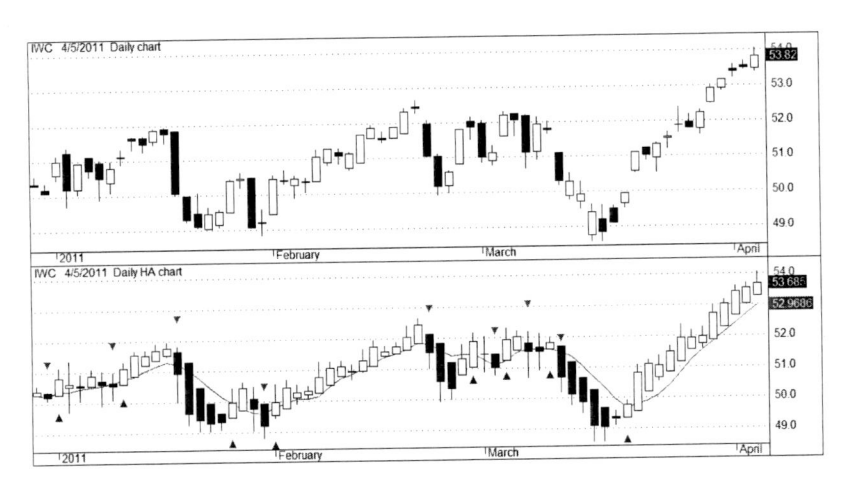

FIGURE 21.2: *iShares Russell Microcap Index Fund ETF (IWC) daily charts with Japanese and modified candles for January through March 2011. A seven-day simple moving average of the regular closing price is displayed on a heikin-ashi chart in the lower pane.*

Does this moving average improve discretionary trading? The trends are delimited now by stricter rules, and a number of false signals are removed. This is an improvement over the basic heikin-ashi visual strategy that requires action when candle color changes.

It is the time and place for an important observation: **Trends with steeper slopes appear clearer on a heikin-ashi chart.** This is the reason why financial instruments that historically display trends, such as FX pairs and technology stocks, are more suitable for heikin-ashi trading.

30-Second Summary

- The heikin-ashi visual strategy builds on long entries (short exits) when modified candles change color from black to white. Exits (short entries) are triggered when candle color switches from white to black.

- A moving average of the regular closing price introduces an improvement over the basic strategy and removes some false signals, but the trader is still exposed to whipsaws during price consolidations.

- One of the methods used to combine heikin-ashi candles with averages is to trigger entries and exits when haClose crosses the average of the closings.

- The slope of the price or/and average is relevant; a stronger trend leads to clearer heikin-ashi charts and signals.

- Instruments that historically displayed trends are more suitable to heikin-ashi trading.

CHAPTER 22

HEIKIN-ASHI AND MULTIPLE TIME FRAMES

In an old fable from India called the "Blind Men and an Elephant," six blind men are asked to determine what an elephant looks like by feeling different parts of the elephant's body. The first blind man feels a leg and says the elephant is like a pillar. The second one feels the tail and says the elephant is like a rope. The third blind man feels the trunk and says the elephant is like a tree branch. The fourth man feels the ear and says the elephant is like a hand fan. The fifth blind man feels the belly and says the elephant is like a wall. The last man feels the tusk and says the elephant is like a solid pipe.

After hearing their observations, a wise man says to them: "All of you are right. The reason every one of you is telling it differently is because each one of you touched a different part of the elephant. So, actually the elephant has all the features you mentioned."

This story and its wisdom apply exceptionally well to trading. Like the six blind men describing different parts of the elephant, traders frequently see only a small piece of the bigger picture by using a single time frame for analysis and decisions. They neglect the bigger picture that may (and very often does) hide risks. Not only are decisions incomplete, but poor risk and capital management kills when an adverse move hits.

Multiple time frame analysis and trading draw increased attention because of the better odds in catching trends in their infancy and remaining in them longer. Obviously if an uptrend is just starting in daily (TF1), weekly (TF2), and monthly (TF3) time frames, the winning odds for a long entry now are far bigger than when the entry is initiated in a daily time frame with weekly and monthly charts casting bearish clouds. The ideal scenario is to have trend alignment in all three time horizons and to initiate the trade *as early as possible* in the trend. As a compromise, two consecutive time frames may replace the ideal scenario.

The core of the heikin-ashi charting technique consists of visualizing trends and reversals with modified candles built with the five simple rules described in Chapter 2. An uptrend is identified with higher probability when a modified candle changes color from black to white. Generally, downtrends start when candle polarity reverses from white to black.

These basic observations lead to a first multiple time frame strategy involving heikin-ashi:

- **Buy (exit short)** when the current modified candle color changes from black to white in all three time frames chosen.

- **Sell (enter short)** when the current modified candle color changes from white to black in all three time frames chosen.

(Note: All transactions are initiated at the close of the price bar.)

Obviously this scenario is ideal, but too strict to ever occur; so some negotiation must take place. One option is to work only with two consecutive time frames (TF1/TF2 or TF2/TF3) instead of three and to apply this strategy:

- **Buy (exit short)** when the current modified candle color changes from black to white in the two consecutive time frames chosen.

- **Sell (enter short)** when the current modified candle color changes from white to black in the two consecutive time frames chosen.

Another alternative is to wait for a color shift in TF3. Action should be taken in TF1 *only* when the color in this time frame changes as in TF3 and the same color is in TF2:

- **Buy (exit short)** when the color of the modified candle in TF3 changes from black to white *and* the modified candle color changes from black to white in TF1 *and* the color of the modified candle in TF2 is already white.

- **Sell (enter short)** when the color of the modified candle in TF3 changes from white to black *and* the modified candle color changes from white to black in TF1 *and* the color of the modified candle in TF2 is already black.

Since entry and exit conditions are not usually symmetrical, the sell (exit long) condition can be modified to ensure a safer profit. One option is to sell when the color of the modified candle in TF3 changes from white to black.

We apply this strategy in evaluating the charts and time frames for SPDR S&P 500 ETF (SPY) in Figures 22.1 and 22.2:

- Looking at Figure 22.1, **buy** when the color of the modified candle in TF3 changes from black to white (4/30/09) *and* the modified candle color changes from black to white in TF1 (4/30/09) *and* the color of the modified candle in TF2 is already white (4/30/09). The result was that this security was bought at a close of 86.96 on April 30, 2009.

- Looking at Figure 22.2, **sell** when the color of the modified candle in TF3 changes from white to black (2/26/10). The result was that SPY was sold at a close of 110.16 on February 26, 2010 for a gain of 26.67%.

HEIKIN - ASHI

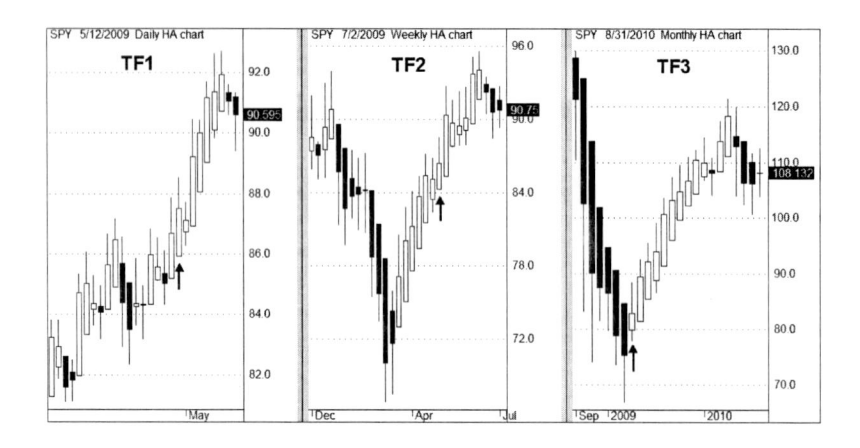

FIGURE 22.1: *SPDR S&P 500 ETF (SPY) with heikin-ashi candles in three time frames between 2009 and 2010. A long entry signal is given when the monthly modified candle changes color from black to white and the other two time frames TF1 and TF2 display the same white color.*

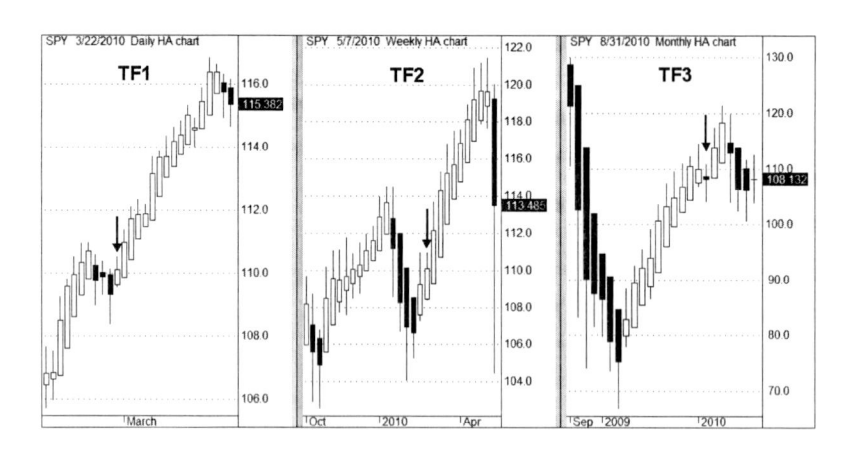

FIGURE 22.2: *SPDR S&P 500 ETF (SPY) with heikin-ashi candles in three time frames between 2009 and 2010. A long exit signal is given when the monthly modified candle turns black.*

HEIKIN-ASHI AND MULTIPLE TIME FRAMES

In the previous chapter, we discussed how moving averages can be used as a filter to reduce false signals on heikin-ashi charts. We can easily build new strategies adding a moving average.

- **Buy (exit short)** when the color of the modified candle in TF3 changes from black to white *and* haClose crosses above the average in TF3 *and* the modified candle color changes from black to white in TF1 *and* the color of the modified candle in TF2 is already white.

- **Sell (enter short)** when the color of the modified candle in TF3 changes from white to black *and* haClose crosses below the average in TF3 *and* the modified candle color changes from white to black in TF1 *and* the color of the modified candle in TF2 is already black.

Since entry and exit triggers are not usually symmetrical, the exit long (sell) condition can be modified to ensure a safer profit. One option is to sell when the color of the modified candle in TF3 changes from white to black *and* haClose crosses below the average in TF3.

This strategy applied to SPDR S&P 500 ETF (SPY) gives the following results, as shown in Figures 22.3 and 22.4:

- Looking at Figure 22.3, **buy** when the color of the modified candle in TF3 changes from black to white *and* haClose crosses above the average in TF3 (5/29/09) *and* the modified candle color changes from black to white in TF1 (5/29/09) *and* the color of the modified candle in TF2 is already white (5/29/09). The result was that SPY was bought at a close of 92.05 on May 29, 2009.

- Looking at Figure 22.4, **sell** when the color of the modified candle in TF3 changes from white to black *and* haClose crosses below the average in TF3 (6/30/2010). The result was that SPY was sold at a close of 102.68 on June 30, 2010 for a gain of 11.54%.

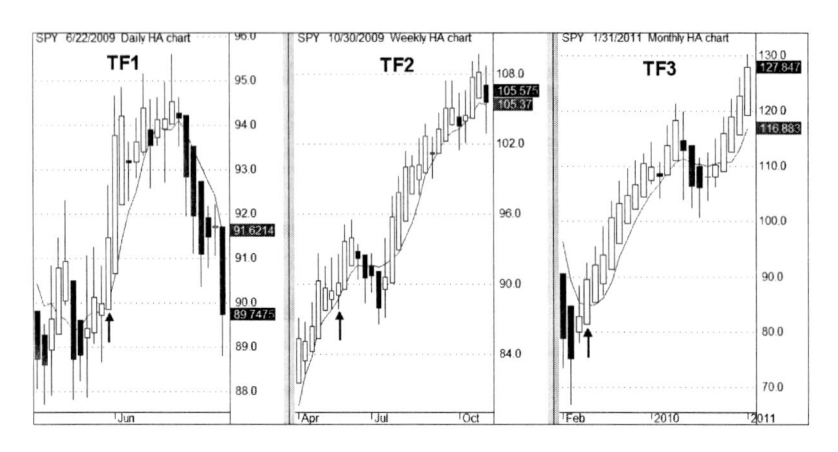

FIGURE 22.3: *SPDR S&P 500 ETF (SPY) with heikin-ashi candles in three time frames between 2009 and 1010. A buy signal is given in TF3 when the monthly modified candle changes color from black to white and haClose crosses above the average of the close. The heikin-ashi candles in the other two time frames TF1 and TF2 are white, too.*

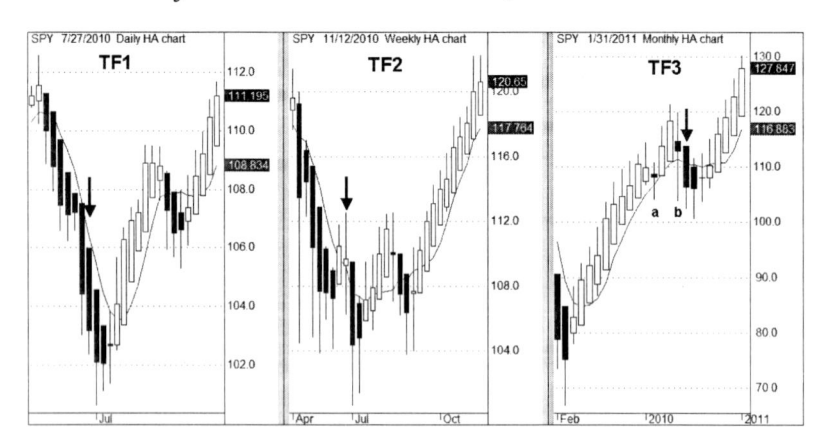

FIGURE 22.4: *SPDR S&P 500 ETF (SPY) with heikin-ashi candles in three time frames in 2010 and 2011. A sell signal is given in TF3 when the monthly modified candle turns black and haClose crosses below the average of the closing.*

HEIKIN-ASHI AND MULTIPLE TIME FRAMES

The examples in this chapter show methods in which the heikin-ashi visual technique is used: color change, and crossings between haClose and the seven-bar close average. Results of these two strategies are slightly different, but false signals are removed using the average in Figure 22.4's TF3 a and b (February 26, 2010 and May 28, 2010). Note that only heikin-ashi candles have been used. A door left open is the inclusion of haDelta and its short average with these strategies.

30-Second Summary

- Looking for and trading the same trend in multiple time frames is a well-known technique that improves the odds for better timing and for staying longer with the trend.

- The heikin-ashi visual technique fits very well with multiple time frames trading.

- The best scenario involves the simultaneous buy or sell signal in all three time frames. This is an ideal situation; as a compromise, the highest time frame rules and the next two lower horizons are used for fine tuning.

- Entry and exit conditions are not symmetrical. The exits are more restrictive if you prefer safer profits or smaller losses.

- Two basic strategies defined in this chapter involve taking advantage of the change of candle color and applying the seven-bar close average to modified candles.

- Despite the temptation to use these rules for mechanical trading, it is advisable to adapt them to discretionary trading.

- If you are looking for powerful signals the next time you are about to trade, heikin-ashi with multiple time frames is an option worth applying.

CHAPTER 23

HEIKIN-ASHI AND NEXT DAY FORECAST

On a heikin-ashi chart, the *next* open (haOpen) of a modified candle is already known at the close (C) of the current bar. In other words, we are able to calculate *in advance* where the modified candle will open the next heikin-ashi candle on any chart and time frame. Since the open is one of the two elements used to measure the size of a candle body and determine its color, we focus on the close (haClose) of the next heikin-ashi candle.

Can we approximate haClose just *before* the end of the current bar? If the answer is positive, we are able to know the color of the heikin-ashi candle and the position of haClose vis-à-vis the average of the closing price (C). This could improve the trading by taking positions *before* the end of the current bar in any time frame.

Here is an example that speaks for itself. Figure 23.1 shows a Dell Inc. (DELL) daily chart for December 2010 and January 2011, with a Japanese candlestick chart in the upper pane and with a corresponding heikin-ashi chart below it. The dates of interest are December 31, 2010 and January 3, 2011, marked 1 and 2 respectively in the figure.

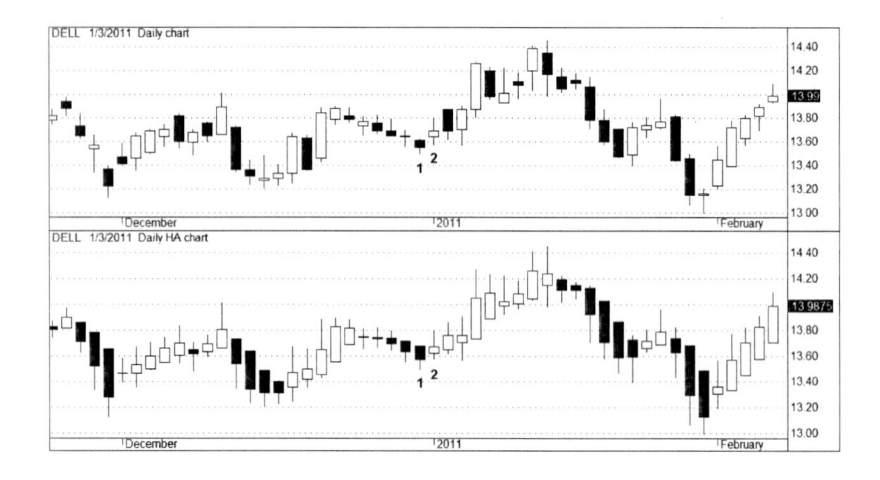

FIGURE 23.1: *Dell Inc. (DELL) daily chart with Japanese and modified candles for December 2010 through January 2011. What is the value of the closing price on January 3 required to reverse the downtrend?*

The attention moves to the last day of 2010 with a closing price (C) of $13.55. We do not know anything about how the first trading day of the new year will be. At this moment, we know only values for haOpen and haClose of the black modified candle ($13.67 and $13.57, respectively) on December 31.

We look forward to the first trading day of 2011 (January 3) and plan to buy, using heikin-ashi strategy based on change of the candle color.

There are good odds that we will witness a trend reversal if the color of the modified candle on January 3, 2011 is white. This is equivalent with haClose greater than haOpen. Since haOpen for January 3 is known already at the end of the day on December 31, 2010 as $13.62 [(13.67+13.57)/2], haClose on January 3 must be greater than this value in order to have a white heikin-ashi candle (and a start of an uptrend).

How is haClose computed? It is simply the average bar price calculated by summing all four prices (O+H+L+C) and dividing the result by four. The only price element we know with certainty on January 3 *during* the trading day is the open (O) at $13.64. The high (H) and the low (L) will be known when trading day ends. To calculate haClose for this day, we make the assumption that the high and low values are known sufficiently well *near* the end of the day. The keyword here is "near," which we can define as in the last minute(s) of the session.

Near the end of the session, the high and low values were $13.80 and $13.57, respectively. After computations, the lowest close (C) required to generate a white heikin-ashi body (haClose > haOpen) was $13.50. Since the final close (C) was $13.69, a long entry near the end of the day had very good odds to be at a value higher than $13.50. If the price near the end of the day remains below $13.50, buying should be avoided. As with any trade, a stop-loss is mandatory to protect against uncertainty until the end of the trading bar.

This calculation is easier when made either with a simple spreadsheet (see Figure 23.2) or by hand, observing in real time the last price (C) near the end of the current trading bar.

	A	B	C	D	E	F	G	H
1	Spreadsheet to determine the closing price that generates a white heikin-ashi candle							
2								
3	Previous bar							
4								
5	HAOpen	13.67		input				
6	HAClose	13.57		input				
7								
8	Current bar		(HAClose > HAOpen generates a white heikin-ashi candle)					
9			(HAClose < HAOpen generates a black heikin-ashi candle)					
10								
11	HAOpen	13.62		(B5+B6)/2				
12	HAClose greater than HAOpen	13.62		SUM(B11:B16)/4				
13	Open (O)	13.64		input				
14	High (H)	13.80		input				
15	Low (L)	13.54		input				
16	Close (C) should be greater than	13.50		(4*B11-B13-B14-B15)				
17								

FIGURE 23.2: *This spreadsheet calculates the lowest closing price (C) required to have a white modified candle (haClose > haOpen).*

For a long entry, the strategy combining both color changes and crossings between haClose and the seven-bar close average requires haClose to cross above the seven-bar simple average and remain there at the end of the bar. The scenario in Figure 23.1 is now replicated in Figure 23.3, the only difference being the average of the close (C) displayed on the heikin-ashi chart.

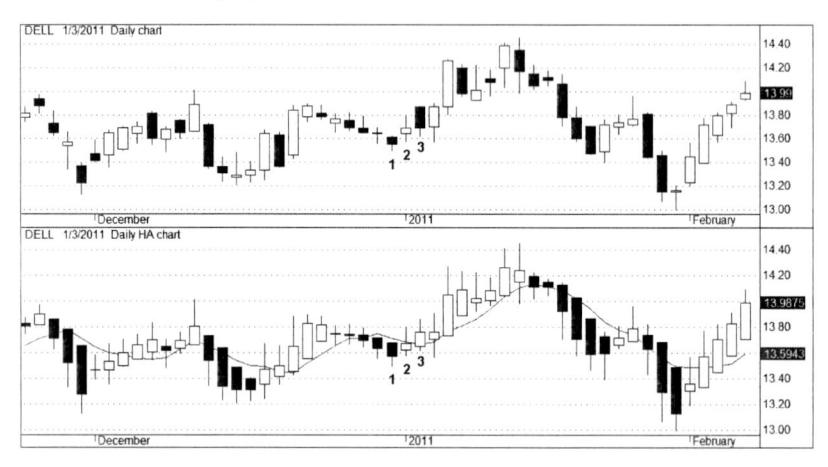

FIGURE 23.3: *Dell Inc. (DELL) daily charts with Japanese and modified candles for December 2010 through January 2011. What is the lowest value of the closing price on January 3 needed to reverse the downtrend if we require haClose to end the day above the seven-day average of the closing price?*

The spreadsheet in Figure 23.4 summarizes the calculation of the lowest close required with this strategy.

The outcome of this approach is different from the previous example. Here the minimum close (C) required to generate a bullish setting on January 3 is $13.85. The close was only $13.69, below the required value. The buying decision is postponed for the next bar (3) when we can rerun the spreadsheet computation described in Figure 23.4.

HEIKIN-ASHI AND NEXT DAY FORECAST

	A	B	C	D	E	F	G	H
1	Spreadsheet to determine the closing price that generates a heikin-ashi candle with							
2		a close above 7-bar close simple average						
3	Previous bars (bar -2 to bar -6)							
4								
5	Close	13.79		input	bar -6			
6	Close	13.77		input	bar -5			
7	Close	13.69		input	bar -4			
8	Close	13.65		input	bar -3			
9	Close	13.65		input	bar -2			
10								
11	Previous bar (bar -1)							
12								
13	HAOpen	13.67		input				
14	HAClose	13.57		input				
15	Close	13.55		input	bar -1			
16								
17	Current bar (bar)		(HAClose > SMA(C,7) generates a bullish signal)					
18			(HAClose < SMA(C,7) generates a bearish signal)					
19								
20	HAOpen	13.62		(B13+B14)/2				
21	HAClose greater than SMA(C,7)	13.71		condition to have a bullish signal				
22	Open (O)	13.64		input				
23	High (H)	13.80		input				
24	Low (L)	13.54		input				
25	Close (C) should be greater than	**13.85**		(4*(SUM(B5:B9)+B15)-7*(SUM(B22:B24)))/3				

FIGURE 23.4: *This spreadsheet computes the lowest closing (C) required to have a modified candle close above the seven-bar average of the close (C) (haClose > SMA(C,7)).*

30-Second Summary

- The body of a heikin-ashi candle is important mainly for its color, which is associated with the trend.

- It is possible to approximate an entry/exit in any time frame to meet a bullish or bearish heikin-ashi condition.

- haOpen for the next bar can be easily calculated at the end of the current bar.

- haClose for the next bar can be approximated near the end of the next bar.

- The examples in this chapter provide two simple strategies where the trader takes action based on higher probabilities to occur *near* the end of the current bar.
- The lowest close required to meet bullish or bearish conditions is easily computed with a spreadsheet or by following the price in real time near the close.
- Stop-loss is a must even with this strategy; there is always a real risk in having big price swings until the end of the trading bar.

CHAPTER 24

HEIKIN-ASHI AND Z-SCORE

Prices go up and down in trends delimited by minor or more relevant reversal points. Catching tops and bottoms is an extreme sport for many traders who use different techniques and strategies. One of these techniques involves Bollinger bands, which are widely used to take more gains from the trend.

The main idea with Bollinger volatility bands is that prices remain inside the bands for a certain percentage of their occurrences. For example, closing prices stay 95.4% within two standard deviations from a moving average. For excessively extended instruments, prices remain 99.7% within three standard deviations above and below a mean. In other words, we *expect* the bands to act as support and resistance for prices.

Lesser known is that z-score, an old statistical measure of volatility, can be used instead of Bollinger bands. Personally I see a visual advantage since z-score measures the distance, in standard deviations, of the price from the average.

Figure 24.1 shows a compare-and-contrast chart of Oracle Corp. (ORCL) for November 2010 through March 2011. In the upper pane, prices are displayed together with Bollinger bands with two standard deviations from a 20-day moving average. Just below, z-score shows how far—measured in standard deviations—closing prices are from the same average.

When closings go above the upper band, z-score extends over +2; when prices dip below the lower band, z-score crosses below -2. In this chapter we will be using z-score for its visual advantage.

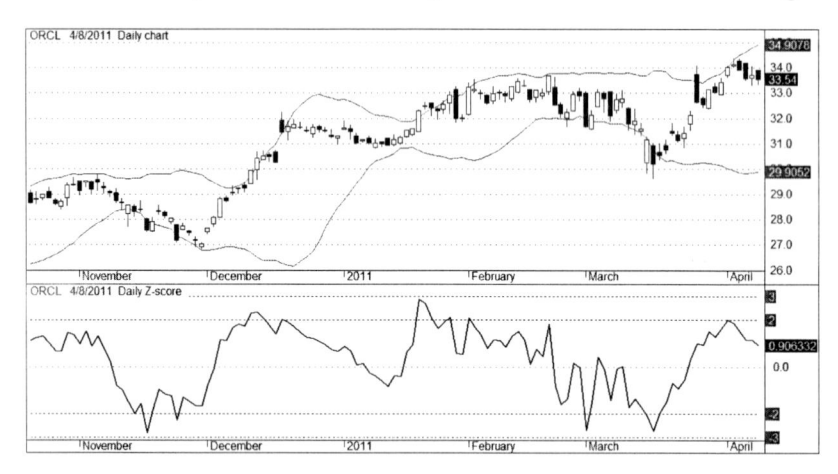

FIGURE 24.1: *Oracle Corp. (ORCL) daily chart for November 2010 through March 2011, with Bollinger bands and a better visual perspective offered by z-score indicator.*

Figure 24.2 gets a little more complex with the introduction of haDelta and its three-bar simple average. Why do we need these indicators? Part Two discussed extensively how haDelta and its average demonstrate that Japanese candlestick patterns can be easily translated using modified candle quantification. For our analysis, we are looking for haDelta confirmations when closing prices are in extreme positions at, above, and below the bands. With prices approaching or hitting the bands as support or resistance, it would be useful to have confirmation with crossings of haDelta with its average, *if* they occur.

HEIKIN-ASHI AND Z-SCORE

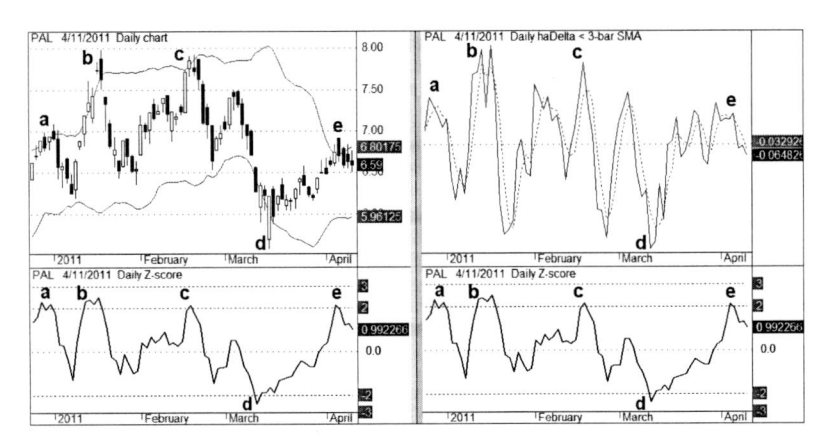

FIGURE 24.2: *North American Palladium Ltd. (PAL) daily chart with z-score and heikin-ashi for late December 2010 through early April 2011. When an overbought/oversold condition appears on the price start, the first impulse is to look for haDelta crossings (indicated with letters) as confirmations.*

On this chart there are five distinct areas (marked a through e) where z-score is at +/- two standard deviations. We will be looking at haDelta crossings to confirm price reversals at these levels of the z-score.

At the end of December 2010 (a), z-score identifies an overbought condition. Is this a reversal or just a false signal followed by a continuation of the uptrend? As in most cases, haDelta helps and sends a compelling message by crossing below its average; a bearish price reversal follows very soon.

Prices get overstretched again in January 2011 (b) when z-score remains above +2 for several days. haDelta offers a false weakening signal during this time, but the confirmation comes when z-score goes below +2 and haDelta crosses below its average; it is time for another reversal.

A third resistance zone (c) emerges after an uptrend in February 2011. Prices close above the upper Bollinger band with the equivalent z-score above +2. Is this a possible reversal or a continuation? haDelta offers a reliable indication when it crosses below its average. The subsequent reversal is further proof that heikin-ashi quantification cannot be ignored.

The second week in March 2011 (d) shows an oversold condition when z-score dips below -2. We look immediately for haDelta crossings above the average and find one occurrence two days later. This is a clear sign that prices will re-enter inside the Bollinger bands.

The fourth overbought indication emerges in early April 2011 (e) when z-score rises above +2 for only one day. At that time, haDelta was already above its average, offering a confusing picture.

The strategy involving Japanese candlestick patterns with Bollinger bands is popular among traders who are looking for reversal candlestick patterns at or near resistance and support levels in anticipation of a trend change.

By replacing candlestick patterns with heikin-ashi charting/quantification and replacing the Bollinger bands with z-score, we get to another level of simplicity with less effort and faster decisions.

Figure 24.3 is another example and a quick exercise for the reader. You can decide whether the use of heikin-ashi is easier and more reliable than candlestick patterns.

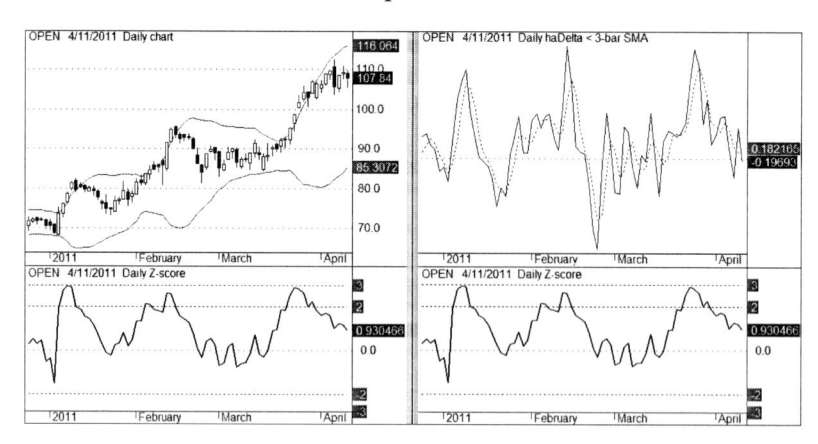

FIGURE 24.3: *This OpenTable Inc. (OPEN) daily chart for late December 2010 through early April 2011 has a very bullish outlook, with closings near three standard deviations from the average. These extreme values are confirmed quickly as reversals using haDelta crossings.*

30-Second Summary

- Volatility bands, such as Bollinger bands, together with Japanese candlestick patterns are widely used to offer confirmations for reversals and continuations.

- Both components of this strategy can be replaced now: Bollinger bands with z-score, and candlestick patterns with heikin-ashi charting/quantification.

- The result leads to faster and more accurate decisions.

- Other bands can be used for the same purpose with the heikin-ashi technique in both formats.

CHAPTER 25

HEIKIN-ASHI AND RELATIVE STRENGTH INDEX

Relative Strength Index (RSI) is a very popular indicator used to determine mainly overbought and oversold conditions.

Since heikin-ashi charting offers sharper images of trends, consolidations, and reversals in any time frame, it can be suitably associated with this indicator. We will be looking for *earlier* signals than those offered by the Relative Strength Index, as well as for confirmations.

Figure 25.1 shows the S&P 500 Index with Relative Strength Index of 14 bars. When RSI approaches 70, the index approaches a top (though not always true) and more caution is required. On the other hand, when RSI is falling and approaches 30, it signals a possible bottom (even this is not always true). The midpoint of 50 is a value of equilibrium; values over it confirm an uptrend while those below 50 confirm a downtrend.

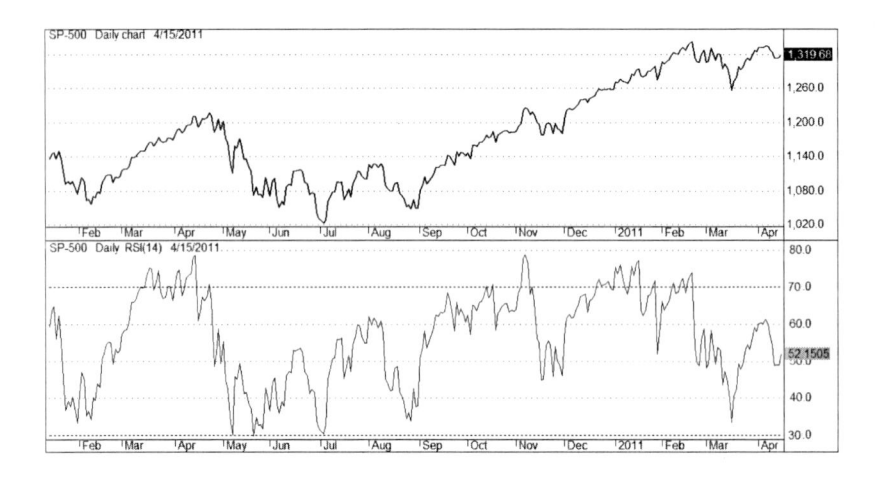

[Chart image]

FIGURE 25.1: *S&P 500 Index (SP-500) daily charts for January 2010 through April 2011 with RSI(14).*

During the period covered on the chart, RSI never went below 30 because the trend was bullish. There were several times when the indicator crossed above 70 with bullish and overbought implications.

Figure 25.2 illustrates a weekly chart of the same index from a heikin-ashi perspective, using modified candlesticks with haDelta and its average. April 23, marked with a vertical line on the charts, has an RSI(14) value above 70 at 72.61. The message is that a possible top may be approaching. Can we see signs of exhaustion or even reversal on the heikin-ashi chart? The corresponding modified candle is white, with an indication of uptrend. One seemingly insignificant detail is actually important in this overbought situation: The heikin-ashi candle has a tiny lower shadow. On one side, the index is in overbought territory with RSI(14) over 70; on the other side, there is a timid indication of a slowdown, visible by using modified candles. This picture requires more attention and tighter stops. haDelta is *below* its average, sending a stronger message for a top/reversal.

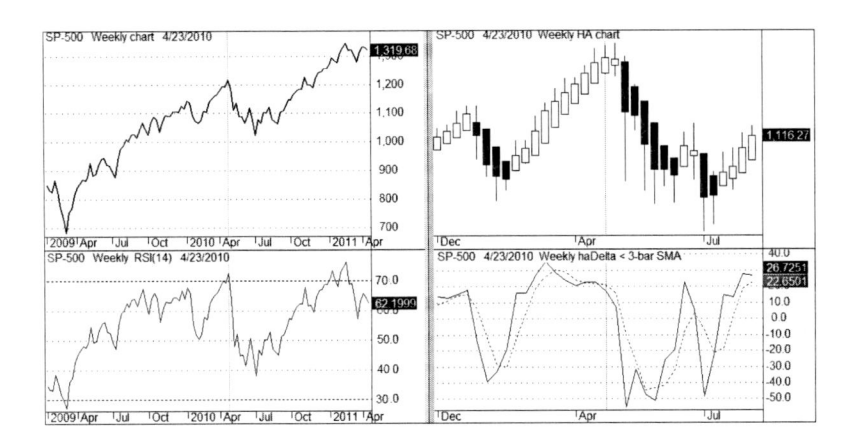

FIGURE 25.2: *S&P 500 Index (SP-500) weekly charts with heikin-ashi charting and indicators for 2009 through 2011. haDelta offers an early negative indication the same week Relative Strength Index goes above 70.*

The following week ending on April 30 confirms the top with a typical heikin-ashi reversal candle. We notice the well-known delay of one bar between a price top and emergence of the heikin-ashi reversal candle. The quantification of heikin-ashi candles makes this handicap manageable, and haDelta shows that the reversal is now a fact.

Figure 25.3 shows the same setting for the US Dollar Index (DXY0) on a daily chart for October 2010 through March 2011.

On the last day of November 2010, RSI(14) crosses above 70, sending a message of a potential top occurring soon. Are there any indications of a top given by heikin-ashi? The modified candle remains very bullish, but haDelta offers a hint at a possible top when it reaches a value similar to that recorded earlier in November. The next day, the US Dollar Index closes lower, RSI goes below 70, and the corresponding modified candle shows a slowdown and a possible reversal (body with two shadows). haDelta comes to the rescue, crossing below its average. A top is in place.

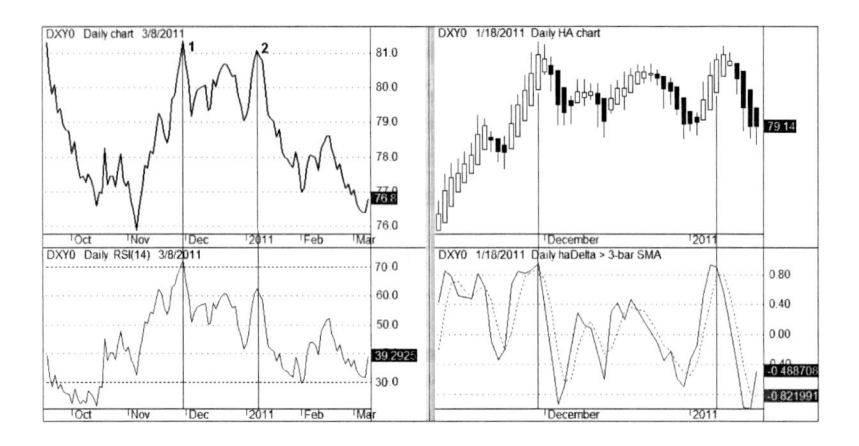

FIGURE 25.3: *US Dollar Index (DXY0) daily charts with heikin-ashi charting and indicators for October 2010 through March 2011. An overbought situation (RSI above 70) is confirmed, with haDelta reaching a resistance offered by a previous high.*

We now look at the second important top on this chart that occurs on January 7, 2011. Technicians consider this value as a resistance and may bet on a high probability reversal. Simple technical analysis proves often to be a reliable tool. We shift focus to heikin-ashi analysis and see no warning on the modified candle chart. Again, haDelta sends a strong top signal when it hits the resistance reached back in November 2010 and January 2011. On the next day, January 8, the US Dollar Index closes lower and the heikin-ashi chart remains bullish, but haDelta is below its average.

30-Second Summary

- Candlestick patterns are already used with the Relative Strength Index to confirm oversold/overbought conditions and reversals.

- Overbought and oversold conditions can be confirmed *earlier* with heikin-ashi tools.

- The association of RSI(14) with heikin-ashi charts illustrates again the one-bar delay that does not prove helpful. Thanks to heikin-ashi quantification implemented with haDelta, this handicap is removed in most cases and confirmations are more accurate.

CHAPTER 26

HEIKIN-ASHI AND ICHIMOKU CHARTS

Like the fashion industry, interest in technical indicators and strategies evolves in cycles. The recent years witnessed a surging interest for older and simpler analysis tools that were able to withstand economic crises, market crashes, and wars. Point & Figure charts, trend analysis, Dow theory, and cycle theory are a few examples of areas attracting traders and investors these days.

Renewed focus has also been seen for Japanese-inspired indicators and techniques, including Ichimoku charts. Developed in Japan before WWII and released to the public in the 1960s, Ichimoku charts—or Cloud charts as they are also known—became increasingly popular in the West.

The simplicity of an Ichimoku chart makes it an attractive trading system. Any Ichimoku chart contains key information that I call "The Fives": trend, entry point, stop-loss, trailing-stop, and possible price objectives. Together with adequate risk and capital management, Ichimoku charting becomes a complete trend-following system that offers better risk/reward for traders and investors.

Before getting into how heikin-ashi and Ichimoku charts work together, we first look at Ichimoku charting with an example in Figure 26.1 showing the S&P 500 Index on an Cloud chart.

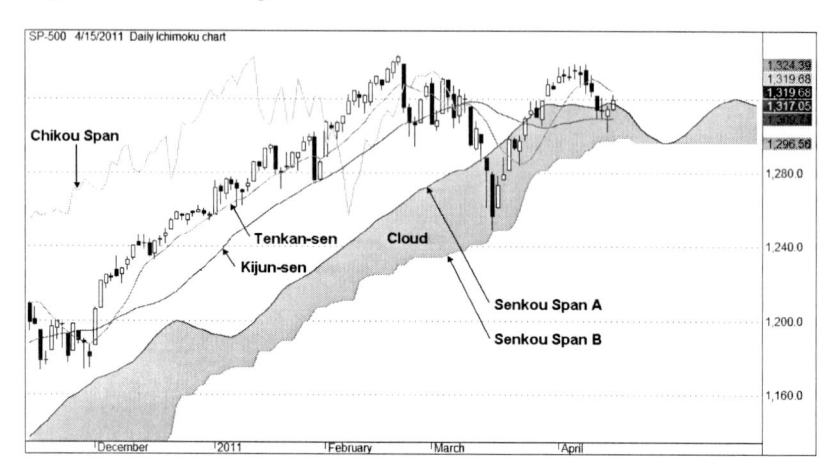

FIGURE 26.1: *S&P 500 Index (SP-500) daily Ichimoku chart for late 2010 through early 2011.*

Any Cloud chart contains the following elements:

- Tenkan-sen (Conversion line)
- Kijun-sen (Case line)
- Chikou Span (Lagging Span)
- Kumo (Cloud) consisting of two lines:
    - Senkou Span A (Leading Span A)
    - Senkou Span B (Leading Span B)

We look at how each component is calculated and describe it briefly. Unlike software packages that calculate Ichimoku averages based on the highest and lowest values during a chosen period, the averages described below are computed as the Japanese do; that is, by using the *midprice* of each bar (high plus low of each bar divided by two).

Tenkan-sen is a nine-day moving average of the midprice while Kijun-sen is a similar average with a longer period of 26 days.

The Cloud is considered the most visible and important element on an Ichimoku chart. It is composed of two lines, Senkou Span A (Leading Span A) and Senkou Span B (Leading Span B).

The Leading Span A is faster and defined as (Kijun-sen + Tenkan-sen)/2 being plotted 26 days into the future. The other line of the Cloud, Leading Span B, is slower and defined as the midpoint between the high and the low of the past 52 days. It is also plotted 26 days into the future.

The Cloud is interpreted as either a resistance or support, depending on where prices come from. When Senkou Span A (shorter line) is above Senkou Span B (longer line), the bias is considered bullish with the Cloud usually colored green. The inverse position of the lines illustrates a negative bias, with the Cloud filled with a color having bearish connotations.

The last element of an Ichimoku chart is Chikou Span, the closing plotted 26 days in the past.

With all components defined, we look now at basic strategies using Ichimoku trading system. The most obvious is the position of the price vis-à-vis the Cloud. When the stock or index closes above the Cloud, the trend is considered bullish; on the other hand, a close below kumo points to a bearish scenario. A closing inside the Cloud sends a message of uncertainty until the exit from the Cloud confirms the next trend.

Chikou Span plays an important role in judging today's trend. If it is above the candle 26 days ago or above the Cloud, today's trend is considered bullish. Inversely, when Chikou Span is below the candle 26 days ago or below the Cloud, today's trend is considered bearish.

With Japanese charting techniques gaining more acceptance, much of this knowledge is altered to fit into existing Western thinking (left-brain oriented). Ichimoku charts are no exceptions, as discretionary and mechanical trading strategies were born using the basic elements of these charts.

For our purpose—the use of heikin-ashi and Ichimoku charting together—we will focus on simple strategies involving support and resistance. Any Ichimoku chart offers multiple levels of support and resistance; therefore, we will be looking for heikin-ashi trend reversal signals *near or at* these levels.

Figure 26.2 shows the S&P 500 Index for November 2010 through April 2011 on an Ichimoku chart with heikin-ashi candles below it. We focus on three instances when the index visited the Cloud: the end of November, March, and April.

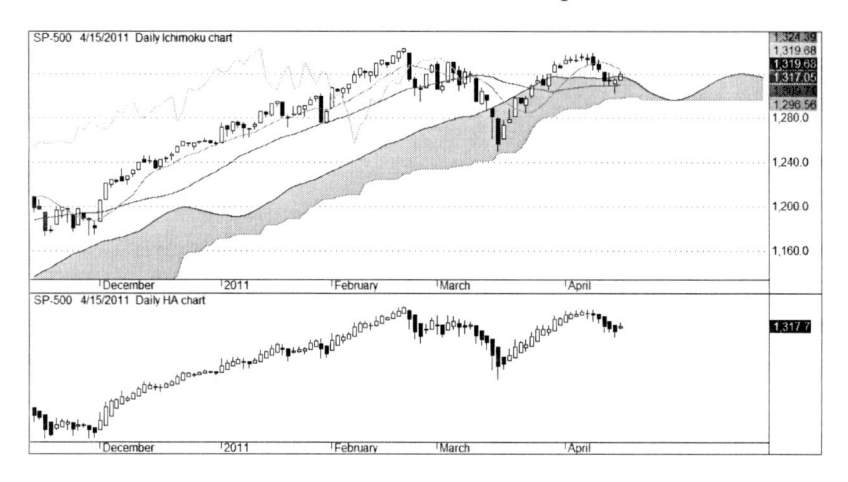

FIGURE 26.2: *S&P 500 Index (SP-500) Ichimoku and heikin-ashi daily charts for November 2010 through April 2011.*

Although the index fell below Kijun-sen and Tenkan-sen in November 2010, the thickness of the Cloud was viewed and acted as solid support. The S&P 500 Index came close to Senkou Span A, but before touching it, the downtrend reversed with a series of high-energy white heikin-ashi candles.

The second and more delicate moment was in March 2011 when the index penetrated the first level of support, Senkou Span A. The hammer above the Cloud was translated as a black modified candle (a sign of continuation for the downtrend). The next two days inside the Cloud had corresponding black heikin-ashi candles with no foreseeable trend change. March 16 marked a low near the bottom of the Cloud (Senkou Span B). Will the next day break the support? Following the Japanese candlestick theory, the bullish harami pattern that developed on March 16 and 17 offered indication of a trend reversal. The heikin-ashi chart also shows a slowdown of the current downtrend (body inside body).

Although the following day, March 18, closed below the bullish harami high, the corresponding modified candle pointed to a trend reversal, changing color from black to white. As a déjà vu, we notice the one-bar delay between price reversals and heikin-ashi visual confirmations. This is something we must live with, but luckily haDelta offers timely signals to compensate for the lag.

As it stood on April 15, 2011, the close above the Cloud showed a positive bias for the markets. The heikin-ashi chart also provided a positive signal with the white candle emerging after the pullback.

We have seen that haDelta and its short average provide in many instances advance indications for trend reversals and make Japanese candlestick interpretation redundant. Figure 26.3 shows an Ichimoku chart with haDelta indicators.

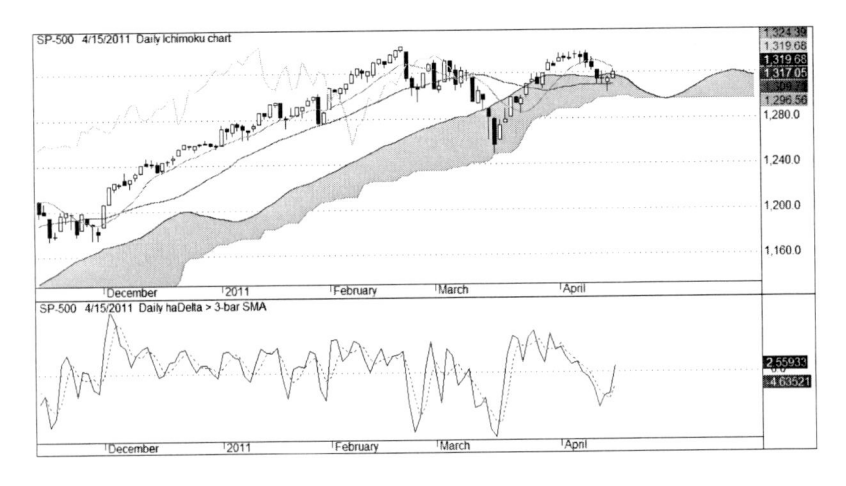

FIGURE 26.3: *S&P 500 Index (SP-500) Ichimoku daily chart with haDelta and its average for November 2010 through April 2011.*

With the first approach at the end of November 2010, haDelta was slightly below its average with a positive divergence between the price and indicator during the month, a sign that the index was ready for a bounce. Later, the low in March 2011 had a haDelta value similar to others that historically pointed to market lows. This was a sign of downward exhaustion for both price and indicator and was followed by a reversal at support. The last intention to visit the bottom of the Cloud was in April 2011 when haDelta was above its average, displaying a positive behavior. The reversal followed soon after.

The last two examples illustrate the advantage of using heikin-ashi quantification over the original heikin-ashi charting technique. **When you use heikin-ashi with Ichimoku charts, you should be looking for crossings between haDelta and its short average** *near or at* **important support and resistance levels identified by Senkou Span A, Senkou Span B, Kijun-sen, and even Tenkan-sen.**

The monthly Ichimoku chart for the S&P 500 Index in Figure 26.4 shows a nascent long-term bullish trend as a result of the close above the Cloud in February 2011.

FIGURE 26.4: *S&P 500 Index (SP-500) Ichimoku monthly chart with haDelta and its average for 2001 through 2011.*

In April 2011 haDelta is below the average with an indication for a possible market top. Looking forward 26 months, the index has a first support at 1,121 followed by a level just above the 1,000 mark. *If and when* these values become closer, we should look for haDelta bearish crossings on the monthly chart. Until then, the bullish trend remains healthy from the perspective of Ichimoku theory and with some twists from the perspective of the heikin-ashi technique.

The weekly chart for World Gold Index (XGLD) in Figure 26.5 exhibits a perfect uptrend, with Kijun-sen acting as trailing-stop since gold closed above the Cloud back in January 2009. Gold bounced back seven times at this support in the past (as indicated by the circled areas on the Ichimoku chart), and we would like to see if heikin-ashi offered bullish indications on these occasions. To make things easier and faster, we use haDelta and its average with the Ichimoku chart.

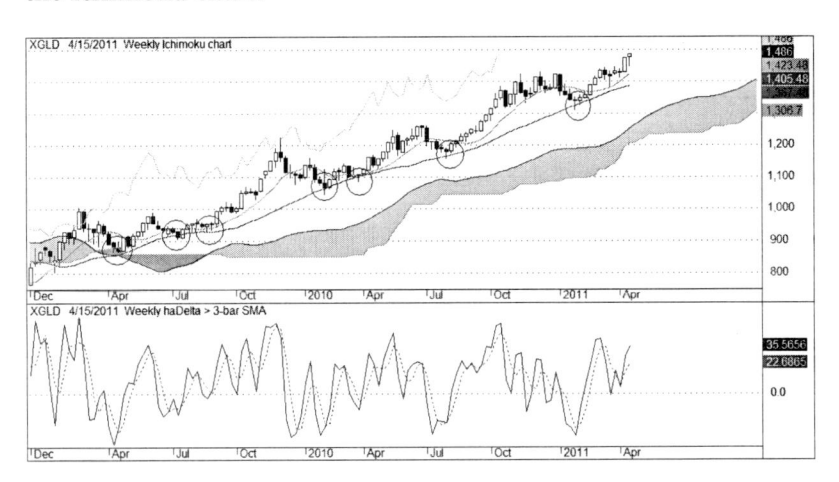

FIGURE 26.5: *World Gold Index (XGLD) Ichimoku weekly chart with haDelta and its average for December 2009 through April 2011.*

Although people are tempted to look for specific candlestick patterns at support, we look for faster and more reliable indications as crossovers of haDelta above its average.

The seven instances when gold found support at Kijun-sen are associated with a majority of positive haDelta crossings. This is an important statistical message for future pullbacks of the gold price to Kijun-sen.

30-Second Summary

- Ichimoku charts are increasingly used as a complete trading system.

- Any Ichimoku chart provides "The Fives," five elements required for any trade: trend assessment, entry, stop-loss, trailing-stop, and possible price objectives.

- Ichimoku charts have several components with indications for support and resistance.

- Many traders and investors use Ichimoku charts with candlestick patterns for price confirmations at or near support or resistance.

- This approach can be easily modified by replacing candle patterns with heikin-ashi tools such as haDelta and its average. It is a fast and reliable approach and requires no need to look at Japanese patterns.

CHAPTER 27

HEIKIN-ASHI AND MARKET BREADTH

Market breadth is used to determine the character of a market and measure its level of bullishness or bearishness. The Advance/Decline line, percentages of stocks above/below averages, 52-week highs and lows, and the McClellan oscillator are some indicators used for this purpose. A popular gauge of the market strength is the percentage of stocks in a market group trading above the 200-day moving average. As it stood on April 21, 2011, this indicator showed 76.81%, which is above the threshold of 75% used to indicate a strong bull market. The indicator can be easily modified to use other periods for the average.

Various types of market breadth indicators can be designed if we could count the percentage of stocks meeting other criteria, such as percentage of stocks in the oversold or overbought areas. Oscillators are good candidates for this job.

In previous chapters in which we have discussed heikin-ashi and its quantification, we have defined triggers for bullish or bearish reversals. Can we count the number of stocks in a market or sector meeting one or several of these heikin-ashi conditions? If so, we will be able to measure the strength of the market or sector using heikin-ashi quantification.

One of the criteria we can use to measure market bullishness or bearishness is the position of the heikin-ashi close (haClose) vs. the seven-bar simple average of the regular close (C).

We look at how this heikin-ashi qualification applies to the S&P 500 Index, the benchmark of the U.S. markets tracking 500 stocks. Figure 27.1 shows the S&P 500 Index and the percentage of stocks above the seven-day close average included in the index %HAup.

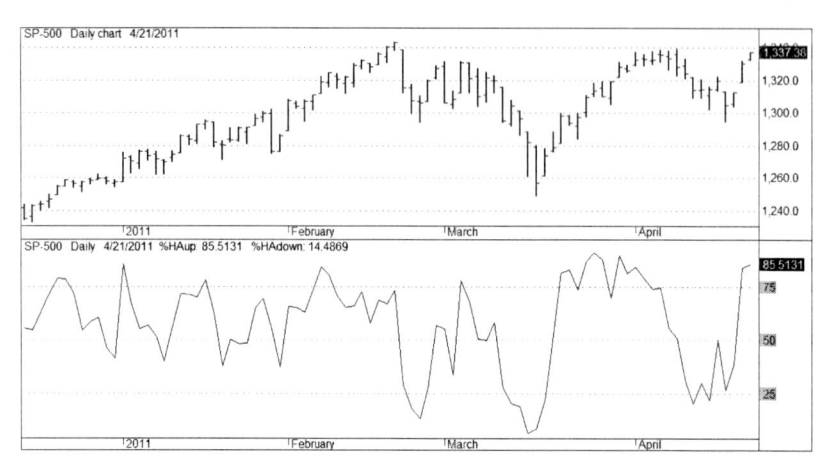

FIGURE 27.1: *The S&P 500 Index (SP-500) daily chart for late 2010 through April 2011, with percentages indicating heikin-ashi bullishness (%HAup) or bearishness (%HAdown) of the market [haClose above MA(Close,7]).*

As the names suggest, %HAup and %HAdown show percentages of stocks above and below the moving average, respectively. Since the sum of the two percentages is 100, we focus on %HAup, which points to a healthy market as long as it remains over 50%. An overbought market is exposed when %HAup goes over 75. The same methodology applies for any time horizon, with stronger results in a weekly or, better, monthly time frame.

The second pane displays only %HAup, the percentage of stocks with haDelta above the average MA(C,7). There are two thresholds drawn on this chart: 25 and 75. Below 25 corresponds to a market condition when we expect an important low of the index. On the other hand, when the %HAup is above 75, the market is very bullish and a top is possible. Note that the negative divergence in February 2011 between the index and the %HAup indicator led to a steeper decline of the market.

In Figure 27.2 we move to a weekly time frame, keeping the index and the indicator.

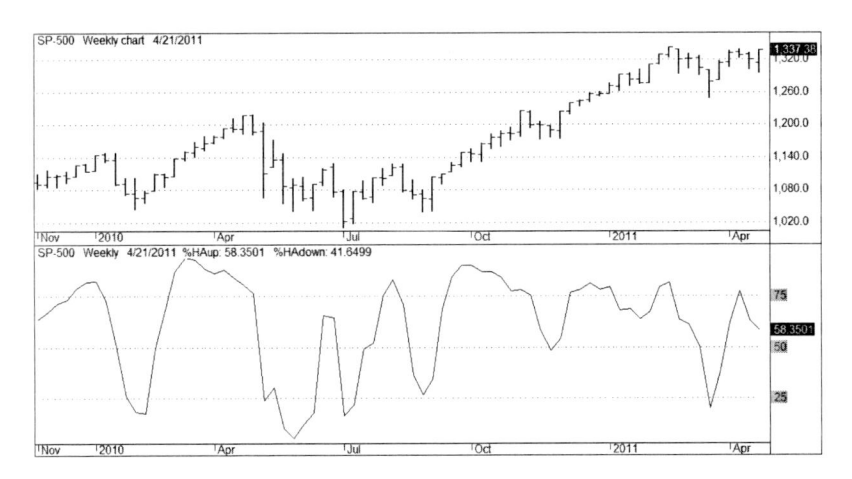

FIGURE 27.2: *The S&P 500 Index (SP-500) weekly chart for late 2010 through April 2011, with percentages indicating bullishness and bearishness of the market as seen through the eyes of the heikin-ashi technique (haClose above MA(Close,7)).*

The thresholds are now changed to 20 and 80, respectively. When %HAup moves above 80, we *expect* a market top. A market bottom is in focus when it falls below 20. The percentage for April 21, 2011 does not favor another reliable medium-term rally of the markets since the value is only 58.4%, despite the S&P 500 being near its recent high.

We look now at the second criterion identified in the previous chapters: bullishness when haDelta is above its three-bar simple average and bearishness when haDelta falls below average. Figure

27.3 shows the market index and the percentage of stocks included in the index with haDelta above its average MA(haDelta,3).

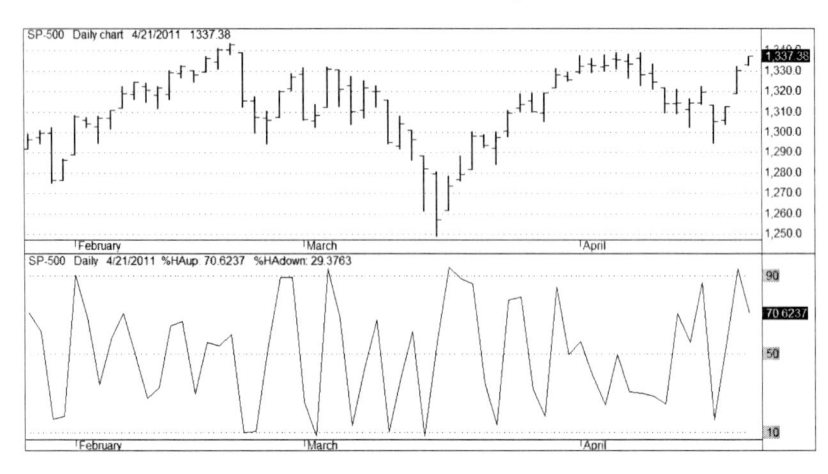

FIGURE 27.3: *The S&P 500 Index (SP-500) daily chart for February through April 2011, with percentages indicating heikin-ashi bullishness of the market (haDelta above its short average).*

Two relevant thresholds are now drawn on this chart: 10 and 90. When %HAup falls below 10, we expect a market low due to excessive bearishness. On the other hand, when the %HAup is above 90, the market is ready to make a top. The negative divergence established between the index and the %HAup in February 2011 led to a steeper market decline on February 22. On that day, %HAup hit 9.8% with anticipation for a low that occurred two days later.

The market rally from mid-March to the first week of April 2011 was not fueled by real strength. During this time, %HAup was falling—a sign that the market internals were deteriorating. On April 6, when the S&P 500 closed at 1,335.54 (very close to its recent high of 1,343.01), the bullish percentage indicator %HAup showed a mediocre value of 49.6%. This disagreement was a bearish sign for the index, and the result came immediately

HEIKIN-ASHI AND MARKET BREADTH

when markets fell. As of April 21, 2011, %HAup was 70.6%, despite the index making a higher close; this is another sign of a rally running out of gas.

How does this approach work in a higher time frame? Figure 27.4 shows the S&P 500 Index over an extended period of time, from February 2010 through April 2011.

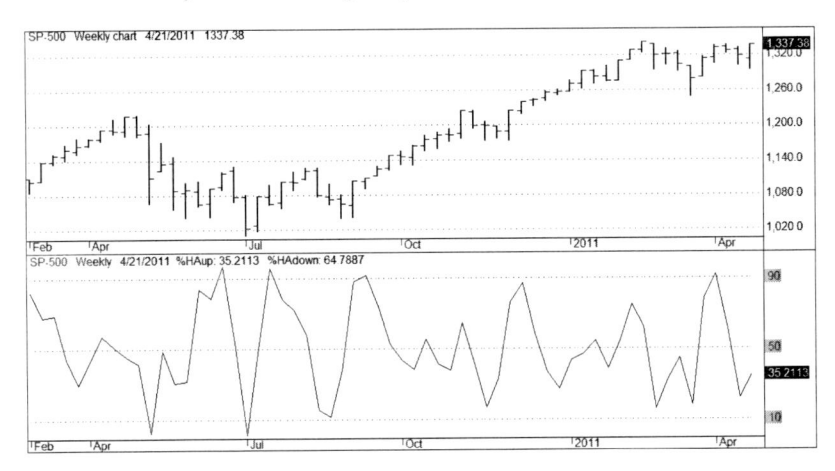

FIGURE 27.4: *The S&P 500 Index (SP-500) weekly chart for February 2010 through April 2011, with percentages indicating heikin-ashi bullishness of the market (haDelta above its three-bar average).*

This chart shows a healthy market over this period, with the bullish percentage indicator %HAup dipping twice below 10%. These extreme moments correspond to expected lows of the index. Given the overall positive bias of the market, %HAup over 90% indicates either energy gaps (February 2010, September 2010) or anticipated tops (June 2010, July 2010, and possibly April 2011).

30-Second Summary

- Market breadth indicators are used to describe the character of the market and gauge the strength of the market.

- Traders and investors can build their own market breadth indicators by quantifying levels of bullishness/bearishness in a market or sector.

- In many cases heikin-ashi and its quantification indicators offer leading reversal signals. Using the heikin-ashi technique to count the number of such indications in a market or sector leads to a new group of market breadth indicators.

- Two criteria have been used in this chapter to measure market bullishness:

- Heikin-ashi close (haClose) above the seven-bar close average MA(C,7).

- The height of the modified candle haDelta above its average MA(haDelta,3).

- The new percentage indicators %HAup and %HAdown can be used in any time frame. One extremely useful indication emerges when bullishness or bearishness is extreme in all time frames.

CHAPTER 28

HEIKIN-ASHI AND PIVOTS

We all dream of buying as low as possible and selling at the very top. The personal profile is a decisive factor for the meanings that "highs" and "lows" have for each trader and investor. However, trends between these extreme points are in focus for the majority; the longer the favorable trend, the bigger the potential gains. This is the main reason why so much effort and capital have been invested in finding new ways to anticipate and confirm minor/major lows and highs in the markets.

In this chapter we define a pivot as an inflection point, a point that marks a change of direction from up to down (sell pivot), or from down to up (buy pivot), as illustrated in Figure 28.1. It is evident that on any chart there are many such points, so applying a filter improves the selection of more relevant points. We should observe here that all pivots are confirmed later than they are ideally shown on charts.

FIGURE 28.1: *Sell and buy pivots, as indicated by the bars marked with the number 2.*

In technical analysis and trading, there are many ways to determine more or less reliable pivots. For our approach involving the heikin-ashi technique, we define pivots as follows:

- **Sell pivot**
    - The high of bar 2 is above the highs of bars 1 and 3.
    - The low of bar 2 is above the lows of bars 1 and 3.

- **Buy pivot**
    - The low of bar 2 is below the lows of bars 1 and 3.
    - The high of bar 2 is below the highs of bars 1 and 3.

Figure 28.2 shows buy and sell pivots on a monthly chart for the S&P 500 Index for 2005 through 2011. Although pivots emerge in any time frame for any instrument, we chose a higher time frame to better illustrate pivots (arrows) and their confirmations (small circles).

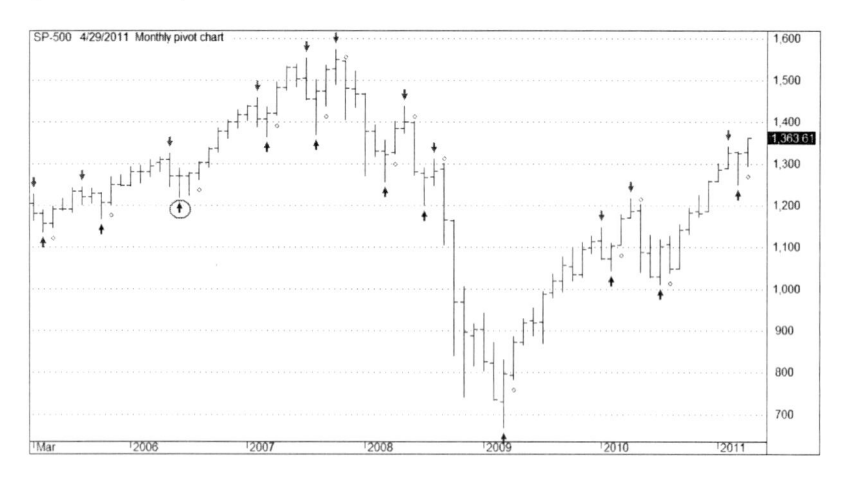

FIGURE 28.2: *The S&P 500 Index (SP-500) monthly chart for 2005 through 2011, with pivots and their confirmations.*

On this chart, pivots follow the definitions with the exception of the buy pivot in June 2006 marked with a larger circle. By the rules, this pivot (identified as bar 2) is valid, but its confirmation comes two months later in August (new bar 3) instead of the end of July (old bar 3). The reason for this is that July 2006 was an inside bar and did not count as confirmation (bar 3). It was simply ignored. The next bar at the end of August meets the requirements and becomes the new bar 3.

The small circles on the chart show pivot confirmations. They appear only at the end of the period identified by the rules as bar 3. In other words, only at confirmation time is the pivot (arrow) drawn on the chart.

Given the usual delay of at one bar between pivot and its confirmation, it is worth looking into how the heikin-ashi technique in both formats—visual and quantification—could help with *earlier* confirmations. Any advance sign of a trend reversal has great financial value and should be given serious consideration. This is what we will be doing with the S&P 500 market index, as shown in Figure 28.3.

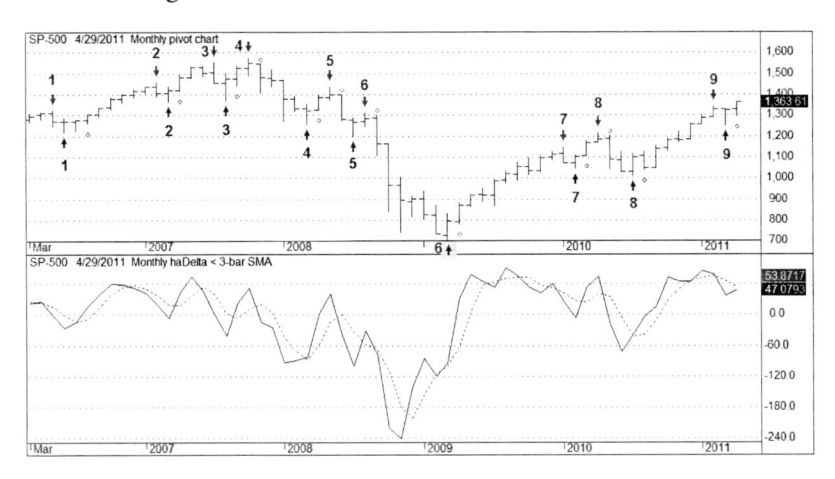

FIGURE 28.3: *The S&P 500 Index (SP-500) monthly chart for 2006 through early 2011, with pivots and heikin-ashi quantification indicators.*

For each buy and sell pivot on the chart, we look at haDelta and its average. If a sell or buy pivot or the prior bar has haDelta above or below its average, heikin-ashi offers a clear advantage, as shown below:

- Sell pivot 1: Bearish indication (haDelta, average). Advantage heikin-ashi.

- Buy pivot 1: Bearish indication (haDelta, average). The pivot is confirmed two bars later. haDelta crossed above its average one bar earlier than the price confirmation occurred.

- Sell pivot 2: Bearish indication (haDelta, average). Heikin-ashi offered an advantage already two bars earlier when haDelta moved below the average.

- Buy pivot 2: Bearish indication (haDelta, average). Heikin-ashi offered no advantage. The pivot is confirmed one bar later. haDelta turned above the average.

- Sell pivot 3: Bearish indication (haDelta, average). Heikin-ashi offers an advantage already one bar earlier when haDelta moved below the average.

- Buy pivot 3: Bearish indication (haDelta, average). Heikin-ashi offers no advantage. The pivot is confirmed one bar later, and haDelta turned above the average.

- Sell pivot 4: Bullish indication (haDelta, average). Heikin-ashi offers no advantage. The pivot is confirmed one bar later, and haDelta turned below the average.

- Buy pivot 4: Bullish indication (haDelta, average). Advantage heikin-ashi.

- Sell pivot 5: Bullish indication (haDelta, average). Heikin-ashi offers no advantage. The pivot is confirmed one bar later, and haDelta turned below the average.

- Buy pivot 5: Bearish indication (haDelta, average). Heikin-ashi offers no advantage. The pivot is confirmed one bar later, and haDelta turned above the average.

- Sell pivot 6: Bullish indication (haDelta, average). Heikin-ashi offers no advantage. The pivot is confirmed one bar later, and haDelta turned below the average.

- Buy pivot 6: Bullish indication (haDelta, average). Advantage heikin-ashi.

- Sell pivot 7: Bearish indication (haDelta, average). Advantage heikin-ashi.

- Buy pivot 7: Bearish indication (haDelta, average). Heikin-ashi offers no advantage. The pivot is confirmed one bar later, and haDelta turned above the average.

- Sell pivot 8: Bullish indication (haDelta, average). Heikin-ashi offers no advantage. The pivot is confirmed one bar later, and haDelta turned below the average.

- Buy pivot 8: Bullish indication (haDelta, average). Advantage heikin-ashi.

- Sell pivot 9: Bullish indication (haDelta, average). Heikin-ashi offers no advantage.

- Buy pivot 9: Bearish indication (haDelta, average). Heikin-ashi offers no advantage. This last buy pivot is still open.

This brief analysis, which involves price pivots and heikin-ashi quantification (haDelta and its average), shows the benefit of using heikin-ashi for sell pivots 1, 2, 3, 7 and buy pivots 4, 6, 8. For the remaining monthly pivots, haDelta confirms at the same bar as the pivot is normally confirmed. The last buy pivot in April 2011 is still open.

The results show an advantage for heikin-ashi in 38% of all pivots on this chart (seven out of 18), 10 draws, and one open trade. These numbers are exceptionally good for heikin-ashi.

How does the same analysis perform when we replace haDelta and the average with heikin-ashi candles as shown in Figure 28.4?

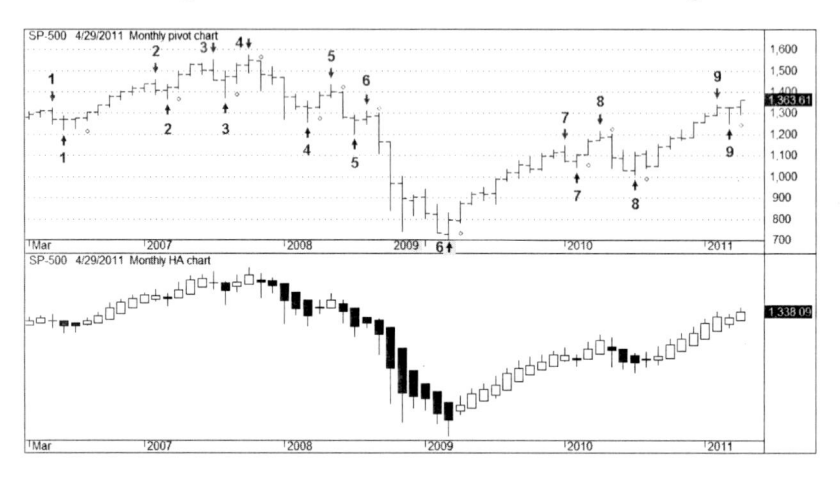

FIGURE 28.4: *The S&P 500 Index (SP-500) monthly chart for March 2006 through early 2011, with pivots and modified candles.*

We repeat the steps based on information in Figure 28.4 as shown below:

- Sell pivot 1: The heikin-ashi candle indicates a reversal from bullish to bearish. Advantage heikin-ashi.

- Buy pivot 1: Bearish modified candle. Heikin-ashi offers no advantage. The pivot is confirmed two bars later, and the heikin-ashi candle is white.

- Sell pivot 2: Bullish modified candle. Heikin-ashi offers no advantage.

- Buy pivot 2: The heikin-ashi candle indicates a reversal from bullish to bearish. Heikin-ashi offers no advantage. The pivot is confirmed one bar later, and the heikin-ashi candle is white.

- Sell pivot 3: The heikin-ashi candle indicates a reversal from bullish to bearish. Advantage heikin-ashi.

- Buy pivot 3: Bearish modified candle. Heikin-ashi offers no advantage. The pivot is confirmed one bar later, and the heikin-ashi candle is white.

- Sell pivot 4 :Bullish modified candle. Heikin-ashi offers no advantage. The pivot is confirmed one bar later, and the heikin-ashi candle is black.

- Buy pivot 4: Bearish modified candle. Heikin-ashi offers no advantage. The pivot is confirmed one bar later, and the heikin-ashi candle is white.

- Sell pivot 5: Bullish modified candle. Heikin-ashi offers no advantage. The pivot is confirmed one bar later, and the heikin-ashi candle is black.

- Buy pivot 5: Bearish modified candle. Heikin-ashi offers no advantage.

- Sell pivot 6: Bearish modified candle. Advantage heikin-ashi.

- Buy pivot 6: Bearish modified candle. Heikin-ashi offers no advantage. The pivot is confirmed one bar later, and the heikin-ashi candle is white.

- Sell pivot 7: Bullish modified candle. Heikin-ashi offers no advantage.

- Buy pivot 7: The heikin-ashi candle indicates a reversal from bullish to bearish. Heikin-ashi offers no advantage. The pivot is confirmed one bar later, and the heikin-ashi candle is white.

- Sell pivot 8: Bullish modified candle. Heikin-ashi offers no advantage. The pivot is confirmed one bar later, and the heikin-ashi candle is black.

- Buy pivot 8: Bearish modified candle. Heikin-ashi offers no advantage. The pivot is confirmed one bar later, and the heikin-ashi candle shows a possible reversal.

- Sell pivot 9: Bullish modified candle. Heikin-ashi offers no advantage.

- Buy pivot 9: Bullish modified candle. Advantage heikin-ashi.

This second analysis uses the visual technique and shows different and less accurate results. The quality of the reversal indications on the heikin-ashi chart is caused by the delay between price pivots and reversals on the heikin-ashi chart. What makes the second analysis different from the first one is that there is no pivot with earlier detection using heikin-ashi candles. Possible trend reversals are indicated for sell pivots 1, 3, 6 and for buy pivot 9.

30-Second Summary

- The dream of buying at the very bottom and selling at the very top can be realistically replaced with buying *near* the bottom and selling *near* the top.

- Price pivots are bars where the current trend, minor or major, changes direction.

- There are many ways to determine such pivots. This chapter discusses and defines pivots as those shown in Figure 28.1.

- To improve buying and selling, we compare price pivots with heikin-ashi charting and its quantification, respectively.

- The main purpose behind relating the heikin-ashi technique with pivots is to look for heikin-ashi reversal indications emerging *before* price pivots. Any successful attempt to identify a reversal before a price pivot is of great financial value to traders and investors.

- Heikin-ashi quantification is superior to heikin-ashi charting.

- Consequently, the quantification (haDelta and its average) of modified candles offers better advance indications for price reversals on a price pivot chart.

- Although pivots can be identified in any time frame, much of the price noise is removed in higher time frames.

CHAPTER 29

HEIKIN-ASHI AND FOREX

With an estimated daily volume reaching four trillion US dollars, the FOREX (FX) market surpasses equity, futures, and bond markets together. Currency pairs show clear trends in all time frames. If you add the increased migration of retail traders towards this very liquid market, the heikin-ashi technique becomes a candidate to consider for FOREX trend trading.

Since the publication of my original heikin-ashi article in *Technical Analysis for Stocks & Commodities* in February 2004, many traders have started using this technique. Several versions of the modified candles were conceived, but very little attention was paid to the quantification of the heikin-ashi candles. This chapter discusses the use of heikin-ashi candles and their quantification (haDelta and its average) to improve FX trading.

Figure 29.1 is a daily chart of the EURUSD pair where both techniques are present: Japanese candlesticks (and patterns) and modified candles on the heikin-ashi chart.

The pattern P1 that emerged on March 10 and 11 may be interpreted by some traders as an invalid bullish engulfing formation because the downtrend was too short and the second body did not engulf the first body. Other traders are ready to accept it if they adhere to very relaxed rules. The existence of loose definitions where personal experience plays an important role leads to subjective interpretation of many Japanese candlestick patterns.

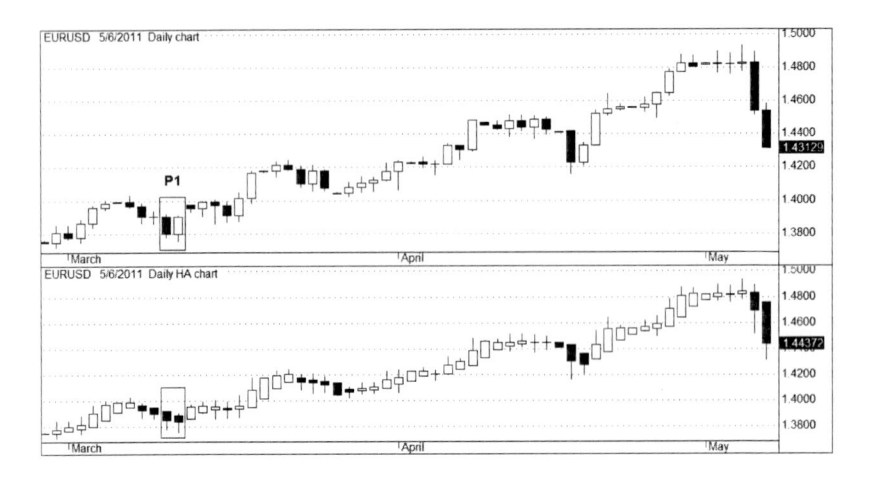

FIGURE 29.1: *Euro/US Dollar (EURUSD) daily charts with Japanese and heikin-ashi candles for March through early May 2011. Key patterns are indicated by boxes.*

Fortunately, we use the heikin-ashi technique which does not look at patterns; rather, it ignores them, looking only at modified candle color, body size, and shadows (see Chapter 2). The second modified candle of the pattern on March 11 is a smaller body with both shadows, which is interpreted as sign of a possible reversal. The subsequent series of white heikin-ashi candles confirms the new uptrend.

We have already seen the clear advantage of using heikin-ashi quantification. We apply it in Figure 29.2 for the same period of time and see the difference: Pattern P1 is now sending a better signal than it did on the heikin-ashi modified candle chart. On the second day of the doubtful pattern (March 11), haDelta is *above* its short average, indicating a higher probability for a bullish reversal. This is an advantage that cannot be ignored.

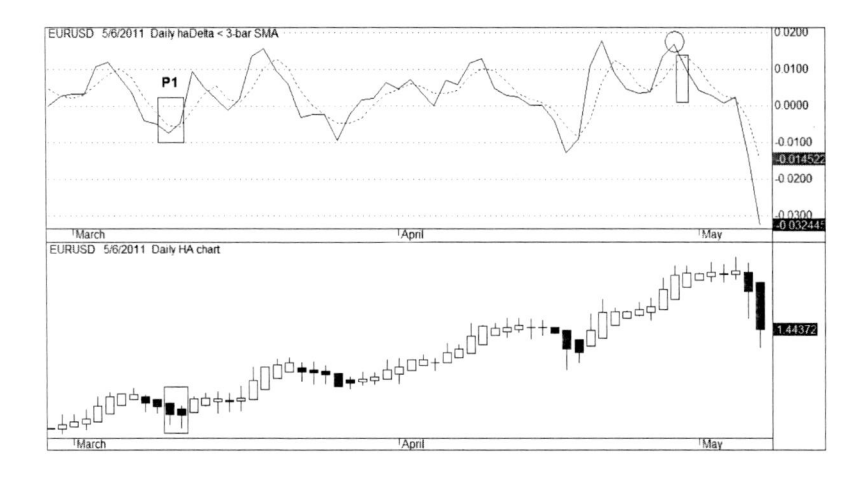

FIGURE 29.2: *Euro/US Dollar (EURUSD) daily charts with heikin-ashi and haDelta for March through early May 2011.*

We go back to the price chart in Figure 29.1 and focus on the consolidation covering the last days of April and the beginning of May. For a period of six days, the price range was very narrow with a close just above the 1.4800 mark. On the price chart in the upper pane, the emergence of longer shadows shows a wait-and-see attitude. Looking at the heikin-ashi chart in the lower pane, we notice a similar pattern of consolidation dominated by small bodies with upper and lower shadows. The EURUSD breakdown comes on May 5. Could the heikin-ashi technique bring any warning?

We shift the attention at haDelta in Figure 29.2 where there are two such signs. First, there was a top of haDelta on April 28 (marked with a circle) comparable with two previous high values in March and April. The second sign of weakness came one day later on April 29 (marked with a rectangle) when haDelta turned below its average just as the price consolidation was starting. Again, advantage heikin-ashi.

Since the heikin-ashi visual technique has Japanese roots, it would be interesting to see how it works for the USDJPY pair in both formats, visual and quantifiable. Figure 29.3 shows these formats on a daily chart with Japanese candlesticks and modified candles.

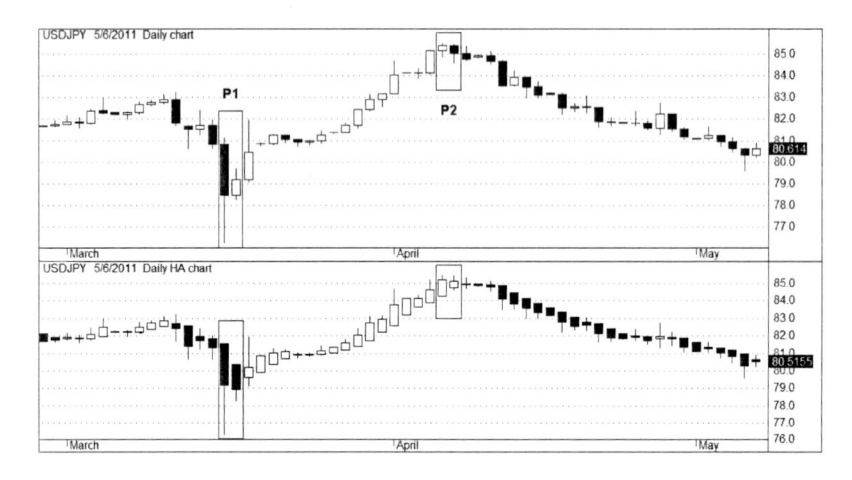

FIGURE 29.3: *US Dollar/Japanese Yen (USDJPY) daily charts with Japanese and heikin-ashi candles for March through early May 2011.*

As expected, trends, reversals, and consolidations are easily identified on this heikin-ashi chart. We now discuss two patterns marked on this chart as P1 and P2. Pattern P1 is a bullish harami with the second body inside the previous body after a downtrend. The candle pattern was suggesting a reversal that became fact immediately after. Conventional wisdom was right about this bullish formation in a downtrend.

Will heikin-ashi succeed or fail? On the modified candle chart there is no reversal indication because both candles show a strong downtrend, with dark bodies and no upper shadows. When the visual heikin-ashi technique does not work, we apply its quantification using haDelta and the short average (see Figure 29.4). The picture is different now, with a positive bias: haDelta is slightly above its average and *suggests* a bullish trend reversal.

Heikin-ashi performs well again, ignoring patterns, definitions, and personal experience.

According to Japanese candlestick theory, pattern P2 in Figure 29.3 is a bearish engulfing formation *suggesting* a trend reversal. The heikin-ashi chart shows an uptrend (white candles) but with a slowdown identified by the second body inside the prior body. The last modified candle of the pattern now has upper and lower shadows as an additional sign of slowdown or even weakness.

Could heikin-ashi help with an advance indication? The focus now shifts to Figure 29.4.

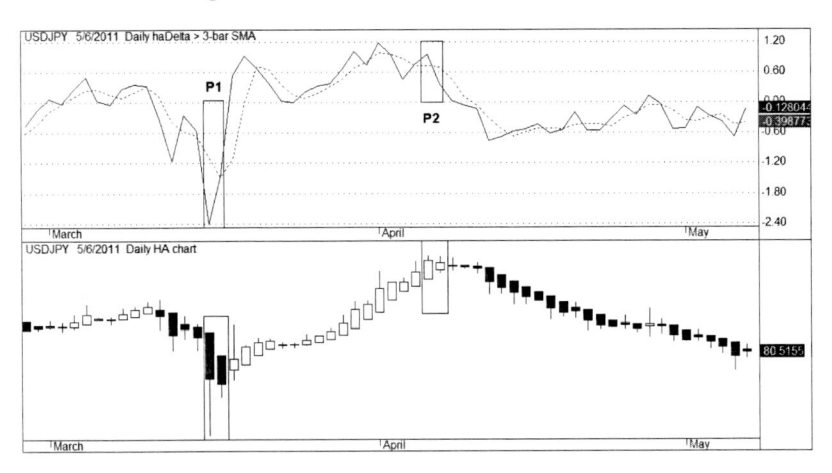

FIGURE 29.4: *US Dollar/Japanese Yen (USDJPY) daily charts with heikin-ashi and haDelta for March through early May 2011.*

The first candle of pattern P2 finds haDelta above its average as sign of continued uptrend. The second candle on April 7 completes the bearish engulfing formation and brings haDelta below the average, indicating a possible slowdown and reversal of the uptrend. The following downtrend confirms the negative crossing. haDelta offered a bearish indication already on the last day of the pattern.

If we look back before April 7, we see that the average peaked on April 1 and haDelta recorded lower values. Although there was no sign of reversal at that time, the uptrend was in danger.

As a general observation, the three-bar average offers good triggers for long and short entries when it turns positive and negative, respectively. There is an inevitable delay, but confidence is high.

How does the heikin-ashi technique work in other time frames? Figure 29.5 shows the GBPUSD pair on a five-minute chart where trends and consolidations are very clear on the heikin-ashi chart, leaving no room for guessing. We discuss the patterns identified as P1 and P2 on the Japanese candlestick chart.

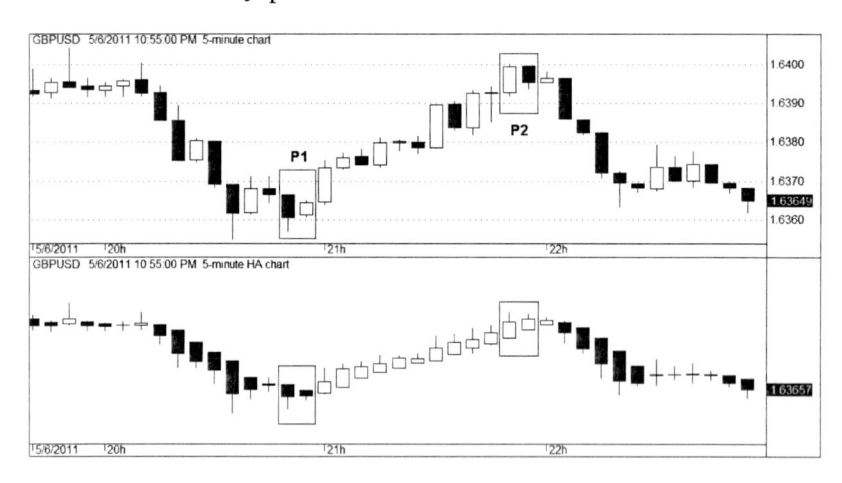

FIGURE 29.5: *British Pound Sterling/US Dollar (GBPUSD) five-minute charts with Japanese candlesticks and heikin-ashi candles for May 6, 2011. Key patterns are indicated by boxes.*

Pattern P1 is a bullish harami emerging in a downtrend. The heikin-ashi chart shows a slowdown of the trend (black body inside black body) and nothing more. Is this a bottom? To get a more accurate answer, we apply haDelta and its average in Figure 29.6 and see that the indicator is above the average twice in a short time. It is a positive sign that confirms the bullish harami and the corresponding slowdown on the heikin-ashi chart. Heikin-ashi wins again.

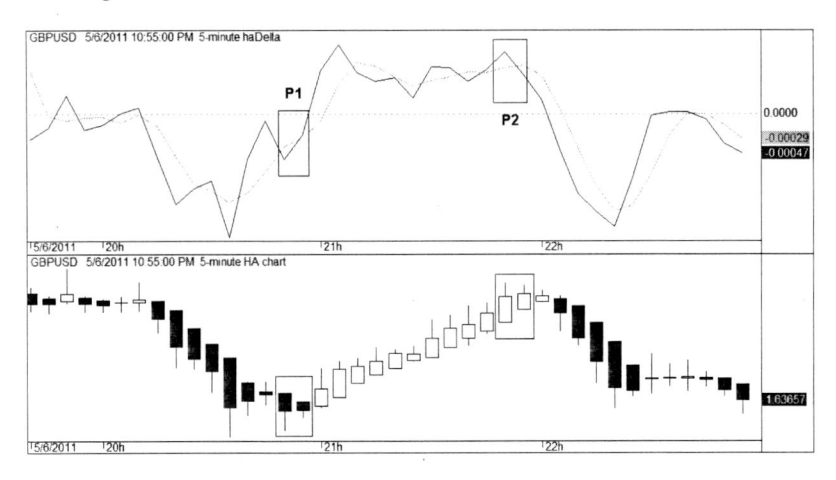

FIGURE 29.6: *British Pound Sterling/US Dollar (GBPUSD) five-minute charts with heikin-ashi and haDelta for May 6, 2011. Key patterns are indicated by boxes.*

Pattern P2 in Figure 29.5 is a questionable pattern. A tweezers top? A more relaxed dark-cloud cover? We underscored that **the heikin-ashi technique in its visual and quantifiable formats does not care about Japanese candlestick patterns**. As a result, we dismiss any doubt about this pattern and proceed to the heikin-ashi chart where the second candle of pattern P2 brings no indications about the future.

Both modified candles are white and show a strong uptrend (a lack of lower wicks), with a single sign of slowdown given by the smaller body of the second candle. For the same pattern P2 in Figure 29.6, things are different: haDelta falls below the average when this pattern is complete. Heikin-ashi does not wait for the pattern to be confirmed; it offers an early bearish signal.

The last example discusses the AUDUSD pair on four-hour charts (see Figures 29.7 and 29.8). Trends and consolidations on the price chart are easily identified using modified candles, but we are more interested in translating Japanese candlestick patterns using the heikin-ashi technique.

Pattern P1 in Figure 29.7 could be considered a bullish harami *if* the first candle was long. Similarly, it could be a bullish engulfing pattern *if* the second body contained the first body. None of these conditions were met, but we use heikin-ashi to see whether there is value in using this technique to further analyze this pattern, whatever its name is.

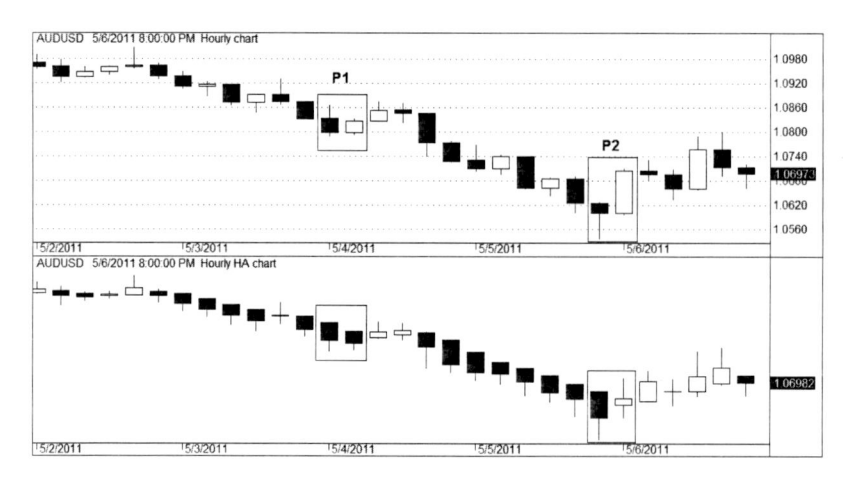

FIGURE 29.7: *Australian Dollar/US Dollar (AUDUSD) four-hour charts with Japanese candlesticks and heikin-ashi candles for May 2-6, 2011. Key patterns are indicated by boxes.*

The first black candle of pattern P1 did not show any sign of trend change on the heikin-ashi chart. Looking at the second candle, we see that its corresponding modified candle is still black but shorter, and with no upper shadow; the heikin-ashi chart offers no indication of a reversal. This is not a handicap since we have haDelta and its average available in Figure 29.8.

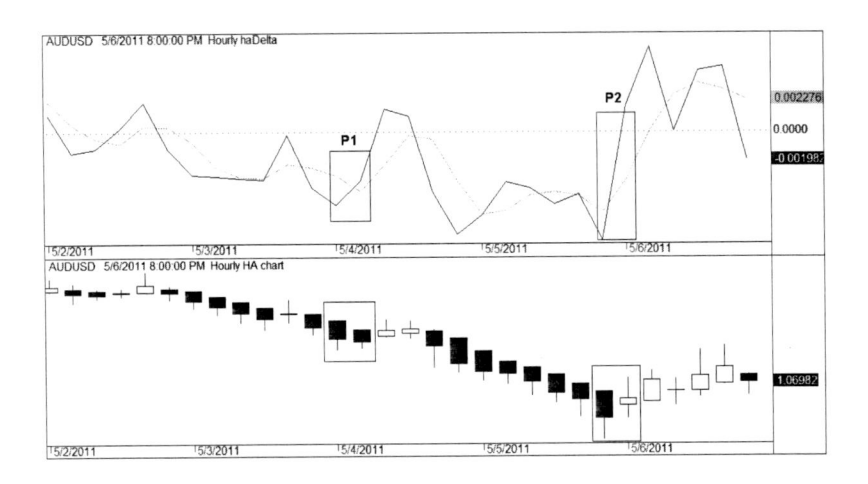

FIGURE 29.8: *Australian Dollar/US Dollar (AUDUSD) four-hour charts with heikin-ashi and haDelta for May 2-6, 2011. Key patterns are indicated by boxes.*

In many cases, heikin-ashi quantification offers advance signals when the traditional heikin-ashi charting fails to do so. Here, the indication is positive, with haDelta crossing above its average at the end of the four-hour bar. The advantage again goes to heikin-ashi. The reaction has been very short; the two white modified candles have small bodies with upper and lower shadows, indicating only a consolidation and no real energy.

Pattern P2 in Figure 29.8 identifies a bullish engulfing pattern. With the hammer emerging in an extended downtrend, the probability for a bottom and reversal grows. This is how conventional wisdom translates this pattern.

How does heikin-ashi look at the same pattern P2? The black modified candle with no upper shadow corresponds to the hammer and points to a strong downtrend with no indication of a slowdown. haDelta is still below the average. The bullish white candle of P2 concludes the candlestick pattern and brings changes to the heikin-ashi chart: A small reversal candle with long upper

275

and lower shadows emerges in the downtrend. It is no surprise that haDelta jumps over the short average, setting a bullish pace.

30-Second Summary

- The FOREX market has features that make the heikin-ashi technique in both formats suitable for currency trading.
- Heikin-ashi works well with any FX pair in any time frame.
- Since many currency pairs display clear trends in various time frames, heikin-ashi is a logical technique to use for trading.
- It is known that heikin-ashi charts display one-bar delayed reversal candles. To mitigate this inconvenience, haDelta and its average are used for more accurate signals.
- When both methods are inconclusive, we look for excessive haDelta values that point to reversals.
- Heikin-ashi ignores Japanese candlestick patterns on the chart.
- It is recommended that you use your own analysis tools with the heikin-ashi technique in both formats.

CHAPTER 30

THE END OF THE BEGINNING

We are almost at the finish line where winners get a trophy and all prepare for the next race. In this case, you are the winner by learning about heikin-ashi and its three powerful features:

- Visual technique
- Quantifiable indicators
- A simple technique to remove Japanese candlestick patterns from your trading.

Although Japanese candlestick patterns display a strong message about how buyers and sellers act together in the market, the patterns lack precise definitions and have too many exceptions and subtleties. As a result, their "correct" translation requires traders to invest more time and money and brings a level of subjectivity that is not appropriate in trading.

These are weaknesses well-known in trading, which have led to techniques where patterns are confirmed with technical indicators.

Heikin-ashi with its two formats, visual and quantifiable, brings another technique that can be used by itself, or in combination with candle patterns if traders feel more comfortable with that option and want to keep their educational investment and routine intact.

Heikin-ashi ignores patterns, definitions, or exceptions; it looks only at each price bar as it develops on the chart and highlights the trend or announces a reversal. This is a healthier approach with no guessing and less margin for error.

This first book on heikin-ashi opens a large door to better trading and more profitable strategies using a simple technique to reveal trends and reversals.

It is time to try and apply it!

APPENDIX A

FREQUENTLY ASKED QUESTIONS

Heikin-Ashi in General

Q: There are over 100 Japanese candlestick patterns well documented. Does heikin-ashi charting provide similar patterns?

A: No. Life is far easier with heikin-ashi. This visual technique has only three types of candle: a white body with upper shadow, a black body with lower shadow, and a white or black body with upper and lower shadows. The first type appears in an uptrend, the second type in a downtrend, and the third candle type points to a possible consolidation or reversal. There are 3 heikin-ashi candles vs.100-plus Japanese candlestick patterns. What do you prefer?

Q: Is there any difference between the heikin-ashi technique and heikin-ashi charting?

A: Heikin-ashi charting is the visual component of the heikin-ashi technique in general and, as the name suggests, refers only to modified candles (colors, bodies, and shadows). The quantification of the modified candles is the other component of the heikin-ashi technique.

Heikin-ashi Technique = Charting + Quantification = Right Brain + Left Brain

Q: I spent many years and big money learning and using Japanese candlestick patterns. Why should I switch to heikin-ashi charting?

A: There is no need to abandon the use of Japanese candlestick patterns. It is up to you if you want to add simple confirmations with heikin-ashi charts and quantification indicators. However, the situation may be different for a newcomer who wants to avoid a substantial investment (time and money) in learning candlestick patterns. The heikin-ashi technique offers a simple, fast, and profitable way to trade and invest.

Q: I am new to heikin-ashi and love this technique. How do I proceed after reading this book?

A: Be sure you have access to a technical platform with heikin-ashi implemented. If you have programming skills, haDelta and its average are great indicators to add to your trading platform. If you do not use candlestick patterns already, you may work only with heikin-ashi charts and traditional indicators. If you are using candlestick patterns, you may start confirming them with signals offered by heikin-ashi charts and modified candle quantification. Send me an email at ha@educofin.com and I will assist you.

FREQUENTLY ASKED QUESTIONS

Q: I love heikin-ashi, but my broker does not offer these charts on the trading platform. Do you have any solution?

A: Yes. The first step is to ask your broker to implement heikin-ashi charts. Many technical analysis software providers added this great feature during recent years. Why should your broker miss the train? Until this issue is hopefully resolved in your favor, you can generate heikin-ashi charts using Microsoft® Excel® as described in Appendix B.

Q: Can I trade only with heikin-ashi charts?

A: The answer is yes. However, as with any trading technique or strategy, this technique should be used together your other favorite technical indicators or strategies. In this book, we discuss some of the combinations that may improve your trading. And remember that the heikin-ashi technique is not the Holy Grail.

Q: I learned about heikin-ashi in 2005, but I have been unable to find much information in the public domain. Where can I get more information?

A: This book is the first successful attempt to describe the heikin-ashi technique and compare modified candles with some of the well-known Japanese candlestick patterns. There is more to add to heikin-ashi as a trading tool after the publication of this book.

Q: Critics say that heikin-ashi charting works with modified instead of real prices. Therefore, the heikin-ashi technique should be avoided. What is your response to these comments?

A: The answer may take many hours of debate. We can start with two basic facts about trading: (1) each of us concentrates on trends, and (2) all technical indicators are *alterations* of the price. If we relate these facts to heikin-ashi charts, we see that (1) trends are very well defined on such charts, and (2) we do not care about working with modified prices as long as trends look so clear. It is very true that reversals on a heikin-ashi chart appear one or two bars later, but this is comparable with any change of trend displayed using traditional technical indicators.

Furthermore, traders and investors can now use heikin-ashi quantification as well. The quality of the signals and the fact that Japanese patterns can be replaced using the heikin-ashi technique make modified candles very attractive instruments for making faster and better decisions.

Q: Is there any relationship between bodies, colors, and shadows on a heikin-ashi chart?

A: The synergy is simple, and it has been discussed extensively throughout this book. Chapter 2 is an excellent start.

Q: What are the strengths of heikin-ashi charting?

A: The answer depends on your profile, flexibility to change, and intentions. The newcomers adopt heikin-ashi charts very quickly because of their strong visual message. The very short learning curve is also an important factor for quickly adding this technique to the trading routine. The quantification of the modified candles will definitely attract more interest with the leading signals provided. With this first book, I am strongly convinced that more people will look into heikin-ashi's potential and use it for trading. There are also die-hards who invested time and money in candlestick patterns. In their case, I suggest using both techniques for confirmation.

Q: What are the weaknesses of heikin-ashi trading?

A: Again, the answer depends on your profile, flexibility to change, and intentions. If you are a gap trader, I suspect that you may ignore heikin-ashi charts, although their quantification measures the momentum and can help. It is up to you. If you use only heikin-ashi charts with no quantification indicator, you will find the short delay between price reversals and those on a heikin-ashi chart as a handicap. However, it is not a handicap since you have haDelta and its average available. People are different,

FREQUENTLY ASKED QUESTIONS

and each technique is far from perfect. But anything leading to a better understanding of trends and reversals is worth looking at. For those who look at shadows and follow strategies based on their length and patterns, the Japanese patterns will continue being their bread and butter. Again, people are different, and so are their expectations.

Intraday Trading

Q: I am an intraday trader. Can I use heikin-ashi on a one-minute chart? And more generally, can I use the technique in any intraday time frame?
A: Yes, you can use the heikin-ashi technique on a one-minute chart—or in any time frame, for that matter.

Q: I am an intraday gap trader. Heikin-ashi charts cannot help me. How can I use this technique with my specific profile?
A: By definition, a heikin-ashi chart does not show gaps because they are hidden inside the modified candles that are generated. One solution is to use bar or candlestick charts together with either heikin-ashi charts (for the trend) or haDelta (for the momentum).

Delay on Heikin-Ashi Charts

Q: I already use heikin-ashi charts with bar charts. The trends are evident using heikin-ashi, but I notice a small delay of one and sometimes two bars between reversals on the price chart and those on the heikin-ashi chart. Do you have any solution to reduce this lag?
A: Yes. You can use heikin-ashi quantification (haDelta and its short average) to reduce the delay. The examples discussed in this book are clear about the advantages of the heikin-ashi quantification.

Q: Some traders complain about the delay between price reversals and reversals on a heikin-ashi chart. How relevant is this handicap?

A: Everybody wants perfection, but nobody finds it. The same applies to this delay; as heikin-ashi charts are defined and built, the delay cannot be removed. However, the quantification of heikin-ashi candles dramatically improves this issue. Please review the examples in this book and try haDelta in your trading.

Heikin-Ashi Chart Specifics

Q: Why does the open of a modified candle (haOpen) start at the midpoint of the previous body?

A: This is how heikin-ashi candles are defined. The midpoint is seen as a point of balance. If you have programming skills, you may try to generate heikin-ashi charts with haOpen at 1/3 or 2/3 of the previous body height.

Q: haDelta is a nervous indicator. How can I make it smoother?

A: One solution is to apply a three-bar simple moving average as seen in this book. Another way is to apply another short simple average to the resulting three-bar average and to remove haDelta from the picture, working only with the two averages. You will miss the leading signals generated by crossings of haDelta and the first short average, but you will improve results in the longer trends. In trading, as in life, you face many trade-off moments.

Q: Regular price charts display candles with shadows of various sizes. Their length is combined with body size and profiles of prior candles to generate patterns of intense study and interpretation. On the other side, heikin-ashi charts have only three candle types. What do the shadows on a heikin-ashi chart imply?

FREQUENTLY ASKED QUESTIONS

A: On a heikin-ashi chart, an uptrend is featured as a sequence of white bodies, most of them only with upper shadows. Inversely, in a downtrend most of the candles have dark bodies with a lower wick. The second heikin-ashi pattern is a smaller body with both upper and lower shadows. This candle pattern points to a possible reversal but also to the start of a consolidation. The emergence of candles with both shadows is a sign of a slowdown while bodies with only one shadow point to a trend determined by the color of the body.

Q: I focus only on the height and color of the bodies of modified candles. Do I miss important information when I ignore the shadows?
A: Please see comments above.

Q: What are signs of a slowdown on a heikin-ashi chart?
A: The emergence of a candle with a body inside the previous body and/or a candle with a smaller body and with both shadows. This is sufficient to alert you about a weaker trend. You may confirm this signal with technical indicators or Japanese candlestick patterns.

Q: When I use heikin-ashi charts in smaller time frames, I still can notice a certain level of noise (short periods of pullbacks or reactions followed by the resumption of the trend). How can I improve this?
A: Switch to a higher time frame and confirm with technical indications there. However, take great care regarding where you place the stop-loss. A second option is to confirm with crossings of haDelta and its average. A third way to increase confidence is to combine heikin-ashi chart indications with a trailing-stop indicator.

Q: Can I build a heikin-ashi chart using only closing prices?
A: Yes, if you populate your file ready to export with O=H=L=C. The purists may be upset with this premise, but trends are very clear even on the new modified chart. haDelta and its average work fine, too. It is worth experimenting.

APPENDIX B

USING MICROSOFT® EXCEL® TO GENERATE HEIKIN-ASHI CHARTS

This section describes a simple procedure to generate modified data and heikin-ashi charts using open, high, low, and close (OHLC) values and Microsoft® Excel®. The procedure follows three main steps:

1. Export OHLC data to an Excel spreadsheet.
2. Generate modified OHLC data (haOpen, haHigh, haLow, haClose).
3. Create a heikin-ashi chart using modified OHLC data.

Step 1: Export OHLC Data

All technical analysis software packages have the feature to export historical price information as text (.txt) or comma delimited (.csv) files. In both cases, the output file can be opened and processed using any spreadsheet software. For this example, we will use Microsoft® Excel® spreadsheet software.

Figure B.1 shows a section of the worksheet containing daily Apple Inc. (AAPL) price data. You can also use intraday, weekly, monthly, or any other time frame to export the data from.

	A	B	C	D	E
1	Date	Open	High	Low	Close
2	1/3/2011	325.90	330.26	324.84	329.57
3	1/4/2011	332.42	332.50	328.15	331.29
4	1/5/2011	329.55	334.34	329.50	334.00
5	1/6/2011	334.98	335.25	332.90	333.73
6	1/7/2011	334.12	336.35	331.90	336.12
7	1/10/2011	338.83	343.23	337.17	342.46
8	1/11/2011	344.95	344.96	339.47	341.64
9	1/12/2011	343.43	344.43	342.00	344.42
10	1/13/2011	345.31	346.64	343.85	345.68
11	1/14/2011	345.94	348.48	344.44	348.48
12	1/18/2011	327.05	344.76	326.00	340.65
13	1/19/2011	348.58	348.60	336.88	338.84
14	1/20/2011	336.15	338.30	330.12	332.68
15	1/21/2011	333.77	334.88	326.63	326.72
16	1/24/2011	327.06	337.45	326.72	337.45
17	1/25/2011	336.41	341.44	334.57	341.40
18	1/26/2011	342.90	345.60	341.50	343.85
19	1/27/2011	343.90	344.69	342.83	343.21
20	1/28/2011	344.28	344.40	333.53	336.10
21	1/31/2011	335.80	340.04	334.30	339.32
22	2/1/2011	341.54	345.65	340.98	345.03
23	2/2/2011	344.45	345.25	343.55	344.32
24	2/3/2011	343.80	344.24	338.55	343.44
25	2/4/2011	343.76	346.70	343.51	346.50
26	2/7/2011	348.00	353.25	347.64	351.88
27	2/8/2011	353.62	355.52	352.15	355.20
28	2/9/2011	355.19	359.00	354.87	358.16
29	2/10/2011	357.82	360.00	348.00	354.54
30	2/11/2011	354.84	357.80	353.54	356.85
31	2/14/2011	356.79	359.48	356.71	359.18
32	2/15/2011	359.21	359.97	357.55	359.90
33	2/16/2011	360.52	364.90	360.50	363.13

FIGURE B.1: *After the export of historical price data for Apple Inc. (AAPL), the .csv file is read with Microsoft® Excel®.*

USING MICROSOFT® EXCEL® TO GENERATE HEIKIN-ASHI CHARTS

Step 2: Generate Modified OHLC Data

The modified OHLC data will be used to draw heikin-ashi charts. The rules to define these values were discussed in Chapter 2. Figure B.2 contains both original (columns B, C, D, E) and altered OHLC data (columns F, G, H, I) for the same period.

	A	B	C	D	E	F	G	H	I
1	Date	Open	High	Low	Close	haOpen	haHigh	haLow	haClose
2	1/3/2011	325.90	330.26	324.84	329.57	325.90	330.26	324.84	327.64
3	1/4/2011	332.42	332.50	328.15	331.29	326.77	332.50	326.77	331.09
4	1/5/2011	329.55	334.34	329.50	334.00	328.93	334.34	328.93	331.85
5	1/6/2011	334.98	335.25	332.90	333.73	330.39	335.25	330.39	334.22
6	1/7/2011	334.12	336.35	331.90	336.12	332.30	336.35	331.90	334.62
7	1/10/2011	338.83	343.23	337.17	342.46	333.46	343.23	333.46	340.42
8	1/11/2011	344.95	344.96	339.47	341.64	336.94	344.96	336.94	342.76
9	1/12/2011	343.43	344.43	342.00	344.42	339.85	344.43	339.85	343.57
10	1/13/2011	345.31	346.64	343.85	345.68	341.71	346.64	341.71	345.37
11	1/14/2011	345.94	348.48	344.44	348.48	343.54	348.48	343.54	346.84
12	1/18/2011	327.05	344.76	326.00	340.65	345.19	345.19	326.00	334.62
13	1/19/2011	348.58	348.60	336.88	338.84	339.90	348.60	336.88	343.23
14	1/20/2011	336.15	338.30	330.12	332.68	341.56	341.56	330.12	334.31
15	1/21/2011	333.77	334.88	326.63	326.72	337.94	337.94	326.63	330.50
16	1/24/2011	327.06	337.45	326.72	337.45	334.22	337.45	326.72	332.17
17	1/25/2011	336.41	341.44	334.57	341.40	333.19	341.44	333.19	338.46
18	1/26/2011	342.90	345.60	341.50	343.85	335.82	345.60	335.82	343.46
19	1/27/2011	343.90	344.69	342.83	343.21	339.64	344.69	339.64	343.66
20	1/28/2011	344.28	344.40	333.53	336.10	341.65	344.40	333.53	339.58
21	1/31/2011	335.80	340.04	334.30	339.32	340.61	340.61	334.30	337.37
22	2/1/2011	341.54	345.65	340.98	345.03	338.99	345.65	338.99	343.30
23	2/2/2011	344.45	345.25	343.55	344.32	341.14	345.25	341.14	344.39
24	2/3/2011	343.80	344.24	338.55	343.44	342.77	344.24	338.55	342.51
25	2/4/2011	343.76	346.70	343.51	346.50	342.64	346.70	342.64	345.12
26	2/7/2011	348.00	353.25	347.64	351.88	343.88	353.25	343.88	350.19
27	2/8/2011	353.62	355.52	352.15	355.20	347.04	355.52	347.04	354.12
28	2/9/2011	355.19	359.00	354.87	358.16	350.58	359.00	350.58	356.81
29	2/10/2011	357.82	360.00	348.00	354.54	353.69	360.00	348.00	355.09
30	2/11/2011	354.84	357.80	353.54	356.85	354.39	357.80	353.54	355.76
31	2/14/2011	356.79	359.48	356.71	359.18	355.07	359.48	355.07	358.04
32	2/15/2011	359.21	359.97	357.55	359.90	356.56	359.97	356.56	359.16
33	2/16/2011	360.52	364.90	360.50	363.13	357.86	364.90	357.86	362.26

FIGURE B.2: *Original OHLC data vs. modified OHLC values for Apple Inc. (AAPL).*

Here are the steps required to enter all information in columns B, C, D, and E:

Step 2.a: Enter the following text information:
In cell F1: haOpen

In cell G1: haHigh
In cell H1: haLow
In cell I1: haClose

Step 2.b: The first day of the modified data section of the spreadsheet (row 2) is different because haOpen does not have a previous value to use. For this particular row, haOpen is the open price of the first day in the spreadsheet.
In cell F2: =B2
In cell G2: =MAX(C2,F2,I2)
In cell H2: =MIN(D2,F2,I2)
In cell I2: =SUM(B2:E2)/4

Step 2.c: Enter the following formulas:
In cell F3: =(F2+I2)/2
In cell G3: =MAX(C3,F3,I3)
In cell H3: =MIN(D3,F3,I3)
In cell I3: =SUM(B3:E3)/4

Step 2.d: Data from cells F3, G3, H3, and I3 is copied down to the end of the worksheet. Columns F, G, H, and I contain the modified OHLC values necessary to generate a heikin-ashi chart for Apple between January 3 and May 2, 2011.

Step 3: Create a Heikin-Ashi Chart

Use the candlestick chart feature in Excel® with dates (Column A) to display on the X axis and the modified OHLC data (F2 through the last value of column I) as the data range. The resulting heikin-ashi chart is shown in Figure B.3 with the X axis from January 3 to March 14, 2011.

ACKNOWLEDGEMENTS

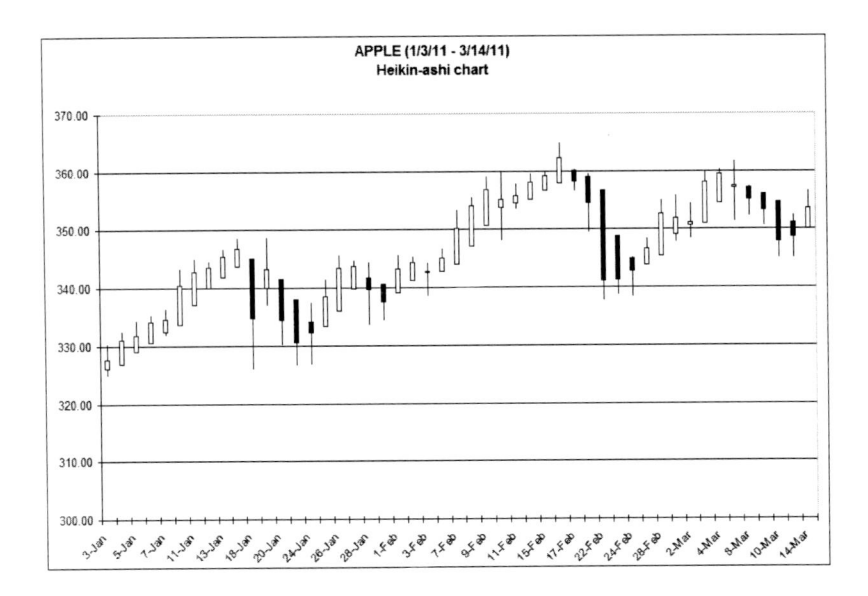

FIGURE B.3: *Heikin-ashi chart for Apple Inc. between January 3 and March 14, 2011.*

ACKNOWLEDGEMENTS

We are all connected.
I am grateful to all traders and investors who are amazed by the simplicity, versatility, and results of the heikin-ashi technique. Their more than 8,000 messages containing feedback, questions, and personal experiences from the world of candlestick patterns and heikin-ashi were priceless input for this book.

My special attention and gratitude go to Mr. Koike, the Japanese trader who ignored the Japanese proverb "The smart eagle does not show his talons" and brought me to the revealing world of heikin-ashi.

The editor makes always a difference from the manuscript to the final product. Many thanks to Chris Keefer from K2 Communications for her invaluable editing and sense of quality.

The charts in this book have been generated with AmiBroker™ with the exception of those in Chapter 5, which have been produced with Metastock® and a heikin-ashi add-on I wrote to make life easier.

Finally, I feel a deep sense of gratitude to Virginia and Veronique for their extreme patience and ideas about this book.

RECOMMENDED READING

Bulkowski, Thomas N. *Encyclopedia of Candlestick Charts.* Hoboken, NJ: John Wiley & Sons, 2008.

Chande, Tushar S., and Stanley Kroll. *The New Technical Trader: Boost Your Profit by Plugging into the Latest Indicators.* Hoboken, NJ: John Wiley & Sons, 1994.

Nippon Technical Analysis Association. *Analysis of Stock Prices in Japan.* Nippon Technical Analysis Association, 1989.

Nison, Steve. *Beyond Candlesticks: New Japanese Charting Techniques Revealed.* New York: John Wiley & Sons, 1994.

Nison, Steve. *Japanese Candlestick Charting Techniques: A Contemporary Guide to the Ancient Investment Techniques of the Far East.* 2nd ed. Paramus, NJ: Prentice Hall Press, 2001.

Valcu, Dan. "Using the Heikin-Ashi Technique." *Technical Analysis of Stocks & Commodities,* February 2004.

Valcu, Veronique. "Z-Score Indicator." *Technical Analysis of Stocks & Commodities,* February 2003.

INDEX

A
above the stomach, 53-54
Advance/Decline line, 251
AGCO Corp. (AGCO), 88-89
Agilent Technologies Inc. (A), 94-95, 98
Akamai Technologies Inc. (AKAM), 80-81, 124-125, 127
AmerisourceBergen Corp. (ABC), 140
AmiBroker, 293
Anooraq Resources Corp. (ANO), 151-152
Apple Inc. (AAPL), 23-25, 43-44, 90-91, 288-291
Arch Coal Inc. (ACI), 137
Arms Jr., Richard W. 37
ashi,
    translation in English, 16

B
Bank of America Corp. (BAC), 156, 173
belt hold line,
    bearish belt hold line and heikin-ashi, 181-183
    bullish belt hold line and heikin-ashi, 177-180
    with heikin-ashi, 177
Berry, Brian 2
Boeing Co. (BA), 85-86, 90
Bollinger bands, 10, 231-235
Braque, Georges 65
Briggs & Stratton Corp. (BGG), 144-145
Broadcom Corp. (BRCM), 110-111

C

candle charts,
    heikin-ashi charts compared with, 51-57
candlestick patterns,
    pros and cons of, 51-57
Candlevolume, 37, 39
    with heikin-ashi, 40-42
Chande, Tushar 45, 295
Chikou Span, 244-245
Chipotle Mexican Grill Inc. (CMG), 17-18
CIENA Corp. (CIEN), 106
Citigroup Inc. (C), 129, 133-134
Cloud charts, *See* Ichimoku charts.
Coach Inc. (COH), 146, 148-149
Commodity Research Bureau Index (CRY0), 199

D

dark-cloud cover, 39, 53-54, 159, 177, 200, 273
    with heikin-ashi, 93-94, 99-104,
da Vinci, Leonardo 5
Dell Inc. (DELL), 225-226
doji,
    variations (types) of, 143
    with heikin-ashi, 143
doji-like candle, 7, 16-18, 22, 29
Dow Jones Utility Average (DJ-15), 73, 75-76
dragonfly doji, 143, 150-151
    with heikin-ashi, 152-153

E

EarthLink Inc (ELNK), 160-161, 166-167
Elan Corp, plc ADR (ELN), 165
Elliott, Ralph Nelson 2
Elliott Wave theory, 2
engulfing patterns, 64, 79, 85, 91

bearish engulfing pattern and heikin-ashi, 80-81, 85-88, 90, 119, 138-139, 182-183
bullish engulfing pattern with heikin-ashi, 53-55, 82-85, 87-88, 146, 161-162, 171, 274-275
last engulfing bottom, 88-89
last engulfing top, 90
EPIQ Systems Inc. (EPIQ), 170-171
Equivolume, 37-39
with heikin-ashi, 40, 42-43
evening star, 113, 169, 177
with heikin-ashi, 53-54, 113-119, 121

F

Financial Select Sector SPDR ETF (XLF), 202
Finish Line Inc. (FINL), 136
FOREX (FX) pairs,
AUDUSD, 274-275
EURUSD, 267-269
GBPUSD, 272-273
USDJPY, 269-271
with heikin-ashi, 267

G

Gann, William Delbert 2
Gann strategies, 2
General Electric Co. (GE), 25, 108
Genzyme Corp. (GENZ), 115-116
Gilead Sciences Inc. (GILD), 101
Google Inc. (GOOG), 188-190
gravestone doji, 143, 153-154
with heikin-ashi, 154-156

H

haDelta, 31
crossings with short average, *See* use of haDelta.
definition of, 31
interpretation, 32, 35

moving average of, 33
smoothing, 283
use of, 68, 72-74, 84
hammer,
variations (types) of, 123
with heikin-ashi, 123
hanging man, 128-129
with heikin-ashi, 129-131
harami,
bearish, 67
bullish, 67
with heikin-ashi, 67-72, 74-75
heikin,
translation in English, 16
heikin-ashi candles,
change of color, 55
construction and interpretation of, 21
five rules for translating, 22
haOpen with midpoint of previous candle, 284
quantification of, 31
relationship between bodies, colors, and shadows, 282
with shadows, 284
three types of, 16
heikin-ashi charts,
anticipate next heikin-ashi bar, 225-230
building with only closing prices, 285
ideal visual flow of, 26
reducing noise on, 15, 17, 27, 45, 55, 109, 213, 285
signs of slowdown on, 22, 285
strengths and weaknesses of, 282
trading only with, 281
using Microsoft® Excel® to generate, 287-291
heikin-ashi technique,
as a visual technique, 15-19, 277

definition of, 21
forcasting with, 225-230
quantification, 31-35
quantifiable indicator of, 31
strengths of, 15-19
used for intraday trading, 272-275, 283
with moving averages, 213-215
with multiple time frames, 217-223
with other techniques and indicators, 211
high-wave candles, 169-170
with heikin-ashi, 173
Home Properties Inc. (HME), 179-180, 191-192
Howe, Neil 2

I

Ichimoku charts, 3, 8, 11, 243
with heikin-ashi, 246-250
in-neck, 185, 188
with heikin-ashi, 185, 189-190
Industrial Select Sector SPDR ETF (XLI), 120
International Federation of Technical Analysis (IFTA), 307
International Paper Co. (IP), 178
inverted hammer, 53-54, 123, 131-132
with heikin-ashi, 111, 126-127, 133-134
iShares Russell Microcap Index (IWC), 213-215

J

Japanese candlestick patterns,
challenges in using, 63-66
gaps in, 56
heikin-ashi and, 52-57
pros and cons of, 55
quantification of, 45
JP Morgan Chase & Co. (JPM), 171-172

K

Kagi charts, 3

Kijun-sen, 244-245, 248-250
Kitchin, Joseph 2
Kondratieff, Nikolai 2
Kumo, 244-245

L

last engulfing pattern, 90
LDK Solar Co., Ltd. ADR (LDK), 99-100, 102-103
Leading Span A, *See* Senkou Span A.
Leading Span B, *See* Senkou Span B.
long-legged doji, 143, 147-148
   with heikin-ashi, 149-150
Lowe's Companies Inc. (LOW), 97-98, 154

M

marubozu,
   black, 181-183
   white, 178-180
   with heikin-ashi, 178-180, 182-183
market breadth, 251
   with heikin-ashi, 252-256
   McClellan oscillator, 251
MetaStock®, 293
Microsoft Corp. (MSFT), 200
Microsoft® Excel®, 281, 287
modified candles, *See* heikin-ashi candles
modified candle prices,
   formulas for defining, 21
   haClose, 21
   haHigh, 21
   haLow, 21
   haOpen, 21
Monsato Co. (MON), 82-83, 85
morning star, 53-55, 105-106
   with heikin-ashi, 106-112
moving average,

with heikin-ashi, 213
Moving Average Convergence-Divergence (MACD), 2

N

NASDAQ Composite Index (COMPQX), 6, 11, 32-34
Netflix Inc. (NFLX), 38-41
New Germany Fund Inc. (GF), 118
Newmont Mining Corp. (NEM), 117
North American Palladium, Ltd. (PAL), 233
NuStar Energy L.P. (NS), 68-72
NuVasive Inc. (NUVA), 126
NVIDIA Corp. (NVDA), 28, 139

O

Officemax Inc. (OMX), 96
Olympic Steel Inc. (ZEUS), 186-187, 197-199
on-neck, 186
  with heikin-ashi, 185, 187
OpenTable Inc. (OPEN), 234
Oracle Corp. (ORCL), 231-232

P

piercing line, 93-94
  with heikin-ashi, 94-99
pivots,
  buy, 257-258
  defined, 258
  with heikin-ashi, 259-265
  sell, 257-258
Point & Figure charts, 1, 2, 59, 243
priceline.com Inc. (PCLN), 84-85
psychological line indicator, 47-49

Q

quantification,
  with the heikin-ashi technique, 31
  with Japanese candlesticks, 45
Qstick indicator, 45

R

Rambus Inc. (RMBS), 162
Randgold Resources Inc. (GOLD), 132-133
Relative Strength Index (RSI), 2, 10, 237
    with heikin-ashi 238-241
Rembrandt, Harmenszoon van Rijn 65
Renko charts, 3
reversals,
    in heikin-ashi charts, 55
    in Japanese candlestick charts, 55

S

S&P 500 Index (SP-500), 46-49, 109, 238-239, 244, 246-248, 252-255, 258-259,
Schlumberger Ltd. (SLB), 181
Senkou Span A, 244-245
Senkou Span B, 244-245
shooting star, 53-54, 123, 135-136
    with heikin-ashi, 136-140
SPDR S&P 500 (SPY), 219-222
spinning tops, 169-170
    with heikin-ashi, 170-173
Stochastics, 2
stop-loss, 179, 227, 230, 243, 250, 285
Strauss, William 2

T

takuri line, 124
    with heikin-ashi, 126-127
Tenkan-sen, 244-245
Thompson, Sir William 13
three black crows, 201
    with heikin-ashi, 202-205
three white soldiers, 196
    with heikin-ashi, 197-200

thrusting pattern, 191
    with heikin-ashi, 192
trends,
    visual aspect in heikin-ashi charts, 6, 15, 17, 22, 28-29
    visual aspect in Japanese candlestick charts, 6, 28-29
trailing-stop, 243, 249-250, 285
trend reversals, 17
    and one-bar lag on heikin-ashi charts, 18, 283-284
tweezers bottom, 160
    with heikin-ashi, 161-164
tweezers top, 164-165
    with heikin-ashi, 165-168

U

Under Armour Inc. (UA), 130
US Dollar Index (DXY0), 52-53, 239-240

V

volatility, 10, 231
volume, 37
    as reflected in heikin-ashi, 40-43
    as reflected in Japanese candlestick charts, 37-39

W

Warner, Charrles Dudley 209
Winthrop Realty Trust (FUR), 182
World Gold Index (XGLD), 249
World Platinum Index (XPLT), 114
Wyckoff method, 17

X

Xiaoping, Deng 61

Y

Yogi Berra 10

Z

z-score, 231
    with heikin-ashi, 232-234

ABOUT THE AUTHOR

Dan Valcu, CFTe, has 15 years of experience in the markets applying technical analysis. His articles and studies have been published in *Technical Analysis of Stocks & Commodities*, *Trader's Magazine*, and other periodicals in the technical analysis community.

Starting his research in Spring 2003, he was the first author to bring from Japan and promote in the West the heikin-ashi technique both as a visual instrument and a technical indicator in 2004. As a result, heikin-ashi is a component of many technical trading platforms today.

Mr. Valcu develops trading strategies based on the heikin-ashi technique and applies modified candles in his trading. This book, a world premiere, is written for the traders who need simple techniques to highlight the trend, reduce the noise, and alert about possible reversals. In addition, this book is a guide for easily translating candlestick patterns.

An active promoter of technical analysis, Mr. Valcu wrote three books about this subject and strategies. He serves on the Board of the International Federation of Technical Analysis (IFTA) and holds the professional designation of a Certified Financial Technician. He offers training, seminars, and trading camps in technical analysis and risk management. More information about heikin-ashi can be found at www.educofin.com.